I THINK I GOT AWAY WITH IT!

A whimsical sail through my life of hosting special events,
escorting wildlife trips around the world, and meeting some
of the fascinating people I touched shoulders
with along the way.

I invite you to treat this book like an old friend.
Enjoy it when you are in the mood, then pick it up again
when you feel in need of a chuckle. Most of all, don't take any
of it too seriously – I didn't!

I THINK I GOT AWAY WITH IT!

Published by Golden Bee Publishing
info@goldenbee.org.uk

Printed in Great Britain and distributed by Ingram

ISBN: 978-1-7399766-0-6

This book is dedicated to the many people who
have been kind to me throughout my life,
and in so doing have taught me the incalculable
value of kindness, both in receiving and giving.

Contents

Forward *by Jasper Carrott* OBE

Clive Thomas is probably the least known person I know. Why he has written a book I have no idea.

Who is going to buy it, the same people who buy The Telegraph because they like the pictures? Or the residents of Wales because his surname is Thomas.
His friends and family will buy it, so there's three and if he promotes it as a book and doorstop it will get to double figures, just.

He is clearly hoping for a miracle, which is why I am writing the foreword, it's the initials you see.

It is all a bit sad because it is a half decent book, well, a bit more than that actually. I won't praise it too much because I have my own books to sell and some of his writing can raise a half-hearted smile.
Ok, belly laughs dammit!

I have known Clive for far too long, and we have some memorable times to talk about. I met him when there was such a thing as The Celebrity Squash Team, where we drank gallons of Robinsons Barley Water in between crucifying the noble sport of the same name. He did not play as there was not enough room for Clive and an opponent in the court at the same time.

A lot of the escapades we got up to are featured in the book, but I get very little praise for instigating the events in the first place or indeed starring in them for very little reward. In between his organising my events he had me involved with charitable occasions where I was expecting stuffed brown envelopes full of cash for the charity, "Destitute Entertainers of Birmingham". My favourite charity as there is only one recipient.
The envelopes were pristine, brown and empty.

In the book Clive will tell you of his life in events and travel and I will grudgingly admit it is an impressive recall of some the people he has met, known, served and irritated. While they didn't know him he indeed met up with Royalty, super stars, the mega rich and Big Issue sellers.

He lives life on the edge, always taking risks, coming up with wonderful ideas that are frankly bonkers. Success and failure are secondary though, it's creating something new that counts. Now that takes courage, like writing this book.

There is a very generous side to Clive that I have seen put to work in many different areas over the years. They are in the main away from the back slapping and publicity causes. They feature obscure peoples/children in unfashionable places, the deserving and needy he encounters on his journeys. Always touched by the distress of others, he gives.

He's a big softy really and that is part of the reason I love him so much. When you buy this book in the Pound Store, if it is unsigned remember, it will be very rare. Like mine.

Jasper

Welcome to MY world

It's a well known saying that 'everyone has a book in them', and whilst it might not be true (as anyone who's ever admitted to reading Fifty Shades of Grey will attest) I have been told it so many times that I feel like a Public Library.

For years when standing in bars or sitting at dining tables telling people stories of the extraordinary characters I've met, of the amazing places I've been and the wonderful things I've seen it won't be long before I hear those words... 'you really should write a book, Clive'. And even if this is a polite way of saying... "you really should bugger off and leave me to finish my drink/meal/crossword puzzle in peace" ...when you are told something repeatedly then you do start to believe it. But books don't write themselves, and besides, time has always been the enemy.

Until the pandemic.

Having spent my life in the hospitality business, where success relies on getting people together and mingling, with our government coming up with ever more ingenious ways to keep people apart and singling, it dawned on me that I finally had my golden opportunity to set myself down at the desk and get cracking putting pen to paper.
It was a now or never moment!

Obviously, like every new writer, I spent the first few weeks ordering and then neatly setting out all manner of stationery: pens, pencils, notepads, rubbers, binders, folders, index cards, paper clips, treasury tags and so on until finally, having had a wonderful time, spent a small fortune and written not a word, I decided that physically writing north of 90,000 words was for the birds! So I then spent more money on a fancy new laptop and even more time setting it up, deciding on the font, the line-spacing, alignment, indentation and... you get the idea. Because, like so many before me, I was discovering that the hardest thing about writing a book was to avoid all the million and one things that conspire to distract you from actually sitting your backside down on the chair and actually writing it.

But again, as so often in my charmed life, events conspired to help me out and as the national lockdown dragged on and on and life as we all knew it ground to a halt. Finally there was nothing happening anywhere and so with no distractions or excuses left to me, I started. And once started, I found I couldn't stop.

Until I reached the end, that is.

And as I wrote I discovered that rich and wonderful as the English language is – Gyles Brandreth (about more whom later) once described English as "the Lingua Franca of the world" – but like those so many other writers of the past, I found there are times when it failed me. I would be searching for a descriptor but couldn't find the word I wanted because the word didn't exist. And so I've just had to use my powers of invention and invent the word I wanted.

William Shakespeare invented hundreds of words, such as bandit, lacklustre, green-eyed and dwindle and Charles Dickens wasn't above making up a fair few: butterfingers; flummoxed, squashed and kibosh to name but some. And even though they must have been a nightmare to play scrabble with, if it was good enough for them it's good enough for me. So if you come across any unfamiliar words please don't immediately jump to the conclusion that I couldn't afford a proof-reader and that they are typos. Or that I'm *unkeyboardordinated**.

And so, here it is - my life so far condensed into this little volume. And little isn't usually an adjective used in connection with me. If you are one of those people who have ever told me that I have a book in me, I sincerely thank you. It is now out of me and in your hands.

I hope you enjoy it.

Chive

Footnote:
*Unkeyboardordinated. Unable to type without ~~frequently making mistakes~~ making frequent mistakes.

Life's train
Hakey, Beefy
& Porky

Another events person, my friend
Sam Spillane told me that she believes
"Some people come into our lives for
a reason, some for a season and some
for ever" on balance I reckon she's right.

I've always tried to make sense of life by picturing my journey through it
and my interaction with the many different people I've met as being like
a train on a long track. I think the idea came to me from some Buddhist
philosophy I picked up on my travels, or maybe it was Hindu, Socrates
or from the back of a cereal box, but in any case it has stayed with me.

As I see it, each of us is the engine, pulling OUR four carriages: one
for family, one for friends, another for work or business and a fourth
for local community including neighbours and church (or similar).
As we pull the carriages along the tracks of our life, though the decades
and across continents, we pass through various watersheds, crossroads,
crisis and celebrations, which are the stations, where some people get off
whilst new people climb aboard. Others move between the carriages: as
business associates become friends and sometimes friends become family,
but together they make up OUR story, and each has a part to play: large
or small. They are all important. And whilst this is happening in our
carriages, we are getting on and off other people's trains, as we in turn
become part of *their* story.

The journey will have its delays, its accidents and sometimes a change
of route. It will also bring happiness and sorrow: expectations both high
and low and there will be hellos, goodbyes, and final farewells. In time
will come our own final farewell, and we never know at which station
we ourselves will end our journey.

Think about it. Do you agree?

Well, one person who jumped onto my train years ago and has moved
carriages from 'Vague Associate' to 'Firm Friend' is my pal Hakey.

His given name is Colin, which translated into French is Hake...
You get the drift. Hakey is thought by some to be a 'man's man'.
A low handicap golfer and accomplished sailor, successful businessman,
quick witted, knowledgeable about wine and can hold his drink (mostly).
Actually, he is he is a consummate 'people's man', able to get on with
anyone and everyone.

Early on in our friendship I mentioned how much I loved the Channel
Islands and Hakey told me that he had a house in Alderney and promptly
invited Kay and I to come over for a weekend. Never needing to be
invited twice, that summer we packed and went.

Although Alderney is the third largest of the Channel Islands, it is only
about 3 miles long and a mile and a half wide, so many of the residents
and summer's visitors know each other. There is an old pub on the island
by the harbour at St Anne's called *The Divers* where, during the summer,
Hakey and his mates would meet from around 5.30 for a few 'gentle pints'
before departing promptly at 7, back to hearth and home. At least that's
how Hakey told it, although he did warn me that one of his chums who
had a house on the island was Ian Botham, who isn't a chap known for
'gentle' pints – as I was to discover.

But we didn't expect the ex-England captain would be around for the
'5.30 Club' on that particular hot August evening, as just the day before
he and fellow England cricketer, Allan Lamb, had lost what the press
described as *the most expensive libel case in cricketing history*. Botham and
Lamb had brought a libel action against ex-Pakistan Captain, Imran Khan,
accusing him of labelling them as ball-tamperers and racists. Their case
had been thrown out in the High Court and Botham's share of the cost
of the lost trial was said to be in the region of £300,000. However as
Hakey and I sauntered into the pub, Ian was at the bar ordering
a round. I was amazed he had any money left!

He called us over, getting Hakey his usual pint of bitter and asking
me what I'd have. It was still around 30 degrees and my thirst needed
quenching so I opted for a pint of lager.

"You don't want to drink pints in here mate... they'll make you fat!"
chimed Botham, to a chorus of laughter from his buddies all
gathered round.

This was clearly a lad's club and banter was the order of the day and so I thought I'd join in. "I hear you have a pretty nice boat here," I said to Ian who, as everyone on the Island knew, owned a magnificent craft which was his pride and joy.

"Yes" he replied proudly, pointing through the window to *the* magnificent craft, lying at anchor, "it's the one with the blue hull. It was a gift from the Sultan of Brunei"

I gave it a quick, unimpressed glance and looking him directly in the eye said,

"I've heard Imran Khan's is twice the size!"

Time froze. Absolute silence from the assembled cronies, including Hakey who was for once lost for words. You could have heard a High Court Judge's wig drop. I held Botham's gaze. He turned and raised his right arm. I thought he was going to smack me one on the nose as his fist moved as if in slow motion towards the general direction of my head. And who could have blamed him? The tensions of the two week-long trial must have taken their toll. We'd only just met and I'd surely gone too far. But he was simply putting his arm round my shoulder, smiling broadly as he said, "you're alright mate. I'll buy you a pint. My friends call me Beefy – I shall call you Porky!"

And so it was set and has remained to this day.

We've shared a few times together over the years, including the launch of two books – the first was "Botham's Century" where Beefy writes about the 100 people he's most enjoyed meeting. I particularly enjoyed his account of his time with Nelson Mandela. The Elton John and Eric Clapton stories are a good read too. I didn't make the cut but, to prove I'm not bitter, I'll share a couple of 'Bits of Beefy' with you in *my* book.

The first was an occasion when Ian and I had a few things to discuss and he suggested that Kay and I get ourselves up to his house in Yorkshire for a barbecue. Given the distance, a guest room had been thoughtfully prepared and whilst Kay and Kath caught up, Ian took me outside to "help him get the barbecue going". But before we did that, we had a beer and a chat... and then another beer... and another beer... and then finally when all the beers had gone, Beefy finally pulled out the lighter fluid... but decided against that and opened some wine instead.

Now normally, where alcohol is concerned, I am a man with a whim of iron, but I'd had a long drive, no lunch and I was starving. And as the wine started sloshing down over the beers, the barbecue might not have been getting lit, but I was.

"Beefy, shall we get the food going?" I suggested, hopefully.

"'Course! Absolutely. I have some fantastic, dry-aged, rib-eyed steaks" he told me.

Thank God!! I thought.

"Which reminds me, There's some wonderful Rioja Gran Reserva to go with it."

Oh God!! I thought, as the corks popped and more wine was poured and I start thinking about making a start eating the charcoal briquettes.

Anyway, cut to later... much later... and very cut. The wine was finally and briefly interrupted by the food – which Kay assured me was superb and I have no reason to doubt her word although I cannot recall a single mouthful – which for me is very unusual. Back in the house we settled down to chat over a couple of digestifs.

So I was sitting on a soft, slippery leather sofa, next to Kay, Kath was in a chair opposite as Beefy was busily pouring brandy, whisky and God knows what else (it could have been ethanol for I knew) into a never-ended stream of glasses at my elbow. Now, there was no way I could be a bad guest and refuse... that would be rude and bad form. But I did rather wish that my hosts had a few handily-placed potted plants that I pour the stuff into rather than down my throat. But I persevered and I was doing okay until the room started slipping. I was sure that I was sitting still but somehow the room was moving. Up past my eyes and then the carpet ascended until it nestled against my face.

I think I heard Kay say something about, "Clive appears to have slipped onto the rug" but rather than correct her on the point, and run the risk of causing a scene – which *would* have been rude and bad form – I thought it best to remain quiet on the subject and continue to let the rug rest itself against me.

But it was when Kath, Mein Hostess, appeared to agree with Kay that I began to suspect that maybe I was, not to put too fine a point on it, pissed! And so I resolved to do something about it – and promptly rested my head on my hands and fell into a deep sleep.

But when I regained consciousness some minutes later, I realised I'd have to try a different tack to retrieve the situation and resolved to rise from my prone position, walk in an elegant and dignified fashion across to Mrs Botham, take her right hand in my left and kiss it in as gallant way as possible, look earnestly into her eyes, say "My dear Kath, your hospitality has been as warm and as lovely as you are, however I fear I may have become slightly over-refreshed and so, if you will forgive me, I will now retire and leave you with my sincere thanks and gratitude for a delightful evening in your beautiful home."

And with that, I would turn and glide unobtrusively from the room.

So, that was the plan. And went through it a couple of times in my head as I lay there and it seemed pretty airtight to me. So all that was needed was to do it.

Rising from the prone was slightly more problematical that I had first thought, but once I put my mind to something, I can usually see it through. All I had to do was be gallant, elegant and unobtrusive. I took a deep breath in whilst staggering to my feet.

Now, of course, in retrospect, I can see that the deep breath in was a miscalculation on my part. Because as my stomach contracted, my waistline momentarily shrank and my trousers fell down around my ankles.

Possibly, a lesser man would have let this scupper his resolve and abandoned the plan. However, that would have been rude. And bad form. So, I shuffled forward, trousers around my ankles as elegantly and unobtrusively as the circumstances would allow, until I arrived in front of Kath, who I was gratified to see had fallen silent and was staring up at me – being careful to keep her eyes fixed firmly on my face. It was obviously the effect of my warm and genuine smile. But I was relieved to remember that I had chosen a long tailed shirt that evening.

All I had to do now, was get through the speech I had prepared. I quickly ran through it one final time in my head. "Dear Kath... hospitality, warm and lovely as you... slightly over refreshed... retire and leave... gratitude... delightful evening... beautiful home."

That was what I was thinking.

What I blurted out was *"Don't ever leave me alone drinking with that mad b*st*rd husband of yours again!"*

Which, let's face it, is close enough.

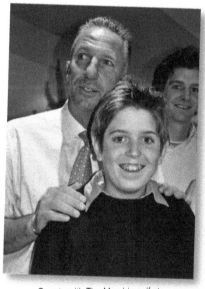

Guests with The Man himself at *Breakfast with Botham.*

But luckily for me Ian is not someone to hold a minor faux pas like this against a chap and I like to that if anything it only served to strengthen our friendship – but then I'm the sort of chap who likes to think all sorts of odd things. But Beefy and I did continue to work together on all manner of projects over the years. One of my particular favourites was "Breakfast with Botham" where, on Lord's Test Match days I gathered together a group of clients and their guests at The Portman Hotel – a mere full-toss from to the ground – to meet Ian and hear his thoughts about the day's play to come, followed by an impromptu and invariably interesting Q&A session.

Beefy was always willing to give candid answers to questions like 'why are the Aussies soooo good at sport?' or 'can England really win this Test?' to very personal inquisition style interrogations, often from women in our audience, about some of the more scurrilous claims made by the red-topped newspapers about what really happened on tour!

On these mornings, Ian and I usually met for coffee and a chat around 7.20 or so, well ahead of the guests. But on one particular day just as I was starting to feel somewhat concerned and anxious when the usually punctual Beefy finally staggered in at about 7.45, bleary eyed and looking distinctly 50:50! He was clearly just coming IN from a long night *out*.

Long after his playing days were over, his drinking capacity was still legendary! I looked at his dishevelled state, thinking this isn't quite what our guests will be expecting from the leading Sky Cricket Commentator and former England Captain.

"Where on earth have you been" I asked.

"You don't want to know," he shot back. "Just be glad I've made it."

I had stayed at the hotel the night before and immediately suggested he took advantage of the shower in my room whilst I ironed his shirt. The hot water seemed to freshen him up. I made a decent fist of ironing the front and the collar at least, and a steaming mug of Kenco Intenso had begun to work its magic as we took the stairs down to the assembled guests at 8.01, all smiles and bonhomie, with Beefy telling me "Thanks Porks, it's lucky you had a room!"

The guests hung on his every word, the Q&A was lively and went on a bit longer than usual, and they didn't suspect a thing. He'd got away with it. WE'D got away with it. But he dared not be late for Sky so as he grabbed a bacon roll I went on ahead to hail a cab to get him to his next appointment in double quick time.

Taxis are plentiful in London, and good fortune was with me as a cab pulled into the forecourt just has he appeared. The cabbie put his window down and Beefy said "Take me to Lords please?" It truly was his lucky morning as the startled cabbie exclaimed

"This one's on me guv'nor! Ian Botham for Lords – that's like gettin' Tony Blair for Downin' Street. Get in!"

As I wrote this, it reminded me of another story about a cabbie and one of my great heroes Winston Churchill. It's well known but I think it's worth another airing.

One winter's afternoon during the blackout, Churchill needed to get to the BBC to make one of his legendary wartime speeches. His official car was delayed and so his long time bodyguard and companion, Walter Thompson, hailed him a black cab and, as the Prime Minister climbed into the back and buried his head in his speech notes, asked to be taken to the BBC.

On arrival Thompson asked the cabbie to wait for them to return in about 40 minutes, telling him "We'll pay you waiting time." Still none the wiser about the identity of his illustrious passenger in the dark, the cabbie replied "Sorry I can't do that guv, I've gotta get 'ome. Churchill's givin' one of 'is speeches at 7. I ain't missed one of 'em since the start of the war!"

Winston was deeply touched by the loyalty of this man and as he stepped out of the cab promptly tipped him a pound which was a great deal of money in those days. The cabbie beamed "Oh go on then, I'll wait. Winston'll just 'ave to do this one wivout me!"

School Days
Small boy, big ambitions

I miss being a kid, it was a golden time when my only responsibilities were running around and laughing a lot. Someone else was in charge of my hair and teeth cleaning; I had no idea about bills, mortgages or income tax, I just loved being outside, jumping in muddy puddles or kicking a football. We lived first in Edgware in the 1960s, then later in Stanmore, both suburbs of North London with stations on the tube. The house was small but comfortable and had a little garden with a greenhouse which I loved. Mum was a school dinner lady and Dad worked in a menswear shop. He was hard working but didn't like spending money, so in winter the house was cold and there was often ice on the *inside* of my bedroom window in the mornings. Getting dressed quickly became a necessity!

Peter would be no more than 6 months old here. Pictured with me in the garden of our house in Edgware.

I spent much of my childhood trying to persuade Mum and/or Dad to let me have a pet. I began by asking for a dog, then when refused a cat, and from there went in decreasing levels through rabbit, tortoise and finally in desperation goldfish, always to be told "No Clive, you won't look after it." But when I was nine my parents did better than a pet,

they gave me a friend for life when my brother Peter appeared at home,

wrapped in a woolly shawl and smiling at me. Looking back it was probably just wind, which he still suffers from, but I was none the wiser and we bonded instantly.

The great thing was that because of our age difference we never had to compete. I was just better then him at absolutely everything and he looked up to me with adoring hero-worship. Would that it were that way now! The little bugger beats me at everything and it's fair to say the hero-worship has faded but the adoration has been replaced with great banter.

School at Stag Lane Primary was a happy time for me. I remember liking art and was very proud to be put in charge of the nature table; which was little more than a collection of acorns, horse chestnuts and an assortment of broken egg shells collected from empty nests. The strange things we remember eh? I'd always done pretty well in classroom tests, but when I was 11 I learnt that I froze in the rigid austerity of the examination room and so didn't pass my Eleven Plus, which meant I didn't go to Downer Grammar School as my parents had hoped but instead was packed off to Chandos, the local secondary which provided further education for hoi polloi.

Big school was an eye opener for me. Having always lived in shorts, summer and winter, I was now compelled to wear long trousers and a blazer and tie for one thing. However, I thought the sports facilities were amazing. We had an enormous gymnasium where I learnt to play basketball and did quite well as I was already 6 feet tall at 12 years old. We had our own school playing field with two full sized football pitches in the winter and athletics in the summer. As well as this there were tennis courts in the park adjoining our school boundary so plenty for us to enjoy.

In my first year there I found myself in class 1C, the C standing for Mr Chandler, our elderly form master. He was known as Chalky, as this is what passed for first year wit back then and was forever writing the names of boys on the black board and how many *lines** they needed to write, often for the most minor infractions.

Teachers who couldn't control their class would send miscreant pupils to The Deputy Headmaster, a fearsome Welshman called Mr Jones (or Jonah as he was known throughout the school).

Jonah seemed to possess a supernatural power to sniff out liars so you had to be honest with him about why you had been sent and if you have been condemned to his tender mercies there was always a better than even chance that you would get a punishment. At best this would be a 30 minute After School Detention but at worst it would be two or three strokes of the cane administered with some vigour to your backside whilst you bent over the back of the chair. In the 1960s this was accepted practice. Common assault on small boys.

I got to know Jonah pretty well during my five years at school attending with great relish his lessons on British Constitution. I can still tell you in great detail about how our parliamentary system is made up and run – but I won't as I want you to carry on reading. I learned that behind the Deputy Head's role of disciplinarian was in fact a very gentle, likeable and approachable man, who could just as easily dispense comforting advice as physical punishment.

In those days Harrow School offered a free scholarship each year to one pupil from the Borough of Harrow. The place was for a weekly boarder, coming home at weekends. All the first year pupils took an exam to whittle us down to just 20 from that intake at our school who would sit the entrance exam for Harrow, which was five exam papers over three days. The exam covered General Knowledge, Current Affairs and questions eliciting opinions testing our powers of argument. We could also chose one of six subjects on which to answer more detailed questions. I chose the natural world which has always been a passion.

Unlike the Eleven Plus exam, where I had felt under a lot of pressure to pass, this time I had convinced myself there was no way I'd get into Harrow and so was much more relaxed. In fact, I rather enjoyed the process – it was like a quiz about which I knew a surprising number of answers. I didn't give it another thought but after some weeks it emerged that I'd achieved the highest marks in the whole of the Borough! So out of the blue it looked like I could be "the one" to get in!

I was amazed, ecstatic and frankly a bit bewildered at the enormity of it all but I was well up for the adventure! Lessons in modern history had already fixed Winston Churchill as a great hero in my mind and Harrow was where he had gone to school. Oh my God! I would be where he had been. I would see much of what he had seen. I may even sit on chairs on which he had sat. I would literally be touching history. I simply couldn't believe my luck.

All we needed to do to seal the deal was for my parents and me to attend Harrow for the formal interview. I was very excited, knowing just what a huge, huge opportunity it was. Chalky couldn't believe it, both the Headmaster, Mr Bellion, and Jonah were ecstatic. But my father was less than keen.

Born in the 1930s, Dad had always been an ordinary working man, brought up to "know his place" and his ambition had been achieved when he became Manager of a menswear shop. To be fair to Dad, he was happy with that; he could look after himself and his family. He explained his reticence to me saying that I would be mixing with boys whose education had begun at Eton or similar and would all be from very different backgrounds to mine – moneyed and privileged. The main, huge, difference between my father and I was that I thought this was a good thing and he didn't. I thought I'd be okay; I was half decent at sport, good at music, quick witted and able to impersonate and do the accents of some of the teachers so I thought I could make myself popular. Dad, on the other hand, worried that I wouldn't fit in, would be bullied, and as a result would be very unhappy. I was horrified when I discovered that he had said as much in a letter to Mr Bellion.

Mr Bellion was young to be a headmaster and ambitious for the reputation of his school and shared my feelings. In fact, he was so convinced that going to Harrow was the right thing for me that he came up to our house one evening to try to persuade my father to change his mind and let me take up my place. As was the etiquette in those days Mother and I were not invited to that meeting in our "best room" but stood with ears pressed the door. My father was a stubborn man and despite all of Mr Bellion's persuasive efforts about the honour for Chandos, an English Public School education being recognised around the globe, the contacts and friends I would make and how these alone would almost certainly set me up for life, he was not to be moved.

After Mr Bellion had left Father and I had a blazing row. He told me that I didn't have a chance of passing the interview and I told him that it was far more likely that HE wouldn't pass, and that I wouldn't get in because of him! I regret to say that we very nearly came to blows.

But Dad's will prevailed and I never walked in those hallowed halls.

I never quite forgave him. It drove a wedge between us from which we never fully recovered. I heard some years later from my uncle, his brother that while the scholarship was free Dad felt he wouldn't be able to keep up with the costs of uniform, evening dress, sports kit, school trips and so on. If only he had confided those worries to me I'm sure in the years that followed I could have seen his point of view. I may have even been able to respect him for a decision which perhaps in hindsight was farsighted but at the time I saw as quite the opposite.

I ask myself now if my life would have been very different if I'd gone to Harrow? Oh yes - of course it would. But would it have been any better? I don't know.

I'll never know. And perhaps it's better that way.

I was stuck at Chandos and so I knuckled down and made the best of it. I've always enjoyed music and played in the brass band. We had a music tutor visit once a week called Harry White, who used to run and conduct the Watford Silver Band. They played on bandstands around London parks on Sunday afternoons and had won a few worthwhile National competitions. I was thrilled when Harry invited me to audition for his band and as one of its youngest members spent many happy Sundays playing the school euphonium at places such as Waterloo Park, Golders Hill and Kenwood. I suppose that's why I was drawn to Herb Alpert and the Tijuana Brass, and the great sound of Glenn Miller's Band. I wasn't totally weird as I loved Elton John, Bowie and later Queen.

Well okay - perhaps I was a bit weird as I was also a big fan of whistling folkie, Roger Whittaker.

I wasn't a great sportsman but was tall and well-built for my age and was a decent basketball player and athletics all-rounder. My dad was keen on tennis and encouraged me at an early age. So what with after school athletics, tennis two nights a week, band practice once a week in summer but thrice in winter; tennis matches on Saturdays and concerts on Sundays in the summer, as well as my regular grass cutting, hedge clipping and car washing in the streets round and about, I didn't really have a chance to get into much trouble, although I was almost led astray by peer pressure to start smoking.

Many of my athletic team chums were seniors whilst I was still a junior, and they gathered for a sneaky drag in the toilet block at break times. In the end the pressure to join in just became too much. I thought I'd have a practice during my 45 minute walk home so I bought a packet of the cheapest cigarettes I could find, five untipped Woodbines, and to save buying a box of matches I asked the newsagent to light one for me. I managed to chain-smoke the five on my way home trying to inhale through my nose down my throat, blow smoke rings and anything else I could think of. I coughed a lot, made my eyes sting and succeeded in making myself violently sick over the wall into a neighbours front garden. (Sorry again Mrs Price!) I must've looked as white as a sheet when I made it home. My mother took one look at me and called the doctor, who still made house calls in those days. Looking back, I'm sure he must've been able to smell the stale tobacco when he examined me and I remember after closing the bedroom door hearing him say to my mother "I can't find anything wrong with him, Mrs Thomas. I'm sure a good night's rest is all he needs but if he is still unwell in the morning just let me know."

Those five untipped Woodbines made me feel so ill that I vowed never to smoke again. And I never have. Of course I was fine the next day and I also somehow managed to escape whatever evil was coming my way from the boys for not joining their gang.

In spite of having a short 'Butterfly' attention span, schoolwork came easily to me and I didn't have to study too hard.

I suppose I did have my own gang but it was very little, only made up of two other people: Colin Shaw, who was also a band member and later became a successful author of business books and an international motivational speaker; and a guy called Julian Posner, a tough stocky little fellow who did weight training and was also in our athletics team. You never got into a row with Pozzi as he was handy with the fists and I was pleased he was usually on my side!

My other chum in the band was Mike Innes. His brother John was a drummer, his dad Don was in the BBC Symphony Orchestra, and the musical heritage running through his blood and in his genes made Mike a fine trombonist. I remember my first visit to the Royal Albert Hall when Mike's dad Don invited me to join them for "Fanfare for Europe" a concert to mark our entry into the EU. Don was up on stage and I was with my mate up in the gods at this amazing venue. It all felt very special, and it must have been as I remember it 45 years later.

Pozzi knew before any of us what he wanted to do with his life; he was going to be a DJ! He passed his driving test the day after his 17th birthday and got hold of a second-hand turntable, speakers, some dodgy coloured lighting and his Dad bought him an old yellow GPO transit van to cart the gear around. He had boxes upon boxes of 7" black vinyl and quickly recruited a couple of us to act as his roadies, thus avoiding any hard physical work himself.

He started his business whilst he was still at school and called it *The Banana Split Discotheque*. Banana Split has grown into one of the most successful party planners in the UK and I know that Julian has booked some of the biggest bands in the world to play at events and parties he's organised for his extremely well resourced household-name clients.

I remember we had a fiery and emotional red headed Irish teacher of English called Mrs Iggulden, who taught us her own, unique version of the English language and definitely had a soft spot for my pal Shaw, who could do no wrong in her Irish eyes.

In one of her poetry lessons we all had to write a poem featuring candles. No, I didn't know why either. But we did. She came up with a theme every time she had us write poetry. While the rest of us were struggling to make head or tail of it, teacher's pet Shaw, bidden by a keen Mrs I (or 'Iggy' as she was also known) to hear what he had come up with, stood up to recite his composition which went: "Goodbye Norma Jean, though I never knew you at all..." with of course the verse ending "...and you lived your life like a candle in the wind, never knowing who to turn to when the rain set in. I would have liked to know you but I was just a kid, the candle burned out long before the legend ever did."

We were in fits of laughter but Iggy, who was clearly not a fan of local-boy-made-good, Elton John, told us to shut up and listen to "the beautiful words Colin has written". We were outraged and now yelling even louder to her "No Miss, it's a song! They play it to Top of The Pops!"

But she wasn't having any of it and gave Colin top marks, telling us

"It's not a song. It's Colin's poem, and it's beautiful!"

I still can't believe he got away with it. I think my old chum's cheek has stood him in good stead ever since. I vaguely remember writing some rhyme which included *candle flickers and see her knickers*. I was never teacher's pet material!

On my last day at school after some classmates and I had removed the life sized skeleton from the biology lab and sat it on one of the toilets in the master's staffroom which was strictly out of bounds, clutching a toilet roll in one of its bony hands, I remember Mr Bellion (also known as Roy the Boy) who drove a shiny Ford Capri sometimes spinning its wheels a bit like a boy racer would, which we thought was very cool, wishing me well and telling me to go and make my fortune, and that he thought I would "either make a million (which was a lot of money in the early 70s) or end up in jail".

Since then I've done both but only one night in the cells... so far. We had a careers advisor come to visit the school and he was most uninspiring to say

the least. I can't even remember his name.
He had lots of "handouts", which were as dull as he was.

Our interpretation of it all was:

Apprenticeship = Forger
Army = Kill or be Killed
Insurance = Die of Boredom
Postman = Better than walking the streets (marginally)
Bank = (See Insurance) although we didn't know about banks in the City and how you could scam yourself a fortune! Apparently legally.

I paid little attention to it all because
I already knew what I wanted.

I wanted to be like Alan Whicker!

If you're too young to remember Alan Whicker, his TV show which ran for years was called "Whicker's World" and was all about this dapper English gentleman in horn rimmed glasses who travelled the world, describing where he was and interviewing interesting people along the way. What a life!

 I knew that AW had begun his career as a war correspondent so I was determined to follow in his footsteps and become a journalist. I was already writing reports of my tennis club matches for two local papers and when I left school one of them, The Harrow Observer, offered me a job as a cub reporter. It paid very badly but as a Middlesex County junior tennis player I was earning extra money coaching tennis and I'd kept up the car washing, which was a nice cash generator and so life immediately after school was pretty good as I set the sails and cast off from my safe mooring.

I was heading through the harbour and out through open sea, with my parents chant ringing in my ears,

"Yes, okay, but when are you going to get a proper job?"

Tennis
<small>in the</small>
Big Apple

The average weekly wage in 1976 was £72. My fee for my first *proper reporter's job,* for a national newspaper was £35 a day plus expenses. Not quite in Jim Rockford's* league at $200 a day, but it wasn't half a bad start. What's more I was to do it in another country, and like Jim I had expenses.

1976 was the year of the Incredible Heatwave: the hottest British summer for 350 years when, basically, the nation wilted. But I didn't see the standpipes in the road, people watering the roses with their bathwater or swimming in the fountains at Trafalgar Square

Me with my droopy moustache inspired by Australian tennis legend John Newcombe, with fellow tennis coach (the other) Richard Geere.

to cool off because that summer I left the country for the first time, with more on my mind than in it bound for... America!

It's a trip I have done countless times since but it's difficult to describe the excitement I felt that first time. America was the land of big cars, Hollywood stars and flowing with milk and honey and Coca-Cola.

It was a hell of a step up from hot, sweaty, smelly North London in 95°F. I was 18, fit and devastatingly handsome (in the way that all 18-year olds know themselves to be) and heading to a summer camp in the mountains of Massachusetts to teach tennis to the rich and beautiful young things of New England for three long, glorious months. And to make things even better, before setting out I'd done the rounds of Fleet Street offering my services and landed myself a job! Back in those days you could bowl in off the street ask to see the sports Editor and be shown to the lift. These days you'd be shown the door.

The Daily Mirror's head office was an imposing glass and mirrors tower block at the foot of Fleet Street and so I thought I'd start there and work my along but, as it turned out, I didn't need to because, bless them, they immediately saw the benefit of having a young "Special Correspondent" reporting for them from the last US Open Tennis that was to be played on grass at the West Side Tennis Club Forest Hills New York! The obvious advantage for them was that because I was already going to be in the States, they didn't have to pay to fly me out there. But that was nothing to the advantage to me. I was to stay at the Roosevelt Hotel with all the other journalists, get to see one of the major tennis tournaments in the world, file reports on the matches (paying particular attention to the British players) and do some interviews. *And I* was to be paid!

All *very* Alan Whicker! When I discovered that the hotel was on East 45th and Park Lane and my room overlooked the Chrysler Building I couldn't believe my luck! I felt I was well and truly on my way.

The three months at camp flew by. Teaching tennis to young, eager American kids was hardly the most arduous of chores – as doing something that you love doing never is – and I had a ball doing it. There was also lots of leisure time and a particular highlight was the weekend I borrowed a car from the camp chef and made my way to *Tanglewood* to see the wonderful Judy Collins in concert. While I was there I also learnt that it's very true what they say about American girls loving an English accent and I became delightfully popular with the local ladies who were summering at the camp teaching sailing, drama and singing. I sometimes wonder why I ever left.

But eventually my time there was up; the summer was over and it was time for me to get to work and so I got on the Greyhound bus, with my

press credentials proudly in my pocket and headed off to The Big Apple.
I was no longer a child, I felt that I had become a young man and like
most of my friends I wanted to *be someone.* To me it seemed that the
young people I met in New York didn't share that ambition; they wanted
to *be sensational!* I had a bit of catching up to do.

I was a good bit younger than the rest of the press corps and so nightclubs
were new to me. I joined them at a few bars where several were well
known to the staff, and at the Algonquin where Sinatra and Dean Martin
regularly performed although not on the two nights that I visited.
I do remember Buddy Greco, the fantastic jazz pianist and singer,
started his set by saying "if you know the words and the tunes are familiar
to you and you would like to sing along – please don't". I later adopted
this great phrase for myself when introducing opera singers and London
show cast members at our *Music on the Menu* dinners.

My best night out was spent with a few of the American journalists and
we were joined by a couple of the commentators who were covering the
Open. I remember Julie Heldman being particularly entertaining.
She had risen to be world number five in the early 70s and had played
her last US Open the year before and was back at Forrest Hills again,
talking about the tennis rather than playing it. After visiting a few bars,
we'd arrived at a lively Latin nightclub called Copacabana during the early
hours, and Julie told me that she was enjoying the freedom of no longer
playing, as a night out like this would never have done in preparation for
a match the next day. I was later to discover from Ian Botham who would
become a family friend that this was *exactly* the kind of preparation he
found useful during his years as a top ranked England cricketer!

I remember the atmosphere at those clubs being electric and being where
Sinatra and Dean Martin and Sammy Davis Junior performed was
a huge thrill for me, loving as I do, the thought of 'touching history'.
But... these 40-plus years on... the occasion that really sticks in my mind
was when Julie insisted that those of us remaining upright join her for
breakfast at what I was told was New York's oldest delicatessen – Katzs'
on Manhattan's Lower East Side. We arrived just as they were opening
up at 6am and it was there that I ordered my first pastrami on rye.
Julie advised me to add a portion of potato latkes to soak up the alcohol.

I loved it there and it wasn't just the food (which was more exotic and delicious that anything I had ever eaten back home); it was the nostalgia, the pictures of past patrons on the walls, the original wooden floor with the patina of many generations past. Then there were the smells, the sounds and the people, the neon ads for beer and whiskey and the hard wooden chairs which helped keep us awake, at least until the food arrived. It was a loud, bustling fun place in the heart of New York – **I was there** and I'd been out all-night drinking in New York, New York.

What would Mum and Dad have made of that?!

As for the job I was sent to do? Well, it was pure joy because for a sport-mad kid like me who had all the passion of a champ but lacked the prowess, so being a sports reporter was definitely the next best thing. In almost every stadium, for every sport, in every city, the Press Box is a hallowed place with some of the best seats in the house. And here you can get paid to sit in comfort and look down, both figuratively and literally, on both the action and all the punters who have paid hundreds of pounds, dollars or euros for their seats.

In 1976, the US Open was still held at the old West Side Tennis Club in Queens. It was a very beautiful, elegant venue but even then the event was getting too big and outgrowing it. A year later it would more over to Flushing Meadows, a stadium far larger and able to cope with the crowds who flocked to see the stars, like Jimmy Connors, Bjorn Borg, Chris Evert and our own Virginia Wade.

On my first day I'd got myself in the front row of the unreserved press seats. I had a comfy chair alongside many others and there was a curved desk that stretched before us all. This was repeated in tiers behind me and I thought I'd been very clever, getting myself to the front, close to the action but as it turned out, I'd made a rookie mistake.

Back then how sports reporting – in fact, all reporting – worked was that the reporter would write out their piece and then have a mad scramble to find a phone, make a reverse charge call to the office in London and ask to be put through to "copy", where a person in a very noisy room of 30 or so clerks all clattering away on typewriters, would transcribe their words dictated down the phone line. Once they had done this, the typed pages of foolscap would then be rolled, put into tubes which were sealed and sent through a network of pipes, under air pressure I assume, to other parts of the building where the sub-editors received them, and set to work editing the stories so they would fit the spaces available. Some big department stores had this system too. Money in note form would be 'tubed' sent off, and shortly after another tube would arrive back containing the change.

This Heath Robinson way of working was what was called 'High Tech' in 1976. Of course, there was no way for the reporter to check that their report was being transcribed correctly because, what with the shouting over the noise of other hacks filing their pieces in the Phone Room and the transcriber in Fleet Street straining to hear it over the deafening rattle of typewriters in the room, misheard mistakes were inevitable. And so if your carefully crafted report about Evonne Goolagong winning another tournament appeared under the headline NEW CHAMP'S GOOLIES GONE, there was very little you could do about it. It was an incredibly arcane and imperfect system but it was how things were done back then and so I got on and did them.

But it did mean that after every match I would have to leap out of my comfy chair in the front row and battle my way through the mad scramble of other, wiser reporters, who had placed themselves nearer the exits. So I was always at the back of the mad throng charging to the Phone Room to file copy. All professional camaraderie and courtesy went out the window; it was like the Boxing Days Sales meets Rollerball as shoulders, knees and elbows were mercilessly employed to get one to front of the scrum.

It was only after I had done this a few times, and had the bruises to prove it, that I noticed, sitting in his own *reserved* place in the press box and looking as dapper and debonaire as ever in his colourful bow tie and pink trousers, the award-winning tennis journalist from the Boston Globe, Bud Collins. He never seemed to leave his seat. After a match, as the rowdy exodus to the phones began, Bud just sat there, tapping idly away at his typewriter, making the odd refinement to his copy, without a care in the world. I was intrigued and so after the next match I gave my battered elbows a rest and stayed in my seat and watched in amazement as Bud, finally satisfied with his match report, removed it from the typewriter and then fed it into a machine about the size of a small suitcase that sat on the desk next to him.

I couldn't resist slipping in next to him, introducing myself and asking him what on earth this machine was and what did it do? He explained to me that there was a similar contraption plugged in at his office 200 miles away in Boston, and as the paper emerged from the machine here so it was replicated in the office. This seemed incredible to me. It was like science fiction coming to life. He told me it was called a Facsimile Machine. I was entranced. This was the future and it was a future without me having to jostle my way physically through the competition in order to scream my priceless words down the phone, across the Atlantic, where some cloth-eared cockney word mangler was waiting to mishear it all.

Instead, like my new hero, Bud Collins, I could while away my time between tennis matches staring at the clouds and improving my mind with a cocktail or several.

I wanted to know where I could get one of these miracle 'Fax' Machines. Bud told me that were available on the market and a snip at around $20,000.

With a sigh I thanked him and slunk back to a seat several rows back, next to the exit. Maths was never my strongest subject but even I knew that at 35 quid a day, *I was resigned to many more years of elbowing my colleagues and bellowing down the phone.*

I saw Jimmy Connors play Bjorn Borg in a titanic final, which began in the late afternoon sun and finished a little over three hours later under floodlights. I reported that the match had been fought with gladiatorial combat, with highs and lows of great extreme, both players battling it out like prize fighters refusing to be conquered. The players had very differing styles but were very evenly matched. Jimbo (as Connors was universally known) exploding with energy, running everything down in the way he always did and regularly hitting the lines at the corners. Bjorn, the "Ice Man", coolly covering every inch of the court and regularly unleashing unbelievable passing shots from the back of the court as Jimbo stuck to his serve and volley game and ran out the eventual winner to claim his second US Open crown.

The Ladies Final was enjoyable it in a different way. The grace the poise in the rallies between Chris Evert and Evonne Cawley were a masterclass in how baseline tennis should be played, with Chris being with victor on the day. I remember too having the pleasure of reporting that Virginia Wade was also as a winner that year, in the Ladies Doubles with her Russian partner Olga Morozova.

Footnote:
The Rockford Files. Starring James Garner, one of the best detective series of all time I'd say! You must remember?

Jimmy Connors and the Wimbledon dress rehearsal

Through contacts I made when I was in New York I landed a newly created job as Player Liaison Executive for the Beckenham tennis tournament a couple of years later. Although the prize money at Beckenham was not great, and it didn't help that they competed for top players with a well sponsored tournament in Manchester the same week, the Beckenham tournament was just two weeks before Wimbledon and it was played *on grass,* which made it an extremely attractive proposition for a lot of players.

A Wimbledon title has always been the biggest prize in tennis and getting practice on the faster surface of grass for many of the players was more important than the lure of the bigger prize money elsewhere. Hence Beckenham became known as the dress rehearsal for Wimbledon. Nevertheless some of them still had to be persuaded and in 1978 I found myself appointed as the man to do it and set off, travelling to tournaments in Monte Carlo, Düsseldorf for the Nations Cup and to the French Open in Paris with the brief of persuading as many of the top players as I could to sign up for Beckenham. I had a measure of success getting agreement from some of the great names of the day: Stan Smith, Jamie Fillol, Tom Okker, Vijay Amritraj, Roscoe Tanner and Evonne Cawley (nee Goolagong) to name but a few. Sadly I couldn't claim the credit for luring Connors to Beckenham as he'd played there before, knew its value as a Wimbledon warmup and had agreed long before my involvement to return.

During the tournament one of my jobs was to stand in front of the umpires chair with a microphone introducing the players each day.

I had the bright idea of giving the crowd a little bit of background about them as they knocked-up, which had never been done before and it seemed to be popular with the audience. Although it was not without its problems. The first day was fine. First on was Jimmy Connors, although I can't remember now who he was playing in his first round match but I do remember telling the crowd, "At the Foxgrove Road end, we have Jimmy Connors, 24 years old from Bellevue Illinois". There was a warm reception as he was a big star and so I then reeled off a few facts finishing with "Jimmy is currently ranked number two in the world".

With that a tennis ball whistled past my left ear. Jimmy was standing on the baseline, one hand on hip, the other cupping his ear looking at me shouting "What's my ranking?"

I stuck to my guns and replied, although somewhat hesitantly.

"Number two in the world."

He hit another ball at me and I had to duck, much to the amusement of the crowd. "World number one" he said turning to the crowd "I'm going to win this tournament and I'm going to win Wimbledon!" and then went on to win his opening match comfortably.

Afterwards I was sitting in the clubhouse, clipboard in hand, preparing what I was going to say to introduce the next two players when he stalked in, towelling himself down and was obviously looking for me. Now, Jimmy Connors was a fine player but was known to have a rather fiery temper both on and off court, and it looked like I was about to witness it first-hand and so I thought I would get in first.

"Mr Connors" I started, "I really didn't mean to upset or embarrass you earlier but I did double check and your official, current world ranking is..." I didn't get any further as he cut me off with a disarming laugh. "Hey. It's fine, man. I didn't mean anything back there, hitting the balls at you! It was just a bit of theatre, just something to try to get the crowd on my side". He gave me a laugh. "I thought it went well, didn't you?"

Well, yes, I had to admit, it had gone over well I agreed, very relieved not to have his racquet wrapped around my ear. "I think we work well together, Clive" he went on, smiling. "Perhaps we can make a thing of it."

So the following day my new best mate, Jimbo Connors was playing Roscoe Tanner from Lookout Mountain in Tennessee.

Once again I gave the crowd a bit of background, like at the time Roscoe had the fastest recorded serve in the game at 147 miles an hour, however, as he wasn't in the top 10, I didn't mention rankings. I put the mic down and Jimmy stopped knocking up. "Hey Clive!" he shouted over to me "what's my ranking".

"Mr Connors, you are currently world number 2" I replied and immediately ducked as the inevitable flying ball came my way.

"I thought we got this straightened out yesterday!" retorted Connors. "I suppose you could be described as arguably the world's number one" was my compromise. Jimmy was pleased and the crowd were amused and the match got underway.

On the third day Jimmy had been drawn against the Indian number one Vijay Amritraj. An absolutely charming man who I'm sorry to have lost touch with. I started to do the introductions and the microphone gave up the ghost. I don't know what the problem was but it just wouldn't work. So I put it down and simply said as loudly as I could "There is a problem with the microphone, so ladies and gentlemen, please welcome today's players."

But Jimmy was having none of it. He came over to me and said loudly "If you're not going to tell them about me I'm going to tell them about me." Followed by "Go hit some!" He then put his racket into my hand and shoo'd me away from him, towards the baseline. Fortunately for me I'd played tennis to a good standard but only as a junior and here I was in a white suit, shirt and tie, polished shoes holding a top-of-the-range, metal Wilson T2000 racket, the like of which I had never before swung and whose grip was far too big for me! So I stood on the baseline and by now many in the crowd were laughing at the spectacle. Vijay being the gentleman that he is, gently knocked a ball high over the night that landed perfectly for me to play a forehand return. I concentrated hard and remembered what I had said when I was teaching "take the racket back past your face forward by your waist and follow-through".
I did this and the ball made it over the net.

An amazing thing happened. The crowd applauded!

Vijay easily retrieved the shot and played a gentle crosscourt to my backhand. More confident now, I moved my feet, swivelled my hips and lent into the shot with all the power I could muster, hearing some

stitching somewhere in my jacket rip as the ball left the racket.
Now the pace was hotting up. The crowd cheered this time and Vijay
played a forehand back with a little more power. Buoyed by the support
from the crowd I was right up for this rally and I managed to power
it right back. But my confidence got the better of me and I slammed
it straight into the net.

There was a sigh of disappointment from the crowd and Jimmy who by
then had barged the net cord judge in front of the umpire off his seat and
was sitting legs splayed watching our rally, jumped up, ran over to me
grabbed his racket back and told me "Get outta here, you're too good".

Our exchanges during the rest of the week about his ranking carried on
right up to the day of the final where he beat Stan Smith in two sets.
In those days there was a party on the last night. Everyone who was
involved with the tournament was invited including the players, and for
the second time in a week Jimmy sought me out. He was treating me like
and old chum by this stage, which was nice as I thought I'd just been his
on-court stooge! Jimmy was probably the most competitive man I've ever
known. He was famous for his brashness, his bluster and his downright
intimidation of his opponents but that week he showed me a much softer
side as he reached into a folder he was carrying, pulled out a black and
white photograph of himself volleying at the net on which he'd written
"Clive my God, get it right" and had signed it JC. He said,

"Only you and I know what that means right?!"

"Yes of course, and the thousands
who saw us on court this week"

I'm pleased to tell you
that picture survived
I don't know how many
house moves and it is
still one of my treasures.

Footnote: *Jimmy didn't in fact win Wimbledon that year as he had predicted. It was Bjorn's turn to avenge his US Open defeat at Connor's hands in a disappointing one-sided final dominated by Borg.*

Mr Maskell and Miss Navratilova

Another tennis man who treasured his memories from way back is the lovely and generous *Dan Maskell,** who was the BBC's voice of tennis for many decades, cherished for his trademark comments like "Oh I say" and "a peach of a pass!"

I had first met Dan on that scouting trip to Monte Carlo looking for players for Beckenham and, ever on the lookout for a bit of saleable copy, I took the huge liberty of asking Mr Maskell if he would allow me to interview him. No one had commissioned me to do it, but as I saw him every day in the press room and had exchanged a few pleasantries I thought 'why not?' He graciously agreed to the interview and was exactly the gentleman you would expect him to be, immediately putting me at my ease and telling me to call him Dan. Although I never sold the piece, I felt very privileged to have had 20 minutes or so of his company to myself. As he told me of his many achievements and adventures without being the hero of any of his stories, I began to learn the value of modesty. As a child he'd been a humble ball boy, became a decent professional player and as a coach, taught Princes Charles, Andrew and Princess Anne along the way.

Many, many years later in 1991 I was invited by a great industry friend, Andy Hindle, to a National Sporting Club lunch in London to mark Dan's retirement from commentary when he was around 82 years of age. But in spite of his advanced years he spoke most eloquently and animatedly about some of the players he remembered fondly, especially about John McEnroe, a player who was infamous for his on-court tantrums and criticism of officials. But according to Dan "young John just used to get extremely frustrated with bad line calls. But he never won a bad point. By that I mean on several occasions when a point had been awarded for him and he knew that his shot had been out, he tanked (deliberately lost) the next point. John desperately wanted to win, but he always wanted to win fairly".

He also took us back to the time when Martina Navratilova was a 16-year-old playing in the Girls Singles at Eastbourne, the week prior to Wimbledon, during her first visit to England.

She had come from Czechoslovakia with another tennis playing girl of similar age. They were on their own and had only one tennis dress each which they used to wash out each night. Dan decided they needed a bit of English kindness, so he gathered them up and drove them down to dress designer *Teddy Tinling's** shop in Eastbourne, where he hoped that Teddy might give them each a dress or two. He said he did, but I suspect that Dan might have discreetly paid for them.

On the way back to the digs Martina asked him "Mr Maskell, do you think we could stop for an ice cream. We can't get ice cream in Czechoslovakia. I've only had it once and I thought it was wonderful." So they stopped and he bought them two of the hugest Mr Whippy cones for the grand total of six old pence

A couple of weeks later, Martina was playing in the Girls Singles at Wimbledon but had also gained a wild card entry to the Ladies Singles of the senior tournament, where she survived into the second week before being knocked out in the quarter finals. An amazing achievement as she was still only 16. In those days players could elect to have their prize money paid part cheque and part cash. As Martina had hardly any cash left she chose that option. Later that day she appeared in the commentary box and again thanked Dan for his kindness saying, "Mr Maskell here is the sixpence I owe you for the ice creams".

He said "Of course I refused to take it, and the more I refused the more she insisted. I remember hugging her telling her she had a great career ahead of her. He lent forward, his eyes moistened by this fond memory, as he said quietly into the microphone, "and do you know ladies and gentlemen, I still have that sixpence in my box of treasures today".

Us tennis people are quite a soft a lot you know.

Footnote:
Dan Maskell. From 1929 to 1991 Dan didn't miss a single day at Wimbledon. He said that as a BBC commentator he saw it all from the best seat in the house.

Teddy Tinling. Apparently a British spy during WW2 later designed a number of dresses for Martina. His dresses being sought after by many of the leading lady tennis players of all nationalities, Teddy became known as the most prominent tennis dress designer of the 20th century.

The Sargent Men

I had been commissioned by *Club Squash* magazine to write a monthly column called *Clive Thomas' Celebrity Showcase* where I was to interview well-known people who played squash, which was really starting to take off as a popular racquet sport. This was wonderful for a young journalist as I got to meet and hit it off with a good few of them. As well as F1 driver James Hunt*, Wimbledon men's singles semi-finalist Roger Taylor and England International footballer Dennis Tueart, our team included actor Leonard Rossiter famous as Reggie Perrin, Rigsby and as Joan Collins' would-be suitor in those long remembered Cinzano television ads, theatre icon Tommy Steele, Monty Python's John Cleese, TV comedians Jasper Carrott and Don MacLean, actor William Franklin, and ventriloquist Roger de Courcey.

This is the best of the event programme covers produced for me by David Smith, the Sunday Times cartoonist.

Something that I have noticed over my years of meeting and knowing various celebrities is that actors and comedians are a very competitive breed, often even more so than professional sportsmen and women. And squash is an aggressive game that has to be played full-throttle and played to win. Which is possibly why so many of them were drawn to it. And so I soon had the phone numbers of some very well-known faces who, in addition to their professional talents, were also rather good players of one of the fastest-growing popular sports.

I sensed an opportunity.

I admired the work of the Malcom Sargent Cancer Fund for Children (now called Young Lives vs Cancer) and suggested to my new squash playing celeb chums that we create a team called *The Sargent Men*, supporting the charity by playing competitive matches against club teams at their clubs. We attracted sponsorship, charged the clubs for the visit and so raised some much needed money for the charity. All the celebrities were happy to support the cause and charged not a penny in fees or expenses. I'd become friends with a cartoonist called David Smith whose work was regularly published in The Times and Sunday Times, and was delighted when he volunteered to produce programme covers for me.

The evenings were always full of fun. John (Cleese) might come in to a match doing an exaggerated Ministry of Silly Walks entrance, and he was certainly the inspiration behind he and Tommy kneeling on their squash shoes for the photographers, making it look like they were in a funfair at the Hall of Mirrors. Don had a racquet made with not one but

Clockwise, from bottom left:
BBC commentator Ron Pickering interviewing Tommy and Leonard after their Wembley Final.
Don biting off more than he could chew with British No 2 Bryan Patterson.
John and Tommy pretending to be Diddy Men!
Don's famous double headed racket being admired by top Australian pro Cam Nancarrow.

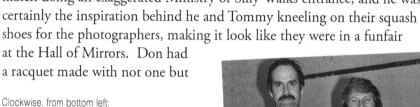

two heads! He could never hit a ball with it in anger as it didn't have the strength of a real racquet, but it must have been photographed hundreds of times. It was quite a revelation to see Len transform from his television character, the shuffling old Rigsby, landlord of some of the dampest flats in town into this dynamic athlete hurtling round the court, with the stamina of a marathon runner winning points with the most deft of touches.

Jasper would even open the door of the court and tell the assembled crowd a story between games. Invariably this took much longer than the 90 seconds interval permitted in the rules, but nobody cared. The audience loved it, and it was his way of grabbing a breather!

Tommy was very fit and practiced most days on the court he had at home. His town car was a mini cooper in British racing green and he told me he had had the boot modified to accommodate his squash bag which contained his shoes, kit, two towels, shampoo, conditioner, Eau Savage aftershave, skin moisturiser, oh and three squash racquets.

James always appeared with his own fan club, usually comprising three or four brightly bejewelled young women almost invariably blonde, who cheered him on with adoring devotion, and he would blow kisses, making *them* all the more excitable, and making the crowd smile and cheer!

The great thing about all the celebrities is that they saw the value of fooling around in doing what they did best, *entertaining,* but they really did want to win! I suppose you don't get to the top in anything without having the drive and a motivation to not give up.

But who was the best? Of the sportsmen, James and Roger. Nothing to choose between them. Of the actors and comedians who played for us the most regularly, Don, Tommy and Len. As proved when we were able to persuade BBC's Saturday afternoon sports programme "Grandstand" to televise the Final of an event we organised where the celebrities played *each other.* Len, having beaten Don in the semi won the event narrowly beating Tommy (who had triumphed over Jasper) in a long exhausting match. At times when the score stood at two games each, both of them considered calling it a day in the deciding 5th game, because as they explained to BBC commentator Ron Pickering after the match, they were completely drained and felt totally debilitated, but to their credit the last few points were the most hard fought of the match, proving that successful people just *don't give up.*

I'm so pleased we did it. We helped a decent charity and had some surprisingly memorable closely fought matches. Glass backed courts had just hit town, so over 100 people could watch in comfort.

*And I made friends for life with *Len, Don and Jasper.*

From left to right
Leonard Rossiter,
James Hunt,
Tommy Steele,
William Franklyn,
Don Maclean.

Footnote:

James Hunt. *Played for us in 1976, the year he was F1 World Champion. These days such an icon would be surrounded by so many layers of assistants, publicists and minders, all of them authorised to say no and few if any with the authority, or the courage to say yes. We live in very different times, and I'm not at all sure we are any the better for it.*

Leonard Rossiter. *Sadly called by the Almighty to join the Heavenly Hosts Team in 1984 when only 58 years of age.*

Prestige - The beginning

By now I had been accepted into the NUJ, I had my Press Card, (London Freelance Branch), and was working as a freelance sports and features journalist for the Daily Mail, which in those days was a decent newspaper appealing to the middle classes of middle England. In addition to this I had my monthly *Clive Thomas Showcase* in Club Squash, and I'd had a few interviews published in Tennis World too. I was travelling extensively to report on a variety of top-class sporting events many of which were sponsored.

On my travels around UK and beyond, as a journalist I was being treated royally, especially by the sponsors, who were desperate to remind my colleagues and I to mention their company or brand repeatedly in our reporting. Traditionally the Title Sponsor of the event received simply that, the title! There seemed to be no industry standard or even a yardstick guideline and I became increasingly aware that some sponsors received an awful lot more from some event organisers than others. It was simply a case of these companies getting not what *they deserved,* but rather *what they negotiated!* This gave me an idea, which in time it proved to be one of my better ones.

But in order to put this idea into action, I realised I needed to learn how to negotiate. So I booked myself onto a three day course given by one of the great negotiating gurus of the 80s, a gentlemen by the name of Roger Davis who taught me the golden rules: there is always more to negotiation than price; how to get more and allow the other party to still feel good about the situation; and, crucially, how to move a deal on if you reach stalemate.

With my past experience of sponsoring companies expectations, my new negotiating skills, my contacts in Fleet Street and my almost suicidal levels of self-belief, I continued my burgeoning career in journalism and as that didn't take up all of my time was able to set myself up as a sponsorship broker and event organiser. I was determined to bring more money into sport and, by acting for the sponsor, earn myself a margin for doing so.

And this was how Prestige Promotions came to be.

On the Toss of a Coin

As time passed and our reputation for doing good work spread I found myself acting for Rothmans, KLM, Mazda Cars and Pirelli and with my secretary Jean Tate, bookkeeper Maureen Hunniford and fellow event manager Jo Teague who had run some big events for the NSPCC now working with me to make my little event company a success, we needed more than my spare bedrooms to work from, so I found some office space to rent in Kings Langley High Street which was within walking distance of home. It was a little old somewhat rickety building down a passageway between a bakers and butchers, which was owned by the butcher, and attached to the back of his shop. Apparently it used to be the slaughterhouse and I reckon they used to freeze the poor things to death as we always had to wear several layers to stay warm.

The butcher was an affable and cheery red faced fellow called Maurice who always wore the ubiquitous striped butcher's apron to cover the evidence of many an enjoyed porterhouse steak. All that was missing was a straw boater and he would have looked like the picture on a Happy Families playing card: *Mr Bone, The Butcher.* We quickly became friends, often meeting on a Friday afternoon in his office or mine for the opportunity to let off steam, and to share a glass or two of whisky to welcome in the weekend.

The months flew by, and during one of our Friday afternoon sessions Maurice told me that the time had come for him to sell what already in my mind at least had become *my building,* and as I was his tenant he wanted to give me first option. He told me the price he wanted, which of course brought forth from me the mandatory sharp intake of breath! I'd never bought a commercial building before so was pleased I'd done the *negotiating skills* course as it would be another chance to put them to the test. I told Maurice I'd see how much I could raise and would make him an offer.

I knew I was in business for the long haul and thought if I could get the office for a decent price it wouldn't do me any harm. When we started we were about £10,000 apart and by the third Friday afternoon of negotiations we were still going back and forth like traders haggling at a horse fair. Maurice said that if we didn't do the deal that afternoon he was putting it on the market. The whisky was going down fast, with both of us becoming more and more animated. In the end we were just £1,000 apart. But the gap felt as wide as The Mighty Zambezi as neither of us would budge from *his* rock-bottom lowest, and *my* absolute maximum. I suppose £1,000 in those days would be worth about £3,500 now. Bear in mind I had quite a big mortgage on my house and my business was far from well-established. I really didn't think I could borrow anymore.

Then Maurice drained his glass, set it down and said "let's get this done. Why don't we toss for it?!"

"What?" I was stunned.

"You mean that we settle this by gambling 1,000 quid on the toss of a coin?"

"Exactly!" said Maurice.

It was a foolhardy thing for me even to even consider as it had been a struggle to get the bank to agree to the loan at my maximum price, which our negotiations had now reached. I'm not sure if it was the testosterone of a young male, the whisky working it's magic, or what has become a trait of mine over the years in not being afraid to take a chance, but I found myself almost agreeing to do it.

"Come on" encouraged Maurice "this is a chance for you to get your hands on your first piece of commercial property at a great price!"

He was right of course. But it was also a great chance for him to unload his freezing cold little rooms that no one else would contemplate buying, without the need of lawyers, estate agents and having to wait a few months to get his hands on what little will be left of the money after their fees! "Let's go down the middle, I'll give you another £500" I blurted out, wondering how on earth I was going to raise that much extra money. But I think Maurice really wanted the buzz of the gamble. He flatly refused and sat there playing with the coin he was keen to toss.

It was almost an out of body experience when I heard myself saying "Okay how are we going to do this?"

He said, "I'll show you the coin so that you can see it has a head and a tail. I'll flick it up, and you can call while the coin is in the air."

I could be feel myself starting to sweat. Now that it was happening I wasn't at all sure it was the right thing to do. The most I had ever gambled in my life was £5 each way on the Derby. And I'd lost that! But I drained my glass, nodded and Maurice tossed. Whilst the coin was spinning I called *tails!* Maurice caught it neatly on the back of his left hand and trapped it with his right to stop it sliding. He lifted his shielding hand slightly and peeped underneath, smiled, slipped the coin into his pocket and held out his hand saying, "Clive, you are a lucky man!"

In that moment I bought my first office, agreeing the price on the toss of a coin and sealing the deal on a handshake!

It's the way I've liked to do business ever since – with a handshake that is, not by getting pissed and tossing a coin to fix the price.

Maurice hadn't revealed the coin and it didn't occur to me at the time that he had done anything but tell the truth. But then I began to wonder why he *didn't* show me the coin. Could it be because it had landed *heads up!* Over the years our friendship has continued to grow and I now have a sneaking suspicion that this was his way of helping a young man on his way. I asked him about it again recently and he simply said "Cliveski – you won it fair and square."

I'm still wondering.

Maurice wasn't only responsible for that piece of good fortune. It was also through him that I met Kay, who has been the love of my life.

It happened like this. Maurice owned another butcher's shop in the Old High Street in Hemel Hempsted, about 15 minutes from what was now really *my office*. Sometime later he converted the basement into a little carvery restaurant which he called *Piggies* – quite clever for a butcher I thought. I lived on my own and Maurice invited me to dine there at mate's rates as often as I liked. Being a chap that could relish a roast dinner on any day of the week I was a frequent visitor and became friends with all of the staff. Maurice was the evening *Maître d'** so we always had a glass or two together after all the orders had been taken.

When Maurice disappeared off for his family summer holiday he got one of the teachers from his daughter's school to *do the Maître d'ing* for him for three weeks. Her name was Kay and I thought she was the most glamorous teacher I had ever met! She was always full of fun and never short of something to chat animatedly about. I knew her equally chatty daughter Jayne, who had been waitressing at *Piggies* before beginning her career in the police and in a poorly concealed attempt to get to know her mother better, during that three weeks I often appeared at the restaurant towards the end of service which was about the time she was sitting down for a well-earned supper, at which she was happy for me to join her. We quickly became friends and then continued dining out together even *after* Maurice had returned from holiday.

We had a few outings the usual things, cinema, theatre a concert or two, and then a very unusual thing – we spent the day at *Live Aid* together. Everyone who was at Wembley that day is forever united in a common remembrance of being part of something unique and extremely special. That just about sealed it for us! Kay came and spent every other weekend with me slowly moving in dress by dress, pair of shoes by pair of shoes until before I knew it, we apparently were living together.

Not that I was complaining!

Maurice had provided me with an office and a girlfriend – and a grand off to boot!

Kay may tell it slightly differently, but this is *my* book not hers!

Place your bets!

Kay has two children: Jayne, who of course I already knew from *Piggies,* and who was about 20 years of age and Simon a couple of years younger. Jayne was very protective of her mum and it took a considerable time before I earned her trust. Simon was away at college and he quickly came on side via the medium of beer and a meal or two out when we visited, in anywhere but a student fast food joint. Oh and more beer!

Introducing Kay to my world was interesting. One of her first trips to an event was to our box at Ascot Racecourse to look after a group from Marlboro Tobacco, where she told me she was completely confused about the betting. I explained as simply as I could, not even tackling odds-on prices, by saying, "if you put a pound on a horse at 20 to 1 and it comes in you would win £20 and get your pound back; at 10 to 1 you would win £10; at 5 to 1, £5 pounds" I asked her if she followed that, and she replied, "Well I think I do, but what happens if I put the bet on at 1 o'clock?"

Not really understanding the betting continued when we were hosting an evening for Case Poclain whose sponsorship of a night's greyhound racing at Wimbledon Stadium had been negotiated by us. I was occupied with some guests so Kay went off to place her first bet by herself. The race was run and she excitedly jumped up saying "Clive, Clive I've got the winner!" I looked at her betting slip and sure enough she had. Beginner's luck I thought.

Second race was exactly the same, and when she had the winner in the third as well I couldn't help but wonder how she'd done it, as while she was cleaning up, it felt like I was paying off the debt of a small South American country via the Tote. I went with her to place her bet on the fourth. She told me, "I always go to the same window as the lady knows what my bet is." I hadn't a clue how she was being so successful - perhaps she was betting on the same two lane numbers in each race. I know some people do that. "Same again" said Kay, when we reached the head of the queue. She handed over £3 but didn't say which dog she was betting on so I asked her what her *same bet each race* was. She said "I just put 50p on each dog – and always get the winner!

That's the idea isn't it, to get the winner?"

48

Losing her money in the process was more than compensated by the mixture of admiring and envious glances from the rest of our group, as word of her success spread.

It was when Kay's first granddaughter, Ruby began calling her Gaga, (either because she couldn't quite pronounce *Grandma* or knew something that we didn't) and me Papa, that I realised I'd made the giant leap from bachelorhood to grandparenting, without getting married or most importantly having any children of my own.

I realise that in these liberal times many couples skip the formality of marriage, but all the grandparents I've ever met have had to commit a significant proportion of their lives and their income to raise at least one child to achieve grandparent status.

Looks like I got away with it - again!

Footnote:
Maître d' ing. To do the work of a Maître d'.

My first Royal Film Premiere

My friend Mark-Foster Brown who had been up at Cambridge with Prince Edward thought that my event organising skills would add weight to the running of an event or two being talked about to benefit the Duke of Edinburgh's Award. I was flattered to be invited to join their committee which met regularly at Buckingham Palace, and was Chaired personally by the young Prince. This led to my being roped into managing *The Riverbank Ball* for them, an event for 1,000 guests in black tie and *backless straps** on the riverbank at Henley. We were able to use hospitality marquees the week after the rowing finished (and before the Henley Festival had been conceived). Using fancy lighting and borrowing a local

Garden Centre's stock of potted plants, palms and small trees, combined with decorative screens and glorious displays created by my flower lady Athena, we converted these functional spaces into two huge and beautiful tented ballrooms with a stage at each end, kitchens, and dressing rooms et al behind the scenes.

The evening glittered with stars, both in the sky above, and at the Ball beginning with Prince Edward delivering a very amusing speech followed by *Billy Connolly* and top of the charts *Bucks Fizz* amongst others performing after dinner. The excited guests danced, guzzled and gassed, and we served a hot survivors breakfast to over 400 people at around 4.30am, just as the sun was rising, catching the mist on the river and giving the place a spiritual and almost otherworldly conciseness. We really earned our stripes that night.

The Survivors! The mist was rising on the river and we were about to serve cooked breakfast to bring The Riverbank Ball to a close.

One of the first high-profile events of *mine* which received Royal Patronage at my invitation, was the premiere of a film featuring my celebrity squash chum, Jasper. It was a comedy called *Jane and The Lost City* based on the Daily Mirror wartime cartoon strip *Jane*, and Jasper had introduced me to Harry Robertson, the film's producer.

Royal Charity Premiere in the presence of HRH The Prince Edward

Odeon Marble Arch

May 11th 1988

He must have really bigged me up as Harry hired me to make all the arrangements for a sparkling black tie evening: first was the screening of the film at The Odeon Marble Arch, and then a big reception and dinner afterwards at The Dorchester on Park Lane which the cast and a host of showbiz stars were attending. I told Prince Edward about it and suggested that we could use the event to raise more funds for the Duke of Edinburg's Award. HRH thought this was a splendid idea and agreed to come to the Premiere and the party. It was all very chi chi and a big responsibility that I was keen not to screw up!

Now, I don't know if you have ever had any dealing with Buckingham Palace but before they entrust a member of the Royal Family to you, they send you a detailed letter outlining the protocol procedure. It reads... in part:

In order to maintain a sense of spontaneous informality to the occasion, guests should not be in a presentation line but rather they should be gathered in groups or clumps of between four to six people.

When the Prince approaches the clump, you, the organiser, must break into the conversation with the words "Forgive me interrupting your conversation..."

Once the clump has fallen silent you may then turn to the Prince and say "May I present... Name of guest."

Guests are to bow from the neck – or curtsey if they are female (and only if they are female). Then if the Prince extends his hand – and only if he extends his hand – guests can extend their hands but must not initiate the touching of the Royal flesh.

Are you following all this?

The form of address is Your Royal Highness first time and may then relax to the informality of Sir.

(I was also warned by one of the courtiers that when meeting The Queen it is strictly forbidden to say 'That reminds me, I must buy a stamp' or to ask if you can have her Cup Final tickets. Anyway, back to the briefing note.)

It is your responsibility to ensure that His Royal Highness meets everyone he should meet and doesn't meet anyone he shouldn't. General discussion may be opened up but awkward or unseemly conversation must be closed down. Chitchat, nattering, blarney and gossip are to be discouraged and direct questions must be directly redirected with the words "We need to move on now Sir".

Every word of this is very nearly true, you know.

When propelling The Prince from clump to clump, you may place a gentle hand in the small of the back, without goosing, and gently press in order to make him go forward. You can make him go left or right by slightly altering the pitch of your hand.

I wondered if I could bring him to a halt with a cry of "Wooah Boy", and if I had a loose sugar lump in my pocket, whether this may be a good time to use it.

Honestly, this is nearly exactly what it almost says.

The briefing note continued:

Please note that if, whilst propelling the Royal Personage around the reception, you lose control of him, Buckingham Palace is not liable for any damage he may cause.

I set to organising everything so that the big night ran like well-oiled clockwork. I had put to good use what I had learned from my days as a Variety Club Barker serving on several of their charity event committees. I formed a committee of my own, inviting some of my clients and well-resourced friends to be involved.

The committee members all agreed to take or sell some advertising space in the souvenir brochure of the Premiere; take or sell tables of 10 for the after film party which of course would include best seats for the film, and by doing this underwrite the charitable donation that was promised to the Prince's nominated charity, The Duke of Edinburgh's Award. In return they were all invited with their partners to a private reception to personally meet HRH at the Dorchester between the film and the formal dinner. The committee members were generous, most of them taking tables and ad space for their own household name companies.

My friends Peter Brenner and Arif Beyzade had a very small business, but Arif set about galvanising support from, it seemed everyone who did business with him, resulting in 30 guests being there at his behest, and 6 pages of advertising sold. Bravo Arif! You SHALL go to the Ball!

We had all enjoyed the film, in which the script required the lovely Kirsten Hughes to reveal her silk lingerie regularly. Jasper played Heinrich Hein, the supposedly evil, but quite endearing baddie, alongside villainess Maud Adams, probably better remembered for her three Bond film appearances most notably as *Octopussy* in the film of the same name. Afterwards I greeted HRH at the Hotel and escorted him into the reception room. As we arrived, he turned to me and said, "I'm glad you're here, Clive, and that know what you're doing because this is the first time I've done one of these on my own."

"Funny you should say that, Sir" I tell him, "It's the first time for me too."

He looks at me rather accusingly and says "But I thought you told my office that you were an old hand at this."

"I know I did" I tell him. "But we young fellows have to start somewhere, don't we?"

And with that, he grinned at me, I placed a hand in the small of his back and propelled him towards the waiting clumps.

And everything goes splendidly. Everyone relaxes in the informality of calling him 'Sir' and there is no inappropriate touching. And I think "My God, I might actually get away with this" And as we approached the final clump I was starting to revel in thoughts of my forthcoming Knighthood... maybe even a peerage?

But as we arrive at the final group and before I can break in with my practised form of words one of the guests, Arif Beyzade... one of *my* committee... turns from the group, and rather than wait for an introduction or indeed bow from the neck, he bows low from the waist making his upper body almost horizontal to the ground, and as he goes down says to His Royal Highness "Hhhello"

"Do I detect a Greek accent in your voice?" Prince Edward replies

"No, I'm *Turkish*, innit!"

"Oh I do apologise", says the Prince quickly. "And how long have you been in England" he asks.

Without pausing for a second Arif informs him, "I've been here 27 years. In fact I've been here longer than YOU!" He continues, animatedly and with increasing volume, "I remember the night you was born! Me an' my wife were so excited 'bout news of Queen havin' another baby"

Prince Edward is clearly unused to such informal conversation with strangers and is bemused and amused in equal measure. He struggled back with a hesitating, "Well after all these years, here I am".

"And I'll tell you something else" says Arif now in full flow, "We love you we do! Us foreigners are more bloody royalist than most of you English!"

Within a minute I had gone from the Ermine to the Tower. However, throughout my life, fate has usually conspired to smile upon me and it was my very good luck to have found the one member of the Royal family who was guaranteed to see the funny side of a complete and utter protocol meltdown like Arif. Edward was a complete Prince about it and told me afterwards how refreshingly unusual it was for a guest to be so relaxed and unphased by meeting him.

Something I am often asked about particularly after a member of the Royal family has attended a function or been especially supportive of a cause, is "How can I say thank you? Is there anything we can give them or is there anything we can do, to express our thanks?" And apart from not inviting Arif to one of their parties, it is a difficult problem. I mean, if Prince Charles has opened your factory or launched your regatta, what do you give to the man who has Cornwall?

I discovered that over the years that the Royal family has been given some pretty extraordinary and impressive gifts. It all started back when Queen Victoria got India – which, let's face it, set the bar pretty high - but I think my favourite story of a Royal gift was told by one member of the Palace staff, who I'm afraid must remain nameless, who told me that after Prince Charles had played a Polo match in Florida was presented with ruddy great, life size sculpture of himself, sitting on a horse, swinging a mallet and made out of cake! Clearly Mr Kipling is still alive and well in America and making exceedingly mad cakes.

I asked what on earth had he done with this life-sized equestrian cake? Did anyone order a swimming pool full of tea to go with it?

Well, the first thought was that it should be cut up and anyone in the Sunshine State who fancied a slice should be invited round for tiffin but this didn't go down too well with the hosts. And the thing is, that whilst it is true that everyone is very careful that they don't offend members of the Royal family, the same applies to members of the Royal family, who are always very careful not to offend their hosts. And the hosts in this case insisted that the cake was a present for the Prince and that he should take it home with him (in a napkin?).

Or in this case, on a seven-ton refrigerated truck, which drove it hundreds of miles to the coast, where it was loaded onto a Royal Navy Frigate, which sailed it back to Portsmouth where it was loaded onto another refrigerated lorry which drove it up to London to be finally delivered to the Buckingham Palace kitchen, where it was stored in one of their enormous walk-in fridges.

And there it sat... until one day in the middle of the night, when the Duchess of York felt a bit peckish...

Footnote:
Backless straps. The sort of evening dresses ladies wear which bare shoulders, arms and a lot of flesh besides, enabling them to stay ultra-cool, while us chaps are overheating in buttoned up collars and ties, linked cuffs on long sleeves, and formal jackets.

Royal Gala
Performance

'ALLO 'ALLO!

in the presence of

HRH The Prince Edward

"Listen Very Carefully.... You will see this Only once!"

on
8th March 1989
at
The London Palladium
and afterwards at
The Hilton Hotel on Park Lane

Prince Edward joined us again for the first stage performance of the now classic TV series 'Allo 'Allo. At the post show dinner, the cast met HRH and Gordon King auctioned one of his magnificent original watercolours.

Buckingham Palace Menu

A keepsake of a dinner we were privileged to be invited to by Prince Edward at Buckingham Palace where, we enjoyed a performance by the cast of "Cats" after coffee. I was surprised to see that the menu was presented in French. One of the valets told me that it had been this way since the Norman conquests of the 11th Century when French became the official language of the court. It is believed that the Royal Family may have kept this in place because of the respect French cuisine still commands around the world to this day.

MENU

Gleneagles Pâté
———

Suprême de Volaille à la Crème
Courgettes au Beurre
Carottes Glacées
Riz Sauvage
———

Crêpes Islandaise

LUNDI, LE 27 FEVRIER, 1989   BUCKINGHAM PALACE

Disturbing the peace!

The 1980s was a boom time for hospitality. I had sold the little office I bought from Maurice the butcher, and with the willing support of my helpful bank manager, the like of which are now an endangered species, I managed to acquire from a firm of architects a splendid three storey sandstone Georgian town house in *Berkhamsted High Street**. It had a big shiny front door, sash windows and room to expand.

These were good times! The City was flourishing and tax laws were far more accommodating than they are today. Back then it was understood that wining, dining and having a generally fine old time was a vital part of the economic boom – so, who was I to argue? And one of the finest old times to be had, a mere 40 miles upstream from London Bridge, was on the banks of the Thames at the annual Henley Royal Regatta.

Lasting for five glorious days (Wednesday to Sunday) at the beginning of July, it is *supposedly* a rowing competition of head-to-head, knock-out contests, rowed over a straight course 1 mile and 550 yards long. The event attracts crews from all over the world who take it all terribly seriously. However, as anyone who has ever attended knows, it is *actually* a splendid day out where you can eat fabulous grub and drink jugs of Pimms and magnificent wines as you lay back in the sunshine with your feet up and yell encouragement to other people in boats who are sweating their backsides off, doing all the hard work.

Now, we had corporate clients aplenty who saw this relaxed afternoon by the river as a good hosting opportunity, but the official hospitality caterers promoted themselves well and were, naturally enough, very protective of their lucrative business. It was a very difficult event to get into; moorings along the straight mile of the course were well sought after and cost a fortune during regatta week and so I figured that if we were to get a slice of this tempting pie we would need to come up with something different. But that was okay as I was building the business up by trying to be different from the rest of the pack. So I rented some not so sought-after land from a farmer off the course just below the start, built marquee on the riverbank and engaged Trevor a chef I knew from Wembley Stadium to take charge of the kitchen with Anna, a former waitress from Ascot now promoted to my Dining Room Manger, to look after front of house.

Next I hired a passenger boat licenced for 150 people and went about creating our own unique atmosphere by booking the 24-piece *National Youth Swing Band* to fill the deck at the bows! My kinda music!

The Henley scene from our boat, with the National Youth Swing Band in the bows delighting the riverbank crowds.

My plan was that after a relaxed lunch on the riverbank our 100 or so guests would gather on the viewing deck behind the band, cast off from our mooring and cruise gently down the length of the course to the strains of Louis Armstrong, Count Basie and of course the great Glenn Miller. We would then turn after Henley Bridge and cruise slowly back taking in some of the rowing races if anyone was interested but most importantly we would be partying and adding some noise in colour to the carnival atmosphere.

The first day of the regatta was a sweltering English summer's day and the band arrived early to set up with several lorry loads of kit. Not only was it enough for a major gig at Wembley but as it was all loaded into the bow of the boat I was terrified the sheer weight of it would sink us before we even cast off! But it was soon all safely aboard and the band were tuned up and playing as the guests boarded merrily after a very good lunch, and we gleefully cast off from the bank a memorable afternoon in prospect.

I knew I had ordered enough booze but as the mercury climbed I hoped that we had enough coke, water and orange juice! Everyone aboard was soon having a rare old time as we cruised gently down the river but what I couldn't have predicted the reaction from those along the course in those highly sought after marquees adjacent to the incredibly expensive moorings. Doubtless they had previously been highly satisfied with their land-based experience but now many saw themselves as being *stranded on the riverbank.* As we glided past the band were in full swing playing the Glenn Miller classics "Moonlight Serenade," "In the Mood" then straight into "Take the A Train" and "Pennsylvania Six Five Thousand".

The guests on the boat were loving being the centre of attention, showing everyone that they really knew how to party on the river! There were so many people on the bank cheering, waving us on and joining in the dancing (some even calling us to moor up where they were) that I got the distinct feeling that many would rather have been on our boat.

I started thinking about how I could get a banner produced overnight, long and thin, to tie onto the rails on the side of our vessel with the words "I BET YOU WISH YOU WERE ON THIS BOAT!" followed by our phone number. I reckoned that over the next four days of the event we could count on getting a tsunami of phone calls about booking for the following year!

And thus we spent a fabulous two hours at the Regatta. However, as we returned to our unfashionable downstream mooring, there was the sort of solemn grey faced, grey suited visitor that you just know is there to suck the joy from the day; he looked like a Chief Inspector of the Fun Police armed with a warrant for my arrest. He came aboard pompously demanding to meet 'The Organiser', which, there was no denying, was me. Luckily, I was sober as I have a rule never to drink when I'm working, but I had decided earlier that I would have a glass or two with my guests back on land at the marquee to celebrate the huge success of the day. However, this was to be denied me as the grey suited gentleman told (rather than asked) me to accompany him immediately to Regatta Headquarters where the Chairman of the Regatta Committee, Peter Coney QC, required to see me as a matter of great urgency.

I did think that if it were of such urgency *he* could come and see *me* but clearly this wasn't how things worked at Henley and so I didn't press the point. I figured it was best to just get it over with, whatever it was, and the sooner it was done the sooner I could get back and get myself on the outside of a few well-deserved cold ones.

His car was waiting and so we climbed in and set off for Regatta HQ which was at the other end of the regatta course and which, if you were paying attention earlier in the chapter, you'll know was a straight mile and 550 yards away. When we arrived I was made to wait for about 15 minutes before being bidden to enter.

The wood panelled office was long and narrow, with trophies and rowing memorabilia lining the walls and illumined cabinets. Very grand and imposing and clearly home to the sort of people who take rowing *very* seriously. The Chairman, wearing an expression that made me glad he wasn't holding a shotgun, sat at the end behind a huge highly polished wooden desk with head bent, reading a document. He didn't greet me or invite me to sit it but peered disdainfully over his pince-nez reading glasses. I thought it was time for me to turn on the award-winning charm.

"Hello there, I'm Clive. I believe you wanted a word" I beamed at him.

Clearly he was a man impervious to charm. Or small talk.

"The noise from your vessel delayed the start of a race this afternoon by two minutes" he said, speaking more through his nose than his mouth. "When we say a race begins at 3.01 we don't mean 3 o'clock or 3.02 we mean 3.01. Do you understand?"

I nodded to show that this was a concept not beyond my grasp.

"Are you planning to have that racket going on tomorrow?"

Up until now, in spite of being spoken down to like some juvenile delinquent idiot, I had held myself in check. But now, hearing the music of the great Glenn Miller being referred to as a 'racket' by this insufferably pompous ass, I felt the hackles starting to rise.

"Yes " I replied unflinchingly. "I am. My guests like it."

"Well I don't. You'll turn it down." Clearly he was a man who considered the words 'Please' or 'Thank You' somehow beneath him.

"Well, Sir" (I wasn't going lose my manners and I've always believed that it stands a fellow in good stead to call a man like that Sir) "I can't really see how we can turn it down because it's a live band".

He glared at me and stated very firmly, "If you don't turn it down I'll have you towed off the reach." Then sarcastically by way of dismissal

"Good afternoon. Sorry to have troubled you" And with that, his eyes dropped back to the document and the interview was clearly over, with the most transparent *fauxpology** I'd ever heard.

His colossally rude and haughty manner (not to mention his slanderous disparagement of Capt. G Miller) made me consider giving him a piece of my mind but I quickly decided that my mind was too valuable a thing to be wasted and also, no matter what the merits of the case or my feelings about receiving such a bollocking, this feller clearly wasn't mucking about and had the power to kick me off the river, which from a business point of view would be less than good. So I bit my tongue and swallowed my pride and on that mixed metaphor left before I could say anything to antagonise him further.

Popular actress Diane Keen, hijacked by the boys in the band!

There was a nice lady at the reception desk and I asked whether the chap who drove me up for the meeting with Mr Coney still about. I needed to get back to my guests, I explained. She smiled with a peculiar mix of charm and vindictiveness and informed me that he had been sent on another errand.

"Do you have any other drivers?" I asked. Again the vindictive smile as she 'regretfully' informed me they didn't. And... before I asked... the waiting time for a taxi on Regatta afternoon was anywhere between 3 days to never.

The penny had dropped. Walking all the way back on this sweltering July afternoon was all part of my punishment. It must've taken me an hour before I realised the second part of my punishment, which was that in my absence no one would close the bar and the free booze – my booze – would continue to flow to those who remained. And long experience had taught me that as long as the free bar was open everyone remained.

There was a hush as, footsore and sweating like a fountain, I finally walked into the marquee. Those still standing and capable of thought had been wondering where I had been and some even worried that I might have fallen into the Thames.

So I stood, holding court telling everyone what had happened. They hung on my every word and I was rewarded during this story against myself with gales of laughter. And it was a consolation to find that I rather like that feeling making a group of people laugh. I'm still in touch with a few who were there that day some 40 odd years ago, and apparently the story gets retold from time to time.

The following day the plastic banner I had ordered, at no inconsiderable cost, had been produced overnight and delivered by courier in time to be tied to the railings of the boat. We hadn't left the mooring before a launch from The Thames Water Authority (another branch of the Fun Police) pulled up alongside, with a uniformed official jobsworth telling me that I couldn't have that advert on the side of the boat and to take it down immediately.

I politely explained that I had checked with the boat owner who said it was ok and was told, "It's against the by-laws to have a moving advert on the river"

"It isn't moving" I explained. "It is stationary and it's the boat that will be moving".

Officer Jobsworth wasn't impressed and I was more firmly told, "Don't get cocky with me, take it down…" and for the second time in as many days "…or I will have you towed off the reach." This is clearly something that gives the good folk of Henley-on-Thames a lot of pleasure.

Until the previous day I never heard the expression *towed off* the reach and if challenged I would've probably said that *toed off* sounded like some kind of sexual deviation.

Again, I was powerless to resist as I had guests booked for the next three days of the regatta so I humbly did as I was told.

Bloody shame, as I was convinced we would have sold out the following year in that single day!

I didn't relish the thought of another interview with the charmless Mr Coney so I decided that we wouldn't start the music until we had passed the starting line – and for good measure we didn't play at the finish either. We did have a dam good blast in the middle of the course and rather than turn after Henley Bridge went on music making all the way down to the lock.

The ingenuity of people on the river was incredible. We passed a New Zealand contingent in a dug-out Maori canoe with eight guys paddling, four on each side and as they drew level the band busked the iconic theme of 'Hawaii Five O'. On another day we spotted Acker Bilk in his trademark black bowler hat and striped waistcoat (although without clarinet) on the riverbank and the band broke into an out of tune few bars of Ackers great hit "Stranger on the Shore".

In the years that followed we ran two big boats, splitting the 30 musicians between them. By then others had caught on to the congenial atmosphere that could be created with on board music. We had blazed a trail, and now others too were annoying Coney's cronies!

Over the years we ran this package we were joined by captains of industry and commerce hosting their own VIPs, and a number of well-known people of the day including the glamorous actress Diane Keen, Jasper who used to have a table, England Managers Ron Greenwood and on a separate occasion Bobby Robson and a few members of the England team and their wives, rugby Internationals Gordon Brown and David Duckham, eccentric weather man Ian McCaskill (who told the nation the night before the Great Storm of 1987 that 'the next 24 hours will be a bit showery') and the even more eccentric racing commentator John McKririck. You'll remember John had outrageous sideburns that looked like a pair of the bushiest squirrel tails stuck in front of each ear! The real rowing enthusiasts weren't interested in what we were doing – they would go to the Members' or Stewards' Enclosures, or The Leander Club.

To be honest, the racing was almost incidental to our guests. They just wanted to have an extended lunch, a good drink and a great day out and in spite of the best efforts of the Chairman of the Regatta Committee and his assorted officious minions, that's exactly what we gave them, always making sure that we really got them "In the Mood!"

Footnote:
__Fauxpology.__ A completely insincere excuse for an apology.

My office building in Berkhamsted. I discovered that when Clementine Hosier (later to become Mrs Winston Churchill) attended Berkhamsted School for Girls between 1900-1903 she lived in what was to become my building. So I erected a plaque that said so, called it Churchill House, and named my room Chartwell after the great man's home in Kent. Another feature woven into my own "touching history" tapestry.

Operation *Fantasy*

The 1980s were great times to be involved in sports sponsorship, and we acted for Rothmans when they sponsored the March F1 team. They knew they weren't the fastest, so set out to win the publicity battle. For the 1982 British Grand Prix I was charged with getting six glamourous ladies, all well known in different walks of life, from Battersea Heliport down to Brands Hatch, and into Rothman's racing overalls to pose with the car and its driver Jochen Mass. *Not too shabby an assignment!*

We called it *"Operation Fantasy."* Actresses Diane Keen, Brit Ekland and Suzanne Danielle; dancer Sue Menhenick (Legs & Co); singer Lynsey de Paul, and Twickenham streaker Erika Roe (who on the day constantly adjusted her front fastening overall zip *ever lower*) succeeded in sending the motor drives of a pack of press photographers into overdrive! Despite the fact that the race was sponsored by Marlboro and won by Niki Lauda in the Marlboro McLaren; that weekend, we stole some of the back pages, and all of the front pages of our national dailies.

Also pipped to the chequered flag by Nigel Mansell in the John Player Lotus; and Jacques Laffite in the Talbot Gitanes, we didn't come close to winning the British Grand Prix on the race track,

but we sure as hell won the publicity race!

Red wine - red *handed* & red *faced*

High on the list of favourites from my own enjoyment of events I put together have been hosting parties around the vineyards and wineries of France. And not just because I am more than a bit partial to a drop of France's finest... although that is also the case.

I have to confess that my fondness for a decent bottle of wine nearly lead me to ruin early in my career, and to save you falling foul as I did, now share this cautionary tale. This is not a story of alcoholic excess and drunkenness. The fact is, I only drank one bottle; but that one bottle could have cost me a small fortune.

I used to hire some of the boats for Henley from a lovely guy called Steve Harris whose cousin is Charles Sichel, of the famous Maison Sichel in Bordeaux. Their jewel in the crown is Chateau Palmer, one of the real wine making aristocrats, and also one of the few Chateaux *not* open to the public

Steve had often thought that his cousin and I would get on famously and could probably do some business, so when Charles came to England to host a series of tastings, Steve took the opportunity to get us together at a Sunday lunchtime tasting at The London Rowing Club. Charles had invited Steve and his wife Gilly, and Steve invited Kay and I.

There we were, with about 80 or so guests seated either side of a big U shaped table in this splendid room overlooking the Thames, enjoying some canapes and looking forward to tasting this most wonderful selection of fine wine, whilst M. Sichel enthusiastically explained the qualities of each one.

I have to confess here, and I know it may be heresy to some, but I'm not one of the 'Swill and Spit' brigade at these things. I'm much more a 'Glug and Gulp' merchant. To me, it's a shame to waste good food but a crime to waste good wine. So after we'd tasted half a dozen or so of these excellent wines I was feeling nicely contented with the world as our host, M. Sichel, told us that we about to sample what was the vinicultural jewel in his family's crown and started sending round the table, a couple of bottles of Chateau Palmer, saying "for obvious reasons, just cover the bottom of your glasses."

Now, depending on the year, a bottle of Palmer from a wine merchant
is going to set you back from around
£200 to over £2,000.
A superior year in a good
restaurant... well you're going
to just hand over your Platinum
Amex and shut your eyes.
The Palmer we were sampling
that day wasn't the absolute
best vintage, but for me... it was
love at first taste. 'Where have
you been all my life?'

And, I know it was unspeakably bad of me, but we all do mad things
when we're in the throes of young love. Instead of passing it along
I slid the bottle surreptitiously under the table and did my best to look
innocent. Simultaneously Steve attracted the attention of a waiter telling
him that "we don't have any Palmer here" and a new bottle duly began its
rounds with us. After merely covering the bottoms of our glasses as we
had been invited to do, we politely passed it on down the table.
And then, Steve, Gilly, Kay and I happily demolished "our" bottle
in the time it took for M. Sichel to tell us all about it.

All of the Sichel wines were superb and at the end of the tasting, Steve
introduced Kay and I to his cousin. I wanted to take the opportunity to
thank him in person for, not only sharing his marvellous wine with us, but
also for being so knowledgeable in his tasting notes, and amusing in his
talk. But before I could say any of this, M. Sichel fixed me with a steely
gaze and simply said "I saw what you did! You sneaked a bottle of my
very fine, very rare and **very expensive** Chateau Palmer under the table
for yourself."

What could I say? I'd been caught out. Well and truly sussed.
And now my treachery had been revealed, my face turned redder than
the wine. "Please, Monsieur Sichel, you must let me pay for
that bottle..." I said.

But he simply held up his hand and said, "You drank the wine.
That is enough. I want you to know - that I know - what you did!"

And with that he turned his back on me and carried on a charming conversation with the other three members of my party, before kissing Kay's hand in farewell and circulating around the rest of the room.

Well, I felt wretched. I have never been so humbled, embarrassed and penitent in my life. And believe me, those aren't things I feel very often so to have all three together... well, I had to do something about it. No time to *procrastineat!** That evening, I rang Steve and through him found the hotel where Charles was staying. I rung him and said "Look, it's Clive Thomas here, you may remember at lunchtime..."

"Yes, yes. I know who you are..."

"Well, I'm calling to say how bad I feel about that bottle of Palmer... and it's far too good a wine to be spoilt by bad feeling so may I please offer you lunch or dinner at your choice of venue as my guest, before you go home?"

And there was the merest pause and then M. Sichel said "Very well, I appreciate your offer, I am free on Tuesday and will be happy to join you for lunch. You can chose the venue." *Phew!*

I put the phone down and immediately set to booking us a table at Simpsons in the Strand, which in those days was one of my favourite places to eat roast meat. They used to have several silver domed mobile carving trolleys, from which succulent roast lamb or beef would be hand carved at your table. For over a century Simpsons had been popular with chess players and I was fascinated to learn that apparently this tradition of carving at the tables began with chess players not wanting to interrupt their games at meal times.

So, two days later I'm sitting down to lunch with Charles. I start off by saying again how sorry I am and... but he waves this away saying "Please, Clive, let us not spoil more good food and wine by discussing this painful subject. This is your apology and I accept..." and I breathed a sigh of relief *"...on condition..."* he continued, smiling at me

"...that as you chose the venue, I choose the wine."

Well. What could I do? Except agree.

And immediately, like a shark sensing blood in the water, the Sommelier was there at Charles' elbow and handing him a wine list the size of the Magna Carta. And with an expression somewhere between a smirk and a grin, he started flicking his way through it. There was the occasional, knowing gasp of "How much!? For that? I wouldn't pay these prices for a Chateau Margaux. Oh, I forget. It's not me that's going to be paying these prices, is it, Clive?"

All I could do was sit there and suffer. And thumb through the food menu, hoping that whatever bank-busting Bordeaux Charles came up with, went well with corned beef sandwiches.

And then, finally, Charles pointed to a name of the list and said, "This one, I think" and the Sommelier's eyebrows disappeared around the back of his ears at the shock of the choice. "And do make sure it's properly decanted."

Well, I ruminated, it served me right. I had pushed my luck too far this time, had been rumbled and now was getting my just desserts. Although, I reflected, I would no doubt be bankrupt by the time we'd reached dessert. But, I was determined to go down with a smile on my face and enjoy my final bottle of wine in Simpsons.

When selecting Simpsons for our lunch, I had forgotten that it was part of The Savoy Hotel next door, and as such its wine selection went from the ordinary, to the very extraordinary, both in quality and price. Would he have let me off lightly and order the 1992 Screaming Eagle at a mere, fifty thousand pounds? No, that was from Napa Valley and surely M. Sichel would go for something from his homeland.

Something like a bottle of 1945 Chateau Mouton Rothschild, a snip at around forty thousand quid?

Or would he have been spiteful and gone for all out for a 1787 Chateau Lafitte for a nice round hundred and ten grand.

Well, I thought, if he has I'll send it back and ask for a new one. And then the Sommelier was crossing the restaurant, with the measured tread of a hangman approaching the condemned cell, holding a bottle and a decanter. Charles was smiling at me, enjoying the moment like a greedy cat toying with a terrified little mouse. I swallowed hard and turned to watch the Sommelier... who was carefully uncorking... a bottle of... house red.

Charles roared with laughter, I breathed a huge sigh of relief

I sent that bottle back (no issue as they sold it by the glass) and we enjoyed a very fine bottle of Gevrey Chambertin with our lunch that day.
But this episode did teach me a lesson and I hope my telling you the story will teach you too.

'If you're going to pinch a bottle of wine from the man who made it... don't get caught!'

We did become friends and I have visited his family's stunningly beautiful Chateau and vineyard in Bordeaux on many occasions.

Footnote:
procrastineat. *To seek out a snack rather than get on with what needs to be done.*

Bollinger's
Debt of Honour

My other favourite wine trips are always in Champagne. And my favourite Champagne house is not only one of the oldest, it is also one of the smallest houses in the region, Ployez Jacquemart, run by the formidable Mademoiselle Jacquemart.

Over the years I have hosted small, interested groups on our *Gastronomy and Grape* adventures. I like to show people a contrast, so I usually include Ruinart, which is the oldest Champagne House, and perhaps

Mercier or Moet, which are two of the biggest and then maybe Billecart Salmon, another small but very high quality producer whose rosé champagne is a sheer delight!

If you get the chance to visit the champagne cellars at Mercier you'll discover that they are so vast there is an electric railway covering 18km (about 11 miles) of track to ferry people and wine, and which is essential for the management of over 4 million bottles! I can't imagine how many *riddlers** they need.

By contrast the cellars at Ployez Jacquemart, who are a farmer producer growing all their own grapes, take ten minutes to walk around and contain a mere 60 thousand bottles. Although tiny it is one of my very favourite champagne houses because their wines, as well as being delicious are the product of love and a tradition that stretches back generations and my show-rounds at Jacquemart have always been undertaken by the daughter of the House, Mademoiselle Jacquemart herself. She is a formidable lady who always make me think of a Bond Girl. Not the ones in bikinis lounging by the poolside, but the ones with the poisoned daggers in the shoes.

However, in spite of her sometimes stern demeanour, she is actually a very charming, kind and exceptionally knowledgeable lady who has not only managed to keep her family business afloat in the cut-throat world of Champagne production, but has also always conducted some of the best tasting sessions I have ever organised.

Except on one occasion, when I took a small group for an evening visit during the harvest and she was not there, as we had arranged. Now, in the past Madame as we all referred to her, had never been as much as two minutes late. But this day, two minutes turned to five minutes... turned to ten... and after twenty minutes I decided that my guests had waited long enough and as the man who had let us in spoke not a word of English, I decided that I had been there enough times to do the tour of the cellars myself. I reckoned I'd made a decent fist of it and so was prepared to host the tasting as well. However, when we arrived back in the tasting room Madame had finally returned, more than one hour late.

She was clearly agitated and full of apologies but, she told us, there had been a crisis. A crisis of the gravest order. It was the time of the harvest:

the most critical time of the year not just for Jacquemarts but for the entire region. And Madame explained gravely, "There aren't nearly enough grapes for our production, so we will not be able to make anything like enough champagne."

Suddenly I completely forgot my irritation at her tardiness. This was disastrous. A catastrophe that could spell the beginning of the end of the business. After two hundred and fifty years, there may be no more Ployez Jacquemart Champagne. I asked Madame what she was going to do and she shrugged and said she had been doing the only thing she could do. She had just been to Bollinger and asked them to give her the grapes she needed.

Now, this struck me as bit of a desperate gamble, akin to grasping at straws. Modern day champagne production is a highly competitive multi-billion pound business and the large, successful market leaders, like Bollinger, aren't in the business of saving their rivals, even when they are as small and relatively insignificant as Madame's house. So what made her think they would?

She selected a chilled magnum of her finest Ployez Jacquemart, which might suddenly be one of the last of the line and opened it. As she poured us all a glass, she told us a story, taking us back to those dark days of 1940, when Germany invaded France and in two short, bitter months had completely overrun and occupied the country. Her country. The whole of the Champagne region was under Nazi control. The Houses still did their best to operate and produce the best wine they could, but she explained with passion that under the occupation of the Nazis it was an extremely difficult time for everyone to say the least.

Her Grandfather was in charge of the Jacquemart House back then and one night they got word that the Germans had arrested the head of Bollinger on suspicion of being a member of the French Resistance which, as everyone in the district knew, he was. In fact he was one of its leaders.

Back then, in 1940, the full horror of what the Nazis were doing in Europe wasn't yet known but what was very common knowledge was that anyone taken by the Nazis was never seen again. Monsieur Bollinger, having been arrested, was as good as dead.

This, for many of the other, smaller houses, could be viewed as a business opportunity. Except Madame's grandfather had another idea. The very next night, with two of his workers and armed with only a couple of hunting rifles, a world war one pistol and a pitchfork, they stormed the local police station, where Bollinger and three other Resistance members were being held and busted them out! It was a suicidal undertaking which, according to Madame, only succeeded because of its naive audacity and a massive slice of Gallic luck. Because it was the very last thing the Germans expected anyone to do and there was only one guard on duty.

Having got Monsieur Bollinger away, they brought him to the Jacquemart estate and hid him behind fake walls in the very cellars below where we were standing. Many Champagne houses had hastily built and "aged" these fake walls at the start of the war to hide away stocks of their best bottles from the thieving invaders and the spaces later became very useful in hiding escaping airmen who had parachuted out over France, on their journey to the coast, or while waiting for an aircraft to come in the dead of night to get them home.

Madame told us how the Nazis ripped the town apart, looking for the escaped prisoners and the people who broke them out. Not many people knew what had happened, and those who did stayed silent. The Nazis were convinced that the Pol Roger's had something to do with it. But little did they know that Madame Pol Roger's role in the Resistance was to waste the time of the Germans and so she actively attracted their attention and deliberately riled them. She did this very successfully by wearing RAF insignia as jewellery, growing red, white and blue flowers in her garden, laid out as French flags, like a series of Tricolore, but she never ever had anyone secreted within the property. Thus the Germans wasted 48 hours at Pol Roger trying to find the escaped men whilst they stayed hidden in the cellars at Jacquemart, being made comfortable and fed by the family. And when the dust finally settled, M Bollinger make his escape across the channel to Britain, where he stayed until the Normandy Landings in 1944 reclaimed the country.

When he finally returned to his estate he invited M. Jacquemart, the two estate workers and their wives to his home, where their very best vintages were shared at a long dinner, of which apparently M. Michelin would have been proud. During the evening he told Madame's grandfather.

"What you did that night was a crazy thing. You risked your lives to save mine. From this day onwards there will always be une *dette d'honneur* from the Bollingers to the Jacquemarts. Whenever a Jacquemart is in trouble and a Bollinger can help, it will be done. And this will pass from Father to Son, from generation to generation." And he made the same solemn pledge to the other men who had also risked their lives.

And so that, Madame told us, is why she had been late. She had been at the House of Bollinger. "This was only the second time since 1946 that we had asked for their help."

I almost couldn't bear to ask. I knew what I wanted the answer to be; I'd heard of the gravity with which a family debt of honour in France is treated "And... what happened?" I asked.
"What do you think?" she said. "They gave me the grapes of course. Salut!"

We either truly touched history that night – or heard the best excuse ever from someone over an hour late for a meeting. What do you think?

Footnote:
Riddlers. *Towards the end of their resting period, the bottles must be moved and rotated to loosen the sediment, mainly dead yeasts, thrown off by second fermentation. Known as 'remuage', translated as riddling, this age old process is done in a wooden 'pupitre' an A-frame-shaped riddling rack, with the bottles neck down ' sur pointe', causing the sediment to collect in the neck of the bottle in preparation for 'disgorgement': the ejecting of the sediment under pressure which then leaves the wine perfectly clear. A good 'remueur' or riddler can handle roughly 40,000 bottles a day. Amazing. Hence the term "he's got a touch of Riddlers Wrist!"*

Two Chefs

Blood

My travels in France invariably have a culinary imperative and I have had the luck and privilege to have eaten in some of the best restaurants in that country. And that doesn't automatically mean the most famous, prestigious or expensive places.

Of course, as anyone with an appetite, palette and waistline like mine knows, the finest restaurants in the world are the ones that have been awarded Michelin stars. I've always found it somewhat ironic that gastronomy should be judged by a company that makes car tyres and whose logo is a little fat bloke who really looks like he should stop eating and start dieting... but I digress). For all their renown and prestige, from choice I don't spend overly much time into Michelin star places; they are all a bit too fussy for me and whilst I much appreciate good service, I don't like the feeling of at least three pairs of eyes on me whilst dining, these circling waiters ready to pounce immediately on a stray breadcrumb as soon as it hits the starched blinding white tablecloth, whilst keeping my wine glass constantly full, ensuring that I completely lose track of just how much has gone down. I often prefer to go where the farmers and fishermen eat and to benefit from the local knowledge that invariably turns up *another great little find*.

But sometimes... well, the lure is just too great to pass by. And so it was that one year Kay and I decided to take a drive through the culinary capital of Gascony, accompanied by old friends and fellow gastronaughts, Oliver and Mavis, with the sole intention of getting a table at the two Michelin starred restaurant at the grandly named Hotel de France in Auch (pronounced *Oosh*). Michelin food in provincial France is significantly better value than in London and the Hotel de France restaurant was owned and run by the legendary chef André Daguin. He was the man credited with inventing duck steak – or as we know them grilled duck breasts – being the first chef to sear duck breasts like a steak. He was also lauded for his use of regional cuisine and for me, one of his signature dishes of fresh foie gras and langoustines was definitely on my wish list.

Obviously this wasn't the sort of restaurant that you just stopped by at on the off chance as you happened to be passing. So we'd phoned ahead and found the Hotel de France had rooms and so decided to book in for the night, as this gave us the head start we needed in securing a table. Hurrah!

We decided to dine early to fully savour what was to be created by this descendant of seven generations of chefs, hoteliers and charcutiers who took over his father's kitchen in 1959, the year after I was born.
This proved to be a fortunate decision because as we settled in the lounge with a pre-dinner drink, M. Daguin himself appeared, to describe some of his dishes and take our order personally. Mavis and I were both attracted to a lamb dish, his description of which made me visibly salivate.

M. Daguin seemed happy to see my drooling anticipation (unlike Kay who told me not to dribble!) and went into delicious detail about the miracle of cuisine that awaited us and it all sounded wonderful until he ended by saying that the lamb would be "served pink". My response to this, as it would be in any restaurant anywhere in the world, was to tell him that it all sounded masterly and delightful, *"but I don't like blood".*

A small look of confusion passed across his features. M. Daguin was a man who was clearly not used to being told how to serve his food, particularly not by someone who was to be blessed with the honour of eating it. But maybe he had misheard. So he simply repeated "we serve it pink."

So I respectfully suggested that he served mine medium and my friend's pink.

His smile now melted like a *dame blanche* in a Dutch oven and was replaced with a fixed (and non-too friendly) stare and retorted.

"How monsieur, am I to get from one piece of meat one portion of pink and the other medium, eh?"

Well, my culinary expertise isn't that wide. I can do things with mince and a pretty decent full English breakfast, but I did respectfully offer an opinion thus: "Well, perhaps I could have the outside pieces that would not be bloody, and my friend would have the middle; or maybe you cut the meat in half and put mine in the oven ahead of hers."

I gave him what I hoped would be a winning smile but, far from appreciating the quick culinary tips, he literally threw his order pad and pen onto the floor turned his back on us and flounced off. Not at all what I would expect from a hospitality professional but perhaps not entirely unexpected from a highly strung Chef, used to most people coming to worship at his temple of gastronomy and who just happened to be French. One of his juniors appeared, picked up the pad and carried on taking the order as if a M. Daguin flounce was an everyday occurrence – and thinking about it now, it probably was.

We were soon shown through to an impressive dining room, with high ceilings and some stained glass in the windows. The tables were nicely spaced and a combination of a muted conversation from those waiting in anticipation of the succulent gastronomic adventure to come, and the clatter of knives, forks and spoons on the plates and dishes of those already immersed in the current culinary delights provided the atmosphere for proper serious dining. Our starters were exceptional, not least my brochette of foie gras and langoustines and, as is the delightful **French** custom in such establishments, an unordered amuse bouche followed in the shape of a white bean and truffle soup of such delicacy and flavour that I would've happily had a Gentleman's portion as my main course. I was in heaven.

The waiters buzzed about like busy bees; (Napoleon's favourite creature apparently - he had bee designs woven into many of his robes) and after a period designed to allow for digestion, and more consumption of a delightful local rosé from Château le Fagé, the main courses arrived under gleaming silver domes reminiscent of Queen Boudicca's breast plates. The contents of the plates were presented like works of art, but to my *anticipointment** my lamb was, to my way of thinking, underdone. Indeed bloody!

So I simply sent it back. Heresy I know but to my delight it did reappear a few minutes later "sans le blood" as I had asked, and I couldn't help but wonder what vengeful misfortunes it may have undergone in the kitchen between plate and grill. Anyway - it was utterly delightful.

The only local wine from that region I knew at that time was of course the ubiquitous Cote du Rhone and the more expensive Chateauneuf du Pape. But there are some truly delicious wines which in those days they didn't export widely but kept for themselves. We were pleased to work our way through a plate of local cheeses to help us to finish one of them, the Vacqueyras made from vines within a short stroll of Chateauneuf. Magnificent! and a firm favourite ever since, along with Gigondas and Rasteau.

The deserts that followed didn't sound extraordinary but appeared as pieces of art with a spider's web of delicate domed sugar work arching over, making them look and taste simply exquisite. Accompanied by an elegant Beaumes de Venise, (literally sunshine in a glass – well that's my translation) and I was in Heaven for the second time in one evening! Unfortunately in those days we didn't have mobile phones, and my camera was a chunky item not to be taken to dinner so I only have the memory to remind me.

But as the last morsel slipped down and the first shirt button popped, a hush fell over the dining room and M. Daguin appeared from the kitchen in pristine starched whites to begin a tour of his domain. He was like a foreign potentate on an overseas tour of goodwill, gliding like a swan from table to table, stopping and exchanging sometimes more than just a few words with each of the appreciative guests. Some gave him a gentle ripple of applause as he approached, others rose to their feet and gave him a slight bow of appreciation. You could see he was loving being a celebrity. World famous – in his own restaurant at least!

Our earlier contretemps had been completely erased from my mind, such had been my delight at what his kitchen had produced and I had thoroughly enjoyed, even if for one night only, becoming part of the romance of this fabled place. During the evening I had even begun to realise that people came here to be enthralled and delighted by the dishes done in exactly in M. Daguin's own style and he wasn't there to modify his cooking methods to suit the palate of a "rosbiff" who was just passing through. Ours was the last table which was to be graced with the maestro's presence and as he approached I rose and flashed Monsieur my widest, toothiest smile, whilst holding out my hand in the age-old conciliatory gesture. Oliver told me later that I was grovelling, but it was a genuine moment for me. However, at the last moment, without giving us a forward glance, he veered deftly off to his right through the service doors and back into his kitchen.

So I never did get to thank him for a truly great meal, and he never got to tell me just what a heathen he truly thought I was!

But I still won't eat blood.

The chef with no name

The second extraordinary chef I want to tell you about I met on another continent not renowned for its fine dining traditions, but who in spite of his lack of Michelin honours was no less skilled (but much more gracious) than his haughty counterpart in Gascony.

This time our travels had taken Kay and I to America. We had a wonderful itinerary planned out, starting in New York where we were staying with our great friends, Jane and Peter Short, before travelling across to the Grand Canyon, then down to New Orleans and finishing up by visiting another pair of old, dear friends, the Jacksons, who lived in Miami.

Travel stories later but for now we're talking chefs.

And this chef resided in New Orleans where for 40 years, until sadly it finally closed in 2020, the leading restaurant in the Big Easy was K-Pauls Louisiana Kitchen. It was an extraordinary success story that was built around two remarkable chefs, Paul Prudhomme and Paul Miller, who shared a culinary vision and were hailed and revered like our Gordon Ramsay. K-Pauls was in the French Quarter, housed in a two-storey building with lots of fancy iron lattice work out front and was just a short, lovely walk from our hotel, through the streets, past buildings with their Victoriana style balconies with trams rattling past and old jazzers sitting on many of the street corners and giving the city its unique and timeless musical vibe which is so good to be part of and enjoy.

I knew K-Pauls' massive international reputation but had no real idea of just how popular this place was until we approached and saw a queue from the front door snaking all the way around the block – there must have been over a hundred people lining up hoping to get in. I knew you had to book to eat upstairs, but downstairs you just turn up on the day and hope to get lucky! Well, I hadn't wanted to go all the way to Louisiana just to trust to luck and so we had booked a table some three months before leaving home to be on the safe side.

So we by-passed the hungry human snake and, doing our best to ignore the envious looks, were shown upstairs to our table. The atmosphere was laid-back and refreshingly unassuming for a restaurant of such great renown, light years away from the cathedral-like reverence of M. Daguin's high temple of Gallic gastronomy. I immediately felt at home there and Kay and I were in a state of high anticipation by the time menus were put in front of us by a charming girl with big hair, bright eyes and a smile that could light up the darkest bayou who introduced herself by saying "Hi I'm Amy-Lou and I'll be your waitress this evening. How are y'all today?"

The obligatory jug of iced water was set down and we turned our attention to the bill of fare. This was real Cajun and creole cooking, in the very place we were told that had invented the blackening process. Part of the menu sounded like a Carpenters record *'Jambalai, crawfish pie, fille gumbo'* then for starters there were *'dancing crab fingers dipped in popcorn batter;* *'stuffed bell peppers'* which turned out to be the size of small footballs; *'barbeque beanie weenie to make you crazy',* and the modestly named *"the best darned grilled chicken I ever ate."*

It was a big dining room, seating around 80 people and most main course items had been very carefully thought through: a fillet of this served on a bed of that, drizzled with a something and accompanied by another something else - all the spices perfectly balanced and flavours finely tuned. I didn't order completely off menu, but I did ask the smiling Amy-Lou if I could have the meat from one dish, the risotto from another and the vegetables and Debris sauce...

Hadn't a clue what it was but was intrigued to find out

Her siren smile flickered for a moment and she replied "Oh my. I've never heard of anything like that! We don't really do that Sir".

I could feel Kay tense across the table; I was making a bit of a habit of annoying world-famous chefs but I proceeded to explain to Amy-Lou that we had come from England, a culinary desert (I lied) but certainly a country at that stage quite backward in its attitude to service, to the country renowned for its fantastic customer indulgence. Her smile radiated back on and she told me that "she would go and ask the chef" and sashayed (if that's what waitresses do in those parts) off to towards the kitchen.

As she went, Kay rolled her long-suffering eyes and told me "you know she won't go and ask the chef. She'll take an order from another table and then come back to us and say the kitchen is too busy. So why don't you just order one of the dishes from the menu?"

Which was fair enough I suppose. So I picked out something complete. But when Amy-Lou came back she was smiling more broadly then before (which I wouldn't have thought was possible) and said she'd spoken to the chef and he would be happy to do as I had asked. I smiled broadly back at her and then at Kay, who refused to meet my smug gaze.

Well! This plate of food was not only the undisputed culinary highlight of the whole of our three weeks in America, but also ranked as one of my top ten meals of all time – and believe me, I have had some pretty top meals in my time. It wasn't just that the ingredients were delicious and perfectly cooked and presented, which is what one would expect, but it was that everything on the plate *worked* with every other thing on the plate. Tastes, textures and aromas danced around each other in the mouth, complementing and enhancing each other delightfully. I was in food heaven and it was one of those meals that (possibly like a condemned man's final one) I wished would never end.

But like all good things it did and I regretfully swallowed the last of it and Amy-Lou beamed back into view to clear the plates, I was moved to say that I'd like to buy a drink for the chef and anyone else in the kitchen who had been involved in putting my meal together. She said she'd pass the message back and within a few short moments returned to the table saying

"Chef will have a beer. And he'd like to have it with you but he can't leave the kitchen".

For me it's always a great honour to be invited by any chef into his inner sanctum so I duly found myself in a noisy, hot steamy clattering working kitchen, the heart of K-Pauls populated by at least 25 guys who all loudly claimed they had a part in creating my dinner! I was greeted by the head chef, an enormous black man taller than me, wider than me and significantly fatter than me. (He probably looked blacker than he really was - his glistening skin contrasting against his gleaming chef whites, and appeared taller as his toque, the tall, round, pleated, starched white hat worn by chefs, added at least another foot and a half). He was clutching the most enormous pitcher of beer but in his huge hand it look like a half pint glass. We clinked glasses and I thanked him for being kind enough to have accommodated my strange culinary request. "Thanks for the beer man" he said in a thick Cajun accent, following up with "I like a customer who knows what he wants, and it's good to meet a man with collateral". I said, "I'm sorry I don't understand what you mean".

He laughed, put his beer down and clasped both of his hands to the front of his enormous stomach, glancing at mine, saying "in the rest of the worl' they just call this fat, but here in New Orleans, we call it collateral – so it's good to meet a man with collateral!"

That's the nicest way anyone has ever commented on my size and coming from him I was flattered. It felt very good to have something in common with a man who had just cooked me one of the best meals I can remember! I asked him his name, and he said "Jus' call me chef. You don't need to know my name, just to remember my food."
What a modest man. But I wish I'd insisted on knowing his name.

Footnote:
Anticipointment. A 20th century accepted portmanteau for the disappointment felt in something you'd eagerly anticipated falling far short of expectations.*

Portmanteau. A word blending the sounds and combining the meanings of two others.

Driving &Drinking
Rallying around Europe

Monte Carlo *or Bust*

Now, I've never been much of a 'petrol-head'. But probably like every red-blooded bloke I enjoy sitting behind the wheel of high-performance sports car and putting my foot down but it's not something I live for. I also value my licence too much to risk losing it, as I'm sure I would in double quick time if I ever owned a machine that could do 150mph in third gear. However, I am canny enough to realise there is a good market, for classic car enthusiasts and would-be Lewis Hamiltons whose idea of heaven is to hare around various parts of Europe for a week or so enjoying the roads, the sights.

And naturally, this being me, some fine dining.

This is exactly who our Prestige Road Rallies have catered to; people with classic cars and super cars and it helps the general bonhomie if they also have a finely tuned sense of humour! Over the years I've been fortunate in getting us into some particularly nice venues to start and finish these events. A favourite rally is our *Monte Carlo or Bust,* named in honour of the classic 1969 movie. The film is a madcap car race through Europe, during which the all-star cast do everything in their power to stop each other reaching the finish line in Monte Carlo and barely a minute passes without a car crashing, exploding or being buried in an avalanche.

Luckily, we invariably managed to avoid these mishaps but, like the film, we always have a lot of laughs along the road.

On several memorable occasions, the start of the rally has been hosted for us by a unique and charmingly *eccentric** couple, Robert and Tanya Lewis. They own the largest and best private car collection in the UK which is truly magnificent and is spread over several aircraft hangar-type buildings on their land. They have collectables from well before WW2 and from every decade since, including a Gull Wing Mercedes, a 1930s Bugatti a Zonder and a Koenigsegg Regera, the fastest production car in the world at just over 300 mph.

There is also the Formula One car that Nigel Mansell won the world championship in, together with an example of every Jaguar that's ever been built and I think the same for Aston Martin. Oh, and a Dalek, which I'm told does exterminate overly demanding guests.

I'm relieved to have survived so far.

They both have a racing licence, and both drive *proper* racing cars, icons from the golden age; Tanya a 1934 MG K3 called *Jenny M* named after her late mother who, says Tanya, was "small, quick and not much got past her!" Robert's choice from the collection is a 1939 Lagonda Le Mans V12, and whilst Tanya's MG is perfect for the twisty tight circuits, Robert can blast his Lagonda on the straights of circuits like Le Mans with devastating effect.

We enjoy contributing to their chosen charity *Help for Heroes* as our thank you. I congratulate them for having now raised well over £3 million for that very worthwhile cause by organising special days at the museum allowing others to delight in their passion for all things motoring across the years.

Susan Hampshire starring with Tony Curtis in the 1969 film *"Monte Carlo or Bust"*.

Gosh – don't we look fierce, like we are Susan's body guards! Joined here by Chris Collett to whom I am indebted for the Rally route planning.

So this particular morning our intrepid drivers enjoyed a private view of the collection whilst munching bacon rolls before being flagged off by Susan Hampshire, who co-starred in the film which had inspired the event.

We made for the coast and hopped across the channel to rendezvous for our first night stop in Reims, right in the heart of the Champagne region.

After a quick shower and change of clothes, our guests were invited to a reception and dinner in the cellars of what is arguably the most famous of all the Champagne houses, Moët & Chandon.

Legend has it that before every military campaign, except one, Napoleon Bonaparte visited the house of his old school friend Jean-Remi Moët, grandson of Claude Moët, who founded the Moët business, and stocked up on cases of champagne. The campaign that he didn't take the bubbly with him? Waterloo, of course.

And to honour this most illustrious of customers Moët & Chandon named one of its vast cellars after him and it was in the Cellar Napoleon we sat down that night to dine.

I am drawn to places where you can feel the history

And on this occasion we could literally touch it too as we were seated at the magnificent oak table where Napoleon bestowed upon Jean-Remi the Legion d'Honneur, the highest award that the French Government could bestow on a civilian. Jean-Remi was not actually French but Dutch (hence pronouncing his name Moët not Mowayhh) and the citation signed at that table reads that the French Government awarded him the Légion d'honneur Cross for "his distinguished service to France in increasing its worldwide reputation for wine" Now I reckon if you're going to be honoured by a government for anything, this is as good a reason as any. And we were there, in that place, sat at the actual table where *they* had sat and made history, enjoying a sumptuous dinner.

And the next morning we were up with la lark, back on the road and off to our next stop. The rally takes place usually over 6 nights and rather than take the easy route through France direct to Monaco, we make it a meander through no less than 5 countries. So from Champagne we head east for a stop in the Black Forest: then we spend a night overlooking Lake Locarno in Switzerland before driving through some beautiful Italian countryside, all the time avoiding motorways where possible and enjoying the prettiest routes that will fit the driving time target of between 3.5 to 5 hours per day. The drive ends along the Italian and French Rivieras before guests take the chequered flag in Monte Carlo. It's not *really* a rally – more of a drive for *ladies and gentlemen* between one gastronomic adventure and the next historic castle or five star hotel.

The Italian Job!

Another popular rally, inspired by a favourite classic movie of mine, *The Italian Job* ends up at a sumptuous last night dinner in the Museum of Ferrari in Maranello.

Are you starting to detect a theme here?

Of course, as even the most resolute pedestrian knows, Ferrari is a legendary car maker of some of most iconic driving machines the world has even seen. The story of Ferrari is full of historic moments and naturally its museum is crammed full of glories and wonders.

When you take the tour, the last space you visit is a huge circular room with something like 20 brilliant red Ferrari Formula One cars, their backs to the wall and their noses pointing into the centre of the room making a smaller circle. Between the cars are displayed the dozens and dozens of trophies that Ferrari and their drivers have won over the years, together with other fascinating memorabilia. Now, as I admitted at the top, I'm not really a petrol head but my first visit to this cathedral of motoring excellence made my spine tingle. It's a very special, almost magical place. I decided on my planning trip that this was the place to have the last night dinner. But when I enquired about booking it I was politely, but firmly told that they didn't serve food in that room (the holy of holies) and that would have to hold the dinner somewhere else.

Now, I could see their point of view, and whilst I do pride myself on being reasonable as those who know me will testify, I'm also nothing if not tenacious and I had my heart set on offering my valiant drivers who had driven the 900 odd miles, an exclusive dinner to remember.

After much to-ing and fro-ing over several months I finally persuaded the Ferrari Museum that *we* should be the first people to host a dinner in this illustrious room. I don't know for sure, I suspect what might have clinched the deal for me was that the dinner was being hosted by none other than Murray Walker, the voice of motorsport for 50 years on the BBC, one of nature's true gentlemen with a motor-sporting pedigree that even Ferrari was impressed by. More on Murray later.

And so, I am proud to say that Prestige Road Rallies where the first (and possibly even the *only*) people to host a dinner in the fabled circular room at the Ferrari museum, with dear old Murray picking out some of the cars on display and describing where they had won a particular trophy, title or honour in that wonderfully animated voice of his, which actually sounds a bit like an F1 car going flat out. We created our own history that night! And as if that weren't enough, we did it again and that time I ended the evening with a song! It came about because the night before I left for this particular trip I had hosted a musical dinner party aboard The Royal Yacht Britannia. It was one of our *Music on the Menu* evenings, where we provided live entertainment between each course. I worked with a delightful group of professional opera singers from The Royal Opera House Covent Garden, and this particular evening comprised opera's greatest hits. I act as compère at these evenings, and many of the first timers in our audience assume that I'm one of the singers. Little do they know that whilst I may have the build of Pavarotti, I sadly don't have his voice to match. But another tremendous performer of my acquaintance, cellist and virtuoso comedienne Rebecca Carrington, who is the daughter of the late, and wonderful broadcaster Desmond Carrington (The Music Goes Round), loaned me her ingenious culinary send up of Nessun Dorma to use. It was kind of her to share, but she did it in the sure knowledge that I represent absolutely no competition! Just two verses and if you've heard me do it you'll know that it's only ever done for a laugh as when I try to sing I usually use more keys than a jailer.

One of the drivers had heard me do this and, to add to the general last night celebrations and merriment, suggested that I perform it for the assembled gathering. Pavarotti's hometown Modena is not that far from Maranello, and that was inspiring enough for me to be up for the challenge!

At the time I'd been doing some fundraising to try to bring a fresh water source to one of the schools that we support in the Maasai Mara, so I let it be known that if I could raise a few hundred pounds for the project via a whip round amongst the guests I could very probably be persuaded to sing. Someone immediately offered £500 for me *not* to sing but they were outbid by the crazy fools who actually wanted to hear me and so I cleared my throat and let rip.

Holding a white table cloth in the fingers of my right hand, like Pavarotti holds his large silk handkerchief I said, "I don't speak Italian so don't know what the words of Nessun Dorma mean, but I think as Luciano is always holding a huge oversized napkin when he sings it, he's probably singing about food – something like this: *to the melody of Nessun Dorma – go on sing it with me now in your head!*

Chicken korma, chicken korma;
Shall I have salad – no! Some pasta
and then a pizza, maybe two, three, four
and an apple pie and ice cream
and to finish .... a ... whole ... tiramisu
tira - mis - uuuu!!!

It struck me as curious and a little bit bonkers that the revenue generated from my 45 second rendition was greater than the four professional opera singers combined had earned for a full evenings work a few days earlier! They would argue of course that they hadn't been paid enough; I've yet to book any act who complains about being overcompensated for their efforts but I reckon I more than made up for it in supplies for the Green Room. These particular divas always used to tell me that the more I gave them to drink in the Green Room, the better they would sing. However, it was always my contention that the more *the guests* drunk, the better they would sound!

Incidentally, if you want to hear me sing I'm still available for after dinner entertainment. And yes, we did raise enough money to allow us to complete the fresh water project at a school called Aitong in Kenya. I'm delighted to tell you the borehole is still producing fresh water today.

Footnote:

**eccentric. Tanya asked me, "Well what do you get for the man who has everything?" Last birthday she bought Robert a sidewinder missile.
"How do you play with that?" I asked incredulously. "You don't – you hang it on the wall of the museum!" Now **that's** eccentric!*

More memories from the rallies

Back to Monte Carlo

Unforgettable moments for me have usually been about the people rather than the cars. Having Murray Walker along on several occasions was of course very special. For one of our finishes we actually succeeded in getting permission

to erect our Finish Line flags right in Casino Square directly in front of the temporary grandstands which had been erected for the *Grand Prix Historique* which was to take place a couple of days later. Murray was ready with the chequered flag for the arrival of our drivers, much to the amusement and interest of passers by of various nationalities, who all seemed to know who he was.

We had a guest on that trip called Shiraz who amazingly *doesn't* drink! He and his two chums in a Ferrari and Rolls Royce Corniche managed to attract 500 euro speeding fines during their first *hour* in France, and rather than be at all sheepish about it, they wore them like badges of honour!

Well *sometimes* its about the cars as other notable entries were a gleaming and throaty 1962 Lotus Cortina which had previously never been further than Brighton and another oldie, a sort of friendly looking 1960 Triumph Herald in wonderful condition. With just a little tightening, tweaking and topping up of engine fluids from their owners en route, both made it to Monte Carlo, turning heads along the way and taking the chequered flag to cheering and great applause from the rest of the group who had already arrived!

Spain, Portugal
&Tuk Tuks

We organised some memorable tours
of the *Paradors** of Spain and Northern
Portugal. Those countries had been
benefactors of millions of Euros that
had been invested in stretches of silky
smooth tarmac, regularly featuring
long sweeping curves through the mountains, which pleased the boys
with heavy right boots no end! We had *two* nights in Oporto staying in
a beautiful, converted Palace on the banks of the Douro.

On the day off from driving I'd arranged lunch at Graham's Port, which
is halfway up a mini mountain with great views, and I'd briefed the guests
to be ready in reception at 11 as we were going on a guided tour of the
city first. I had told them we'd be going off in a couple of minibuses so
it was a complete surprise for them to see ten Tuk Tuks lined up waiting
for them! Memories of Delhi came flooding back to me. They took us all
around the narrow cobbled back streets, and finally along the river so we
arrived for lunch buzzing up the hill sounding like a swarm of mosquitoes!

I liked the Ribeira area of the city the best. Duarte, the young driver
guide in my Tuk Tuk, was from Oporto and obviously had a great love
for his city. He told us the Ribeira had been Porto's commercial centre
and hub for shipments from across the world for centuries. The place
certainly had a fascinating mix of architecture. But now the Ribeira has
a feeling of decaying grandeur, with many of the elegant buildings that
tumble down the hillside towards the river needing a generous dose of
TLC. And a few
thousand Euros wouldn't
go amiss either.

Washing lines draped
with drying clothes
stretched across
alleyways that would
have been far too narrow for a minibus to squeeze through but from
the Tuk Tuks we could take in the scene.

Wrought iron balconies were filled to bursting with plant pots in full bloom, and we came across hidden gems, like a tiny café serving the locals tucked away down a cramped side street, and a Baroque church, simple on the outside but doubtless ornately adorned with gold inside. Then atop one of the many hills a viewpoint where the buildings drop away and we shared a view worthy of a *postcard** out over the terracotta tiled rooftops across the city, down to the Douro and on towards the sea.

Lunch largely comprised the thickest and most tender beef ribs slowly cooked over olive and vine wood. The fat was beautifully crunchy and oh so decadent. I could almost feel my arteries clogging as I wolfed it down! It was perfectly pared with a fine Ribera del Duero, and followed with a few glasses of Graham's finest of course. I told the guests we'd be walking off our feast as it would be all downhill and then along the river. There were some raised eyebrows as the distance was formidable, but at the time we reached the riverbank I stopped by a Dhow and said casually,

I reckon it is a bit far to walk, so we'll hop on this – the captain said he'd take us!

All arranged in advance of course.

Footnote:

*Postcard. How we used to share memories of our travels before smart phones. They also required a stamp.

*Paradors. Another real word. Paradors are very good quality hotels created within historic buildings like castles, palaces and monasteries, run by the governments of Spain and Portugal, and arranged for us by the ever dependable Gary Drewett.

Whisky *Galore!*

On a rally around Scotland, we had enjoyed a late night at the Torridon Hotel, way up in the Highlands, in the most picturesque of settings by a tranquil loch with mountains reflected in the clear water. The hotel has the distinction of a huge ceiling high cabinet which holds 365 different whiskies. That's right, one for every day of the year. There are two token "foreign" whiskeys featured. One from Ireland and another from Japan. Just to show there are no hard feelings!

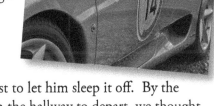

One guest, let's call him *David** to avoid his embarrassment, tried to work his way through a few weeks' worth in that single sitting and was noticeably absent from breakfast the following morning. Despite a few calls to his room on the hotel phone, we'd not heard and seen hide nor hair of him and thought it best to let him sleep it off. By the time guests were beginning to gather in the hallway to depart, we thought we should rouse him, but he'd locked his door, leaving the key in the lock.

No amount of banging produced a response, so the owner reluctantly agreed that we should break in. I honestly thought we'd find the room empty as a result of him slipping out early for some rejuvenating fresh air. Chris thought he'd possibly be bereft of life, but having died happy!

I was praying for the former of course. We discovered that neither assumption was right. He was in bed, snoring softly having slept through the various phone calls and the break in! On waking he struggled to speak, which was not a good sign, and frankly looked awful. A whisky hangover can do that to even the most robust of men!

With our help he managed to put his feet on the floor, and we pulled him upright – and he found he couldn't stand, promptly falling back on to the bed. We tried to get some water into him, but it made him want to puke (a word invented by The Bard, just so you know!) Fearing alcoholic poisoning, Chris, Colin and I got him into a hotel bathrobe, almost carried him down stairs and manoeuvred him as gently as we could into my car, for Colin and me to take him to the local doctor's surgery who had been warned of our imminent arrival. I prayed again – this time that he wouldn't succumb to the need to *glenupchuck** en route.

David was unable to speak coherently so we had told the Doctor the almost certain cause of his distress, but she didn't agree and decided it could be much more serious than a bad hangover. She feared a stroke, or worse (what could be worse I wondered) but confessed that she couldn't actually pinpoint what was wrong with him and announced that there was a very urgent need for him to be in hospital without any delay; and in so saying picked up the phone to summon a Scottish NHS helicopter to take him immediately to Inverness some 65 miles distant. We heard the rotor blades not 10 minutes later and the chopper landed within a few feet of the car park in the adjacent field. This was seriously impressive but David had other ideas. "I'm not going in it" he declared, at last able to string a few words together. "I'm claustrophobic and I can't go in it". We cajoled him. The paramedics insisted, but David would not be persuaded.

The doctor was furious – not only at David's stubbornness but at the waste of thousands of pounds of taxpayers money. However, even in the face of a full on bollocking from the doctor David would not be moved (at least by helicopter). But he still needed to get to hospital and so an ambulance was summoned, as NHS Scotland was not about to give up. I thought perhaps that as their most famous export was the most likely cause of this man's pain, they felt a degree of responsibility for getting him sorted, despite his rejecting their helicopter.

Thank goodness he didn't argue about being confined to the back of an ambulance. Although given the choice of two hours in a tin box over bumpy roads or 20 minutes in a chopper – I know what I would have gone for – a window seat in the helicopter every time.

The ambulance left and finally so did we, heading for our next stop, which was Culloden House in Inverness. And that evening, believe it or not, David turned up in a taxi at the hotel about 6.30pm, remarkably looking

pretty much right as rain, with speech fully restored. He said they'd run some tests and still didn't know what the problem was, so he'd discharged himself telling them, "If you find out what's wrong with me and want me to come back tomorrow, here's my phone number, just let me know. I'm going over to the hotel now to have dinner with my friends!"
The other guests, who by now all knew about the helicopter being sent away couldn't quite work out if this man was very tough, plain senseless, or perhaps a combination of both!

But have dinner he did. No whisky mind! He said he felt 95% ok next morning, and drove on to finish the rally. At the last night dinner on board *The Royal Yacht Britannia* two nights later, having been aided by Stewart Campbell, the even helpful GM at Malmaison in Edinburgh, I was able to present the "Prestige Road Rally Club Special Award" to David. A scale model of a helicopter, as a keepsake from that lucky escape. Rather than show any signs of the slightest embarrassment at what could have been an obstinacy that cost him his life, he beamed from ear to ear and said the "trophy" would take absolute pride of place in his living room, and be the prompt for him telling any visitors the tale of how he came by it.

I think that he and we always knew precisely what has caused his troubles. Perhaps the doctor's training had never included having to arrange these words into a possible diagnosis – *malt, single* and *excessive!*

Footnote:
Glenupchuck. To vomit a night's consumption of expensive single malts.

*David. To avoid potential embarrassment to other Davids who are known to have rallied with us, it was David **Harrison** who sent the potentially life-saving helicopter away.*

Cline's Road Rally **Scrapbook**

The Lord Provost of Edinburgh
loans us Louise, his piper,
to finish our Scottish Rallies.

Forever in my corner, Colin
and Chris. Not really *work*
is it gentlemen?!

Give Beatriz a sweeping
staircase and she'll always
make a grand entrance!

Bob and Glenn –
the Little and Large
of our Road Rally Club

Beware! The Swiss Gendarmerie

Not everyone comes on a Prestige Rally in a fancy or collectable car. Sue Seekens with her husband Ken was a very popular rallier and had the courage to come in her Smart car! She is pleased for me to use her name, unlike thee three drivers who were actually arrested on one of the later rallies and have requested anonymity (so I'll just call them Tom, Nick and Harry).

We do warn people *not* to speed in Switzerland where the gendarmerie can be particularly picky about the odd kilometre or two over the prescribed. We say that if they feel a need, perhaps to let rip in Italy where the police really do *sometimes* stand back and just admire the supercars. These three guys – I think Tom was in a Porsche 911 GT3, Nick a Ferrari Enzo (the one with a nose like an F1 car) and Harry in a Lamborghini Veneno, decided to race – *in Switzerland!* A crazy thing to do as racing carries *much* stiffer penalties than merely breaking the speed limit!

We learned later that the police had been tipped off by a local resident, startled by the *carcophany** as the cars roared past. They sprang into action, *blues and twos,* or whatever the Polizia equivalent is demonstrating their intentions, but couldn't keep up with our aspiring Damon Hills so a road block was formed, forcing them to stop whereupon they were promptly arrested.

The lads arrived very late into dinner that night, just as I was doing my daily post desert "housekeeping talk" only to discover on walking in to an enthusiastic round of spontaneous applause, that they had unwittingly become the heroes of the hour. Taking the mic from me, Tom revelled in explaining that after arrest, they had been dramatically separated by being frogmarched to individual cells, left for three hours, to be then interviewed *individually* and told "We have you on film *racing*!" Now quickly growing into their new celebrity personas they explained animatedly that none of them had cracked under pressure and admitted to racing, even under "intensive interrogation which stopped just short of waterboarding, having our finger nails pulled, and being electrocuted through our testicles!" Apparently.

After several hours they were told that they would be released but each driver would have to pay an immediate 1500 Euro fine and be bound to report back for trial at a later date. Nick apparently told the police that he'd decline to pay the fine and would sort it all out at the trial.

"Yes," said the officer, "You can leave without paying the fine. But we will keep the car."

"And I collect it at the court hearing?" Nick asked.

"No" replied the officer, "We sell it at auction in 15 days' time to pay your fine!"

"Nick's voice went up a full octave," Harry told us.

"Do you take American Express?" He asked hopefully, all the fight gone out of him,

"That will do nicely"

Replied the policeman, coming over to him clutching the card machine.

Harry said to the others, "When we were separated, did any of the police use any sexual interrogation techniques on either of you, apart from the electrocuting of our testicles?" "Well strange you should ask" said Tom. "One of them got very busy in my underpants. Her name is Anna and I'm seeing her again tomorrow!"

You should know, if you are considering joining us on a road trip that this kind of behaviour is unusual, and we rarely have any *real* hooligans or drunkards along!

Footnote:
Carcophany. The loud noise made by the roar of several supercars passing at speed.

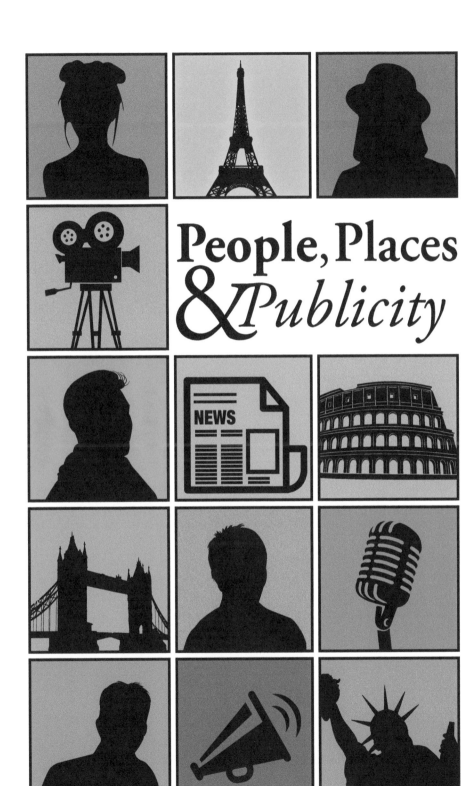

People, Places
&Publicity

The Voice of **Formula 1**

The first book launch evening I organised was for Ian Botham and it set the foundations of a lovely relationship with a lady called Jane Beaton who was head of publicity at Harper Collins. Jane was a genius at shining the light on those whose work she was promoting.

Murray Walker, another Harper Collins author had written his long-awaited autobiography and Jane offered us the opportunity to put on a speaker evening with Murray to promote the book. I thought the RAC in Pall Mall would be an ideal venue. Luckily, they agreed as did a significant number of their members and to my delight we swiftly filled 200 places and promptly opened the booking lines for a second night. Murray and I quickly hit it off, and he proved to be one of the most popular authors we have ever worked with.

The RAC is full of beautiful paintings, most motorsport related and I remember, as the guests were going into the main room, Murray and I stood in a side corridor chatting. On the wall beside us hung a huge depiction of a meeting of the Rolls-Royce Owners Club probably from the 1950s. Every detail of the cars, their owners and the few bystanders had been expertly captured by the artist and I was privileged to have heard at that moment a new, never before spoken, Murrayism as he exclaimed " I would recognise every one of those people – *if I knew who they were!*"

This was typical of Murray throughout his commentating career. He said what was in his head at that moment – even if it only made sense to himself. There are enough to fill a book by themselves but here are a few of my favourites:

- *This is lap 45, and the next lap is lap 46.*
- *And now excuse me while I interrupt myself.*
- *There is nothing wrong with the Ferrari, except it's on fire!*
- *I can't imagine what the conditions are like in the cockpit, they must be unimaginable!*

I've heard Murray's after dinner speech many times since that first book launch, and several things stay with me. He is a man with two voices. His conversational voice is calm measured and with a deep resonance: but his commentating voice which came out as he bounced about excitedly on the balls of his feet clutching the hand held mic, sent his voice higher and his speech ever faster as he often frantically, and always passionately, tried to keep up with telling the viewers about whatever motoring drama was playing out before him.

Even as a man in his 80s, his memory still had a photographic quality. I remember on that first evening in the RAC, one of the guests started a question, rather pompously with "In 1962 when Wolfgang Von Trips won the British Grand Prix at Silverstone, beating John Surtees into second place…."

Murray help up his hand and said, very politely, "Sorry to butt in, but the 1962 British Grand Prix was on the old circuit at Aintree. Von Trips won it in 1961 and John Surtees was second in 1960, 62 and 63."

"Ah yes" said the pompous guest. "I think you are right about Surtees but I'm sure Von Trips won it in '62."

"It was definitely '61" said Murray, still polite but firm. "Von Trips drove a Ferrari and Ferrari dominated the podium that year, and I can be sure because sadly he was killed during the 1961 Italian Grand Prix at Monza."

Someone else chipped in, "But didn't Jim Clark dominate the British Grand Prix in the early 1960s?"

"Well sort of" said Murray, starting to warm to his theme. "Jack Brabham won it at Silverstone in 1960, but Jim Clarke did win it for four consecutive years from 1962, until Brabham broke the spell in 1966 to reclaim his crown."

I was amazed at his apparent total recall. I'd jotted down all these legendary names and dates Murray had remembered, googled "British Grand Prix" when I got back to my room and shouldn't have been surprised to discover that Murray was absolutely right, on every single one of those facts.

But I think Murray really came into his own when telling stories against himself. He had this expression when he was about to proclaim the outcome of a race or even of the championship which was *"Unless I am very much mistaken..."* followed by his prediction of the almost certain outcome. He liked to tell guests about commentating on the French Grand Prix when Alain Prost, who had built up a commanding lead and had even lapped a couple of the stragglers, was approaching the final curve at the Paul Ricard circuit, with the chequered flag almost in sight and only the final bend to negotiate.

Murray said his usual, "Unless I am very much mistaken... Alain Prost is about to win his first French Grand Prix!" To be swiftly followed with *"Oh my God!* I *am* very much mistaken – Prost has just spun off!"

Murray went down very well in Australia and told me that he always enjoyed his trips there, especially the legendary friendliness of the average Aussie. On one occasion when he was on his way to the paddock in Adelaide, he spotted a group of young enthusiastic F1 supporters coming the other way all wearing T-shirts with printed a photo of him and underneath the words *"unless I am very much mistaken..."* He then roared with laughter when in unison they all turned around so that he was able to read *"Yes!* **I am** *very much mistaken!"* printed on the back of each one.

Some of the drivers became convinced that from the commentary position Murray was able to somehow put a jinx on them by predicting some disaster that would strike moments later. Murray frequently told the story at our events that in 1982 at the last race of the season at The Caesars Palace Grand Prix in Las Vegas, Keke Rosberg approached Murray before the race began saying "Murray can I have a word?" Murray always explained to us that commentators and journalists spent much of their time trying to dig the drivers out of their caravans to get an interview or a quote on race days, often unsuccessfully, so he welcomed him warmly and said "Of course Keke, what can I do for you?"

"As you know if I make it onto the podium this afternoon I will win the World Championship" Rosberg said.

"Yes Keke I know" responded Murray. "I've been telling people that since the last race."

"Please don't be offended Murray," the soon-to-be-World Champion said, "but if at any stage it *does look like* I am about to win the World Championship would you please **not say anything about it!**"

The 1996 season was a very special one for Murray. The World Driver's Championship looked as if it could go to one of the Williams Renault drivers, Jacques Villeneuve or Damon Hill, who were nip and tuck at the top of the points table, closely followed by Michael Schumacher driving for Ferrari. Damon had been runner up in the Championship the past two years and had been saying since the start of the season that he felt this was to be *his* year. Murray had been close to Damon's father Graham and his mother Betty, and had known Damon since he was a small boy.

Murray is the consummate professional and always kept his personal thoughts out of whatever he was describing, including some of the terrible accidents which used to be a regular feature of F1 many years ago. But on October 13th, 1996 in Suzuka, Damon Hill, already nine points ahead of his teammate and expected to drive a tactical race, went all out to win. He pipped Michael Schumacher into second place to take the chequered flag at the Japanese Grand Prix and in so doing winning his first World Championship to the delight of almost everyone back home in Britain. And the emotion in Murray's voice was clearly discernible as Damon became the only son of an F1 World Champion to follow in his father's tyre tracks. As he crossed the finishing line Murray had to pause his commentary saying, "I have to stop now as I have a lump in my throat." That lump bought a tear to the eye of many of us who had been cheering Damon home that day. Even after a pause Murray continued "I am, for once, almost at a loss for words" Murray told me that he cherishes commentating on that victory of Damon's as one of the highlights of *his own* career.

Long before *Monte Carlo or Bust* had become our signature bi-annual car rally Murray had agreed to come down and wave the chequered flag at the finishing line in Monte Carlo to make the end that bit more special. I thought I'd push my luck (as usual) and ask if he'd say a few words at the last night dinner. I knew that Murray was a veteran of over 40 Monaco Grands Prix and would have plenty to say. Well not only did he agree to do it, but for my fledgling event agreed to do it for half of his usual fee – a tremendous gesture that enabled me to offer yet another new and unique

Prestige event at a very good price. So successful was our formula that we ran the event every second year, and I'm delighted to say that Murray joined us on four further occasions.

At one of those Monaco dinners I'd invited my chum Jonathan Truss, a tremendous wildlife artist who had by then accompanied many of my wildlife safaris, to sit with Murray and me. I took the lectern to introduce Murray, and having been previously told by him that my impersonation of his voice was "better than most" I felt able to do it in his company, much to the amusement of any assembled gathering. So in his voice I reeled off a few of his Murrayisms. Unbeknown to me until later, Murray turned to Trussy and said "Oh good grief, it looks like Clive's going to be doing my whole speech!"

I would normally host the event from the start, so only link up with Murray once he had arrived in Monte Carlo just a few hours ahead of the guests. But on one occasion I decided leave it to a couple of my very able lieutenants to look after the guests en route and meet everyone at the end. The guests were due in on May 11 so Kay and *I flew down with Murray** on the previous day, which happened to be my birthday. I had booked a table at one of my favourite eateries in Monaco, the *Quai des Artistes* down at the harbour and of course Murray joined us for dinner.

As we drove down from the hotel Murray was saying how different and peaceful it all looked compared to when the F1 cars are flying through the narrow streets, skimming walls and scraping kerbs.

"During the Grand Prix it's like a pressure cooker here," he told us. "The pressure builds, the teams feel it, the drivers feel it, the crowds can feel it too, and that is part of the unique atmosphere of the Monaco Grand Prix".

Part of the route to the harbour took us onto the F1 circuit and immediately Murray became animated, almost in his high excitement commentating mode with comments like "This where Ayrton Senna drove his McLaren into the wall in 1988!" Then, "Here is Tabac Corner where Martin Brundle flipped his car!" Suddenly Murray's voice went up an audible half an octave telling us, "*...and this is Mirabeau, where Brundle crashed again two years later when he drove across the path of Patrick Tambay!!*"

What a great birthday treat to have had our own personal commentary, actually on the circuit in Monaco from the voice of Formula One!

Later at dinner, as we both started to reminisce on our own careers about places we'd been and times we'd enjoyed, I said to Murray "I suppose by now you've ticked all the boxes on your bucket list. You've been everywhere you wanted to go you've met everyone you wanted to meet – and probably become friends with some of them?"

"Yes" he said, picking up a tea-light-in-a -glass thinking it was his drink, "Pretty much, but there is still one thing I'd like to do but you have to be invited to do it, and I haven't been invited"

"What's that?" I enquired.

"I'd like to be a cast away on Desert Island Discs" he said rather wistfully. It apparently had been a long-held wish of his and he confessed that he'd even chosen the seven discs he would play.

At that moment I decided to make it my quest to do all I could to get him castaway on the show and when I got back home I checked Radio Times to get the name of the show's producer and then rang the BBC and asked to speak to her, assuming the air of someone who was expecting to be put through. I was connected to a Deputy Assistant Production Assistant who confessed that she had no idea who Murray Walker was!

I said, "Let me guess. You are twenty-something, a graduate entry into the BBC, and have no interest in motorsport?"

"Yes!" she exclaimed "you're right on all counts".

So I suggested to her that perhaps she mentioned Murray's name to one or two of her older colleagues and if any of *them* had heard of him then maybe she might ring me back. She did and about 20 minutes later rang back saying "I feel so embarrassed. Apparently Mr Walker worked for us for about 50 years!"

I explained just how loved Murray was by the British public and she said she would see what she could do to get him on. When I told Murray he said, "Really Clive you shouldn't".

But I could tell he was delighted.

I'd heard nothing for about three months so I phoned again and this time got the Producer's Assistant – this shows how long ago it was as they were very keen to get Olympians on as we were coming up to the London Olympics. But I was told that Murray's name was firmly on the list for post-Olympics. Well we did so well that post Olympics there were quite a few more Olympians for them to have on.

In a call to Murray about a year later I discovered he wasn't in good spirits. He'd been on a cruise, taken a fall, broken a hip and had spent a period of time in a German hospital which he hadn't enjoyed one bit. I'd never heard him quite so down. But three days later he rang me in a state of some excitement his voice almost at commentating pitch again, telling me that morning the postman had dropped a letter on his mat from the BBC.

"It was an invitation for me to appear on Desert Island Discs! I know that as sure as water wears down a stone this was your doing and I thank you from the bottom of my heart!"

The old Murray was back! Interested, engaged and excited!

He later told me that he had, "a wonderful day and had been spoilt by the *luscious* Kirsty Young", as he described her, and that the experience was every bit as fulfilling as he knew it would be. His first disc was Fleetwood Mac's *The Chain* which

Prestige Promotions proudly presents

A Celebration of
Murray Walker's
60 years in motorsport

The Monte Carlo Bay Hotel
Monaco

September 15th 2010

introduced every BBC F1 broadcast and effectively had become Murray's signature tune, and finished with a classic from a man we both admire, Glenn Miller and *In the Mood*.

That broadcast is still in the Listening Figures top five of any British castaway. Murray had done a lot for me, and I was very pleased to have been able to do something for him, the most modest, genuine of men.

Footnote:
The day before we flew down with Murray, we spent the afternoon with our granddaughters, Ruby and Scarlet. Scarlet was by then about 7 years of age. When she wished us a happy holiday I explained that I was to be **working in Monaco, and she asked what I would be doing. So I chatted her through the weekend – driving Murray, talking to all of our guests making sure they had a good time, and then having dinner with everyone. She looked up at me and said,*

"So you are going to be driving, talking and eating. It's not really work is it Papa?!"

During the writing of this book we sadly lost Murray as he was called to the great commentary box in the sky, but not before he had read several of my stories including the one about him that you have just completed. It was in my conversation with him on his 95th birthday that he spoke the words I'm privileged to have quoted on the back cover.

Champagne *without bubbles*

Like Murray, I have spent many nights staying in hotels of varying standards. For a hotel to establish a reputation as a *great* hotel it needs to be a fabulous looking building in a prime location, offering extreme comfort, an immensely atmospheric bar, and outstanding food. But none of these elements is as important as *the people*. They need to be passionate about every aspect of guest care, provide astonishingly good service, and must work as a cohesive team. For that to happen the person at the top has to himself or herself be an extraordinarily multitalented individual. And if he is, he may become an extraordinary General Manager.

I've known many exceptional hotel General Managers, and several, like Simon Wong, Ciaran Fahey, Tony Murkett, JP Kavanagh and Stewart Campbell, have become personal friends. They all have these qualities in common: clarity, consistency and commitment. The role of the General Manager in a top hotel is amongst other things to be all things to all people. However, whilst wearing many hats, the otherwise astute GM may sometimes miss the obvious.

Whilst still in his early thirties, Tony Murkett became the youngest ever General Manager of Grosvenor House Hotel on Park Lane, then the flagship hotel of Lord Forte's extensive collection, and we became friendly as Prestige held an increasing number of high budget events there. Tony was not only a lovely chap to spend time with, but also a very useful man to know, with a genius for getting things done quietly and efficiently.

One spring, I had just returned from one of my trips escorting a group around a few of the Champagne Houses in Reims and Epernay, when I phoned Tony to tell him about it, and to explain to him that Moët had been pioneering a new ecologically friendly champagne: one *without* the bubbles. I told him that research had shown that just as gas emissions from cows have a detrimental effect on the environment, so the explosion of gas in the bubbles every time a champagne bottle is uncorked, is causing damage and could even be harmful to the ozone layer.

So, with this in mind, Moët had developed a style of champagne which still made that popping sound when being uncorked, tasted the same but miraculously - no bubbles!

"Surely," said Tony, "Champagne without bubbles is simply white wine, isn't it?"

"Moët are afraid that this is what everyone will think" I said. "So they have asked me if I can help them overcome the natural resistance by getting a few bottles into high profile, prestigious hotels in England, like Grosvenor House."

I was in full canter now and continued, "If people see this new bubble-less champagne displayed on bars in *your* hotel, I would think a number of them will be tempted to give it a try. In fact Moët told me that they will allocate me ten promotional cases to give away free of charge, on the understanding that wherever the champagne is being sampled or sold bottles are displayed on the bar."

Ever forward thinking and willing to try new ideas, Tony was intrigued. So I continued, "So if I could get say three cases over to you free of charge would you give them a bit of exposure, encourage your guests have a free taste and let me know what you think? I had a few glasses when I was there and it's delicious!"

"Well fair enough" Tony said, "If you can get them to me without charge of course I'll give it a try - be happy to."

"All they've asked me to do is to produce a purchase order for each of the cases"

I told him. "I guess it's the way they have of knowing I haven't just drunk it all myself or given it away to my chums. Would you do that for me Tony? If you can *get it done today* then I can probably have the cases to you within the next 48 hours." I wouldn't ever describe Tony as an *errorist**, but in that moment I was pretty sure he was going to fall for it

"Yes that's fine" he said, "what do you need me to say on the order?"

I dictated... *"as per our conversation three cases of champagne without bubbles to be delivered free of charge to Grosvenor House Hotel."*

Later that day the purchase order duly arrived, and it was important for me that he did as I asked and had it typed *that day* because

This order for bubble-less champagne was dated April 1st. Got him!

Tony has tried unsuccessfully for the last 25 years or so to have his revenge. So far unsuccessfully. But perhaps this year will be his year. But whether or not it is our friendship endures.

Footnote:
errorist. as a terrorist instigates terror, so an **errorist instigates errors.*

Goldfish and Rick Stein's *dog*

As Prestige grew most our business was arranging events for companies although we were starting to get a few bookings from people who were spending their own money, booking tickets and events just for fun. This was a market largely untapped by our industry and I decided that as these people proved to be a lot more loyal than a number of our corporate clients, this was a new market worth pursuing. But as the private customers only booked two or four places at a time, to make it worthwhile, we'd need volume.

I resolved that as we were such a small business, the best way to get to large numbers of private customers would be to partner with businesses that already reached those people. And the obvious choice for me was credit card companies, as they were in touch monthly with their cardholders and credit card users were the sort of market I was after. So I needed to persuade a credit card company to carry some marketing messages for us.

In those days credit card statements were sent out by post and the paper statement would normally be a single page printed both sides, more sheets if you used your card for business or were a lady who lunched, followed by another sheet that contained a few separated paragraphs of bank offers for insurance, pensions, loans and whatever services the bank was trying to promote. *This* was the part that caught my attention. If we could get one or two of our events on that offers page, we could be cooking with gas!

I'd met the Head of Marketing at Diners Club, a very forward thinking lady called Jane Trotman, and I asked her how successful their marketing via the statement inserts was for them. "Well," she told me "not very, because the challenge is to get people to *read* that extra page. Most just see it as advertising they don't need and ignore it."

I made a bold suggestion by telling her that these sheets are offering people things they probably *need* but that they don't *want*. I went on, "Why don't we mix those up with our offers for interesting things that people might actually *want,* like access to a private book launch with a television author, or a film premiere?" And here was where I was being really cheeky but ploughed on regardless. "On the statement itself, the part of the mailing that you know everyone *will read* in checking their bills, let's trail the lead offer and make it something that is not generally available – access to a theatre first night, hard to get football or rugby tickets, or maybe a private box at racing. And then let's put another similar offer in further down the page but vary the position of it so month on month the *first offer* is something that they want, and then they have to search further down the page to find the second offer, and in doing that will have eyes on your offers which after all is what you really want to achieve."

She took the bait and agreed to give it a try for six months.

Success was slow coming but by month five the response had grown and was starting to be extremely worthwhile for us both and so I wondered if I might be able to get another card company to sign up with us in a similar way. My next approach was to NatWest, as I thought their Gold Card holders would be just our kind of audience. You see, when a business is as small as mine it was not really practical to market research new ideas. We just got them out there, and if they worked we carried on.

After being passed from pillar to post I ended up in front of Carol Lane a senior exec in their Cards Division who due to her complete aversion to using the word "no" and not quoting any corporate boll**ks... sorry, 'guidelines' at me... turned out to be one the most un-bankie people I've ever met in banking.

I'd taken in a couple of offers and pitched the use of the statement offers page like it was a new idea. However, I'd underestimated this lady because she said "this isn't new, Diners are already doing it."

How stupid of me, Why wouldn't these companies keep an eye on what each other were offering? But when I sheepishly told her that we were behind that, to my amazement she replied "That's great. You appear to be something of a specialist! If you make sure that you never offer them anything you offer us I am prepared to trial this. But I don't want to have to do any extra work. So look at our style of writing. Each of your offers needs to be limited to no more than 500 characters. Let's see what happens."

Well it did happen – and *bigly!** I very quickly learned how to write with an economy of words, (although you may not think so reading this book). Our private client base grew exponentially and in those days before Data Protection regulations, if someone made a booking with you there was no issue in adding their contact details to your own database. Or if there was I was never aware of it.

Carol and I really hit it off, so much so that when she moved from NatWest to Goldfish Card she continued to ask us to create and organise new events for them. One of them was to be a hosted company golf day for their top business clients. She wanted it organised on a golf course that people would be so excited about playing that they couldn't possibly resist the invitation. The venue also needed to be within easy reach of all parts of the country and as The Belfry, on the outskirts of Sutton Coldfield in The Midlands, had played host to the Ryder Cup on more than one occasion, it was the obvious choice.

There are three courses at the Belfry but the coveted one is the par 72 Brabazon Championship course. They limited the number of days on which the course can be used to maintain its superb standard but we were able to buy some tee off times, book some hospitality space, and get permission to put quite a bit of Goldfish branding about the place.

The invited guests, all golfers of course, responded with enthusiasm, but as always with corporate guests, even for something as alluring as this, there will be last minute cancellations and Carol told me the night before that she had received four dropouts. Naturally, the charge for the day would still be the same, so her partner Pat called three chums from his golf club to fill the gaps and stepped in to lead the 1st 4 ball the following morning.

Carol said "Clive this has to be very much under the radar. The Board directive was that invites were to be sent to corporate clients ONLY. So we need to be *very* discreet about Pat and his mates. Is that okay?"

I put her mind at rest by saying "Very clearly understood Carol."

The day dawned bright, and there was quite a bit of razzmatazz. We had Goldfish banners all over the course, Goldfish liveried staff supplementing the caterers to pander to the guests every need, and a small gift of a branded leather pouch containing 3 golf balls and a handful of tees was handed to each of the guests as they approached the first tee. Their photographer, recording it all was already sending his motor drive into overdrive.

I knew how to get the best for a host from an event day but I don't know one end of a golf club from the other and recognised that if there were any disputes they needed to be settled by someone of authority with a knowledge of the rules. So my pal Hakey, who was a member of Wentworth and played off a handicap of 4, was appointed Tournament Director for the day, a role which he undertook with gusto. I did tell him he'd have to wear a body size orange goldfish costume for 6 hours but having been a victim of one of my April Fools pranks earlier that year he told me to pi*s off!

Someone described what we had created as more of a golfing pageant and word quickly spread, so by mid-morning we had two reporters and a photographer from Midlands newspapers turn up to see who was playing and what all the fuss was about. This was fantastic for Goldfish and Carol was delighted.

Meanwhile, Carol's partner Pat and his three pals had been first off the tee, the idea being that if anyone asked they were just a 4 going off *before* our event began. But Pat was a very handy golfer and on the par 3 hole chosen for our *nearest the pin* prize, he dropped his ball about 6 inches from the flag! Same with *the longest drive of the day*. Pat's teammate, Dave, hit his ball almost 300 yards. Keeping this under our hats might prove to be a problem.

The Imposters, as they had christened themselves couldn't resit the challenge of playing up on this fabled course. Treading in the footsteps of champions and legends in this golfers paradise, they were inspired to produce their best golf, and played, well, like champions! The silly bug*ers only went and won the event. *And* the nearest the pin competition. *And* the longest drive competition.

Pat admitted afterwards that Carol had indeed told them forcefully to keep a low profile, but *claimed* they thought she meant in the bar and the dining room. Oh yeah??

The local papers wanted to interview Pat and whilst he tried to escape, first by pretending to have to take an urgent phone call and then by feigning illness, the journalists got their interviews and the cat was well and truly out of the bag. Quite what Carol had to face back at the Goldfish Bowl (as we called their HQ) I never knew, but I'm very pleased to say that she managed to keep her job and kept booking things with us. Pat was allowed to keep the elaborate trophy he'd won too. So no real harm done.

Carol and Pat were destined to stay on my *life* train and appeared again on a Prestige weekend at Rick Stein's in Padstow. By then we had organised a couple of book launches for Rick. Most authors are happy to be interviewed on stage after dinner, but Rick's were always book launches with a difference, as he wanted to show the audience how to *cook* the dinner! With something as basic as a simple Bunsen burner or two on a table on the stage, a couple of pans and ready prepared ingredients, he would cook one of the dishes from the book and in that easy relaxed style of his, simultaneously be telling everyone what he was doing and recounting an amusing tale or two at the same time. This often led to him getting something wrong which of course greatly amused the guests and made these cooking demos even more enjoyable. He was always so good-humoured about it and a bit like the slipups in Murray's Grand Prix commentaries, they became a feature of Rick's demonstrations with us.

I asked Rick whether he would be interested in us getting a group of people together to come down to Padstow off-season, stay in one of his hotels with him hosting a reception followed by a cooking demo just for us. He readily agreed, and they were so much fun that we ended up doing several, between Rick's ever increasing demands to go off filming another new series for the BBC.

A lovely client of long standing, Judith White was a massive dog lover and joined us for one of these trips to Padstow. You will remember Rick's little terrier Chalky, who accompanied his master everywhere on his travels around the UK. She asked Rick if he would bring Chalky to the reception. Rick explained that Chalky by this stage was quite old and snappy and could no longer be trusted with people. He thought it would be dangerous for Chalky to be involved. But Judith ever the persuasive, inveigled Rick into believing that she was exceptionally good with dogs, and that all would be well.

Rick somewhat reluctantly appeared with Chalky at the reception that evening. Judith was delighted and in fairness to her did all the right things. Always moving slowly, she crouched down to Chalky's level, let him sniff the back of her hand, spoke gently to him gradually winning his confidence, and then having taken all the time it needed, giving him a triumphant stroke. Amazingly with no disastrous or painful outcomes, and even a wagging tail. The assembled guests breathed a sigh of relief, as did Rick.

Judith rose from her crouched position turned to everyone, and beaming said "there you are, I told you I was good with dogs!"

Then with her newly earned confidence, turned back to Chalky, but rather than go through the 'put the dog at ease' process again, from a standing position she lunged forward, arm extended heading for Chalky's head at a rate of knots and the moment her hand was in range the little devil leapt up and sunk his sharp and jagged teeth into the fleshy part of Judith's hand, right between her first finger and outstretched thumb. Boy did she yelp and shriek!

Chalky hung on. And as she cried out again, Rick somehow managed to untangle them.

It was such a shame as Judith really was good with dogs. *Usually.*

I'm ashamed to say that the incident had provoked some laughter. Poor Judith. She went away to bathe her hand, and restore her dented pride, and by the following morning her souvenir of the experience was extremely swollen and very black and blue.

Shortly afterwards Rick's restaurants, and the pubs all around the Padstow area started offering a very delicious bottled beer called *Chalky's Bite*. Judith always said that it's not everyone who inspires the name of a popular beer!

Cheers to Judith, Carol, Rick and dear old Chalky, now at the everlasting feeding bowl in the sky, where I'm sure visitor's hands are plentiful and within easy reach.

Footnote:
bigly. *Something that happens in a big way, usually a positive thing.*

Bad Publicity!

Having guests bitten by dogs is bad enough from a PR point of view but being put through the wringer by a national paper is worse –
so I discovered.

We took a private box or two at the Benson & Hedges tennis at Wembley Arena and Fenwick's Department Store had booked one to entertain some journalists, one of whom was the editor of *Today* newspaper. *Today* was a middle-market tabloid, now long defunct, whose main claim to fame was being the first British national daily to print photographs in full colour. The editor phoned me afterwards full of praise about how absolutely excellent all aspects of the day at Wembley had been and how she'd like to do an article about Prestige, with an interview with me. She asked if she could send a reporter and a photographer to one of my upcoming events.

Obviously, I was delighted at the opportunity for some free publicity to help raise our profile and invited them to come to our marquee at Ascot so they could see us in action again and take a few good pictures.

The two guys from *Today* turned up and were utterly charming fellows. They were particularly interested in the events we had done with Prince Edward and Prince Charles back in the late 1980s, when we had been on a bit of a Royal roll. We had worked with Prince Edward on a few occasions, and had been involved with Prince Charles too, having organised the sponsorship of a high profile polo day at Smith's Lawn Windsor for one of our airline clients Britannia Airways, in which HRH was to take part.

I was talking about the polo sponsorship and explained to the reporter that unprecedented downpours had occurred every day for a fortnight on the build up to our day. On the afternoon before, Major Ronald Ferguson, the Duchess of York's father and Polo Manager to the Prince of Wales, told me that if the rain stopped overnight and held off the following morning there was a slim chance that one of the pitches at least would be playable. But the rain continued steadily throughout the morning of the match and consequently all the polo pitches were completely sodden, and unplayable.

Britannia had told their guests to turn up as planned given that there was a chance of the day's event going ahead, so by midday our marquee was full of 100 expectant hosts and guests. But by then there was definitely no prospect of play, and therefore the Prince of Wales who was due to have been playing would now not have any reason to appear, which was all very disappointing for everyone, particularly Britannia, who had not only paid The Guards Club the sponsorship fee, but as a goodwill gesture had also made a separate donation of a further £25,000 to The Princes Trust. But it was now looking very much as if their hosting spectacular was going to fizzle out like a very damp squib. I was the man they were looking to, to sprinkle some magic dust to make sure it didn't.

But I wasn't panicking. Major Ferguson had told me of his Plan B, and by the time lunch had been elongated and enjoyed, the Band of the Coldstream Guards in full dress uniform appeared. After all, this *was* the *Guards* Polo Club! We rearranged the tables in the marquee to clear a big space in the centre, and this magnificent band treated us to a fabulous hour of music on the march. Of course when soldiers turn they stamp their boots rather heavily, and the carefully laid wooden floor, never designed to withstand an attack from the British Army disintegrated into splinters beneath the carpet. It was all rather jolly and the guests seemed to be enjoying the music and the spectacle.

But there was more to come. Ferguson had somehow managed to persuade the Prince to put in an appearance after all! This was no doubt in part to show his appreciation for Britannia's generous donation to the Trust but what a gentleman he was! He took his time, laughing and chatting to every single one of the guests, and insisting on spending time with the kitchen staff which made *their* day too. He even took a polo mallet and swung it a few times showing us how it should be done. He was a great sport, and against all the rain soaked odds, we had a success on our hands. Phew!

Well, I told this story to the reporter, only to find myself two days later on Ladies Day, the biggest day of Royal Ascot, to be the subject of a *Today Investigation*.

The headline of the full page article was "SORRY IT'S RAINING BUT WE CAN GET YOU PRINCE CHARLES FOR £25,000!!" There was even a picture of me with Ronald Ferguson and The Prince of Wales, the

caption read: *"Heir of distinction: Clive Thomas's cheque book has been known to conjure up even royalty."*

They had branded me as a sleazy royal fixer who could buy royalty for a fistful of grubby fivers. Oh - my - God. What *had* I done? Not for the first time I could see myself heading for The Tower by the end of the morning.

Damage limitation was the order of the day. First of all I phoned Ron Ferguson. He had seen the paper and said "Clive don't worry a bit. I know more than most what basta*ds the press can be." He had been subjected to some rather unpleasant publicity a few months before when his name was linked to the Wigmore Club in London which had a reputation for somewhat salacious hostessing. He hadn't done anything wrong but the exposure, if you'll forgive the term, wasn't pleasant for him. My next call was to John Haslam the Queen's Press Secretary who I had met on a couple of occasions, and he gave me exactly the same support and comfort saying "The first time you see something like this Clive, you'll be horrified and will feel betrayed. But unless you read that rag, and who does, you weren't to know he was an investigative writer. People will be eating their chips out of those pages by this evening. Please don't worry. No relationships have been damaged."

With this reassurance I was somewhat more at ease with the temporary notoriety the piece had bought me.

But even I, a former journalist myself, had to learn the hard way about taking editors and their reporters at face value.

Elton & Rod

So in spite of *Today's* best efforts, Prestige wasn't out of business and in fact we continued to flourish. One of the annual landmarks in the corporate event calendar is the FA Cup Final. Your very first visit to Wembley for a Cup Final or an England International will almost certainly be your most memorable. Right from the early build-up, the chatter, then the babble of eager anticipation grows and the singing gets louder as more arriving fans join in. As the atmosphere intensifies, the commotion increases; the drumming and the chanting gets ever louder, as a fanfare for the spectacle to come.

And as the teams emerge onto the pitch you lose yourself in the eruption of boisterousness: frenzied clapping, frenetic cheering from both camps, booing, singing and each side ever louder with their encouragement of their team to hopeful victory. And as well as the noise, there is the riot of colour. Scarves, hats and face paint, the waving of flags and the display of banners. The spectacle of 80,000 keyed up and passionate people enjoying one of the best of great days out creates an atmosphere like no other. I still cherish my memories from my first FA Cup Final in '82 when my team QPR, who were the outsiders from Division Two, went up against the mighty Spurs, hot favourites from Division One (now called The Premiership). It was a tense exciting nail-biting 1-1 draw on the day, and we lost 5 days later in the replay, 1-0, to 6th minute Glenn Hoddle penalty.

That was, of course at the *old* Wembley Stadium. The *new* Stadium opened to great fanfare in March 2007 with an England friendly on a perfectly manicured new pitch against Brazil. The new Wembley had been stripped of her iconic twin towers, which had been replaced by a massive arc which in itself, in time would I suppose become the new icon. New Wembley was far bigger and shinier, with capacity increased from 82,000 seated and standing, to 90,000 all seated. But for me the most significant difference was the space underneath the tiered seating for on-site VIP hospitality suites and 160 private hospitality viewing boxes overlooking the pitch.

Old Wembley by comparison had very limited hospitality space. Corporate hospitality just wasn't a thing back in 1923 when it opened. It did boast a wonderful glass fronted restaurant just behind the Royal Box (which I was privileged to be in for *Live Aid* in 1985 - but that really is another story) but on Cup Final days every inch of what hospitality space there was, was always taken by the Football Association. Anyone else wanting to host had to look elsewhere, and the prize venues were those few within walking distance.

A short walk from the stadium was Wembley Conference Centre which had not long been open and I was quick to make sure that we got in for big match days. I staked our claim and were able to hire a big conference suite large enough for about 100 guests. Some theming, plants, screens and up-lighting gave this soulless room some atmosphere, and we called it "The Prestige Lounge".

Our guests, who all had tickets for the big match, were in our care for drinks, followed by a pre match lunch and we always laid on some entertainment, which was to be provided by one of *The Goodies*. I had come to know Tim Brooke-Taylor who had played a couple of matches for my Showbiz Golf Team, and he'd agreed to do a speech after lunch and before the match. There would then be more drinks after the final whistle, and by the time guests were ready to leave the traffic would have died down. A nice package, although I say it myself. But as it happens, it turned out to be far better than I could ever have imagined or arranged.

You need to understand that the Wembley Conference Centre comprised a very confusing labyrinth of corridors and without past experience of getting to the particular suite you needed, or having some helpful North London Sherpa leading the way, you'd probably get hopelessly lost as the signs in the early days weren't that helpful. I remember I sought permission to put some signs up, only to be told that wasn't possible… "Because freestanding signs constitute a trip hazard and wall mounted signage wasn't permitted under sub-section 18468736973974 of local planning law 5975/69734/b…" or some such bureaucratic jobsworths ludicrousness.

I give up!

So I decided to bring a couple of extra people with me on the day especially to lead my guests from the entrance to 'The Prestige Club Lounge'. We were barely 15 minutes into a drinks reception and I had security people coming in saying that guests of ours had wandered into other people's suites and would we collect them. These were the days before mobile phones made everything so much easier for a beleaguered event organiser and so once we had rounded up our wandering guests I thought the easiest thing, as there was still quite a number to arrive, was for me, the most recognisable person on our team, to go to the main entrance and explain the route they should take.

When I got back to the entrance I ran into an old chum, Mike Archer who was the producer of ITV's *World of Sport*, the long running programme fronted by Dickie Davis which used to go head-to-head every Saturday afternoon with Frank Bough presenting the BBC's Grandstand. They were forever trying to outdo each other in whatever ways they could dream up, to attract the best viewing figures and Mike told me that he had pulled off a major coup. He was there waiting to personally greet Elton John and Rod Stewart, who were coming in to be interviewed before the match exclusively on *World Of Sport*. Elton was chairman of Watford FC at the time and Rod Stewart was a famous for being a football nut who had a full size pitch in the grounds of his house. Getting them both was a major feat: a stroke of genius which was guaranteed to annoy the BBC!

Mike and I were passing the time chatting in between me greeting and directing my guests, who now were now arriving thick and fast. His plan was to whisk Elton and Rod straight up to the rooms that ITV were using as their studio and hospitality suite, with cameras geared up for live broadcast, and VIPS waiting to rub shoulders with these star guests. More time passed and Mike needed to go to the loo. He asked if I could stand guard for him. He was very serious and started sounding like a scene from 'Allo 'Allo – "Listen very carefully, I shall say this only once!

"If the boys should arrive whilst I'm away, you must take them directly up to my suite. It's on the fifth floor."

"Yeah of course Mike." I said cheerfully.
"You can leave it to me!"

Mike slipped away from his lookout post and literally 30 seconds later, his two guest Legends arrived. As they came up the steps followed closely by a burly minder the size of a silverback and looking twice as mean, I stepped forward and said to Elton, who was sporting a pink blazer, topped off by a pink ribbon encircling a Henley style boater, "I think you are looking for Mike Archer?"

"Yes we are" he said, "and we need sustenance".

I told them, "Mike's been waiting for a while but was called away and has asked me to look after you. If you follow me I can arrange the sustenance".

Well, the angel on one shoulder was telling me to follow orders and take them directly to the lift and to the 5th floor. But the devil on the other shoulder was telling me that I'd never have an opportunity like this again and was daring me to take them to "The Prestige Club Lounge". Naturally, the devil won;

I just couldn't resist the opportunity.

I took them to my suite set them and Mr Silverback at the bar, told the barman to give them whatever they wanted – I think it was diet coke, beer and champagne, and slid some rather delicious canapés in their direction.

Of course what I *should* have done is left immediately to get Mike. But what I *actually* did was went round several of my guests saying, "we have Elton John and Rod Stewart at the bar. They're dying to meet you so if you want a word I'll get over there now."

I also took Tom Northey, my star client and PR Director of Pirelli, over and introduced him personally. I think that guaranteed Pirelli's patronage for the foreseeable future and almost certainly earned me a set of 5 new P60s for the Merc. Come to think of it, we did organise the Pirelli Calendar Launch the following October and so for that alone I must belatedly thank Rod and Elton.

Now that everyone was happily ensconced, I sent one of my event managers to get Mike who was back at the front door probably wondering where I was, and now more than a bit concerned about the very late arrival of his guests. He eventually appeared in our doorway with a face like thunder and I greeted him with a broad smile and "I was beginning to get worried that you weren't going to join us. Your guests are very relaxed and of course I couldn't take the risk of getting lost in the labyrinth of corridors so thought it far better that you collected them from my room where we've kept them safe" and I added, "out of sight of Frank Bough and any other BBC scoundrels who might have seen the opportunity to hijack them".

There was no doubt about who Mike thought was the scoundrel and who had done the hijacking.

But that wasn't the time or place.

Well Rod and Elton by this stage were having a great time with some of my guests who were all of the football, rather than the pop, fraternity and seemed in no hurry to leave. I overheard the end of one of the conversations where Rod was saying that he'd been quite a handy player in his teens. He told us "I wasn't committed enough to become a professional footballer but did have trials with Brentford" He went on "I've discovered there are only two things I can really do in life – play football and sing!" He started laughing "Elton loves football as we all know, but he couldn't kick a ball straight if his life depended on it!"

They didn't know Mike by sight and weren't to be swayed by his gentle cajoling to leave. I remember Elton saying, "look we've got at least half an hour before we're due on, and we might as well stay here."

I knew that Mike had some serious VIPs waiting to meet these guys, probably some of ITV's best advertisers and whilst I was revelling in my good fortune, I didn't want to be single handily responsible for their advertising income to suddenly plummet. I could almost see the headlines *"ITV revenue down 70% due to advertiser's disappointment at Cup Final!"* Nor, did I want to land my old friend, Mike, in the brown stuff. And so I quietly explained to Elton what had happened, and, gent that he is, he laughed and said to Rod, "we really should go with Mike now, come on dear, I'll help you up the stairs!" And good as gold the pair of them went off with a very relieved looking ITV Producer who would still have his job on Monday morning.

I met Elton again some years later at the Royal College of Music where a few of us had been invited to the Trade Launch of *Billy Elliot* for which he had written the music. Knowing that a lot of Elton's life had been a bit of a blur, I was very surprised that he remembered that day. He told me he it had stuck in his mind because it was so refreshing to be able to relax amongst people who just wanted to enjoy a glass or two, talk about football with not one of them asking for autographs (it was long before selfies). He said that he and Rod had been able to relax because they weren't 'being paraded' as happened with ITV after they left me.

He smiled and said they both had happy memories of that time with me.

It couldn't happen **now** – *could it?*

If Elton and Rod were to be arriving there *today* for a TV commitment, I wouldn't have been allowed anywhere near the front door until they had gone through. They would be surrounded by – what's a collective noun for a group of bodyguards I wonder? A "thug of minders" perhaps, and I wouldn't have got close enough to talk to them – let alone have Elton John tell me he needed feeding. How times change!

Another example of how more relaxed things were back then is that Ron Greenwood, who was Manager of the England football team in the early 1980s, used to pop into the Patron's Bar at QPR from time to time and I was one of the people he chatted to. The week before the 1982 FA Cup Final he had the England Team together at The Hendon Hall Hotel for a training week and being not too far from my home he'd invited me over for a drink and to meet the team one evening.

The FA had given him tickets for the final for all the players, and Ron was bemoaning that the FA had made no arrangements for anywhere private for the players to be before and after the game. I told Ron that we had a private suite at the (then) Esso Hotel at the Wembley complex, that if he and the players wanted to come in and relax they'd be most welcome. I didn't dream for a moment they'd come and thought no more of it.

On the day, after the last of the guests had been checked in, an ominous security man called me over with

"there are some gentlemen at the door asking for you"

And there was a smiling England Manager followed by almost the whole squad, including Peter Shilton, Graham Rix, Kenny Sansom, Trevor Francis, Trevor Brooking, Ray Clemence, all relaxed, chatty and very happy to mingle with our guests who could not have been any more surprised or more highly delighted. I'm sorry to say that I could only find two of the photos from that day - a daughter of one of our clients sitting on England Captain Kevin Keegan's lap, and the son of another with striker Paul Mariner, and the next England Captain Bryan Robson. And I became a legend for the afternoon, as the man who got the England team in for a beer or two on Cup Final Day!

THE FOOTBALL ASSOCIATION

LIMITED

Patron: HER MAJESTY THE QUEEN
President: H.R.H. THE DUKE OF KENT
Chairman: F.A. MILLICHIP

General Secretary:
E.A. CROKER

Telegraphic Address:
FOOTBALL ASSOCIATION, LONDON, W2 3LW
Phone: 01-262 4542/402 7151
Telex: 261110

16 LANCASTER GATE, LONDON W2 3LW.

Our Ref: RG/JC/11814   *Your Ref:*

C.B. Thomas Esq.,
Director,
Prestige Promotions,
184a Kenton Road,
Kenton,
Middlesex.   HA3 8BL.

24th November, 1981

Dear Clive,

Many thanks for your letter.

I am glad to hear that everything went well for you the other night after the game and I am pleased some of the players were able to enjoy your hospitality. I, myself, went to bed very early and I am sure you can understand the reasons for that.

Look forward to seeing you in the near future.

Yours sincerely

Ron Greenwood
England Team Manager

Registered Office 16 Lancaster Gate, London W2 3LW
Incorporated in London   Registration Number 77797

I can't imagine this happening today, at least not without extremely large sums of money being involved, administered by agents and lawyers who would have drafted a hefty tome of terms & conditions, image and naming rights, disclaimers and health and safety requirements. The only two requests, not requirements, that Ron had were a hassle free atmosphere for the players and access to the buffet and cold drinks. Simple. Everybody was very happy, and he even wrote and thanked me. Different times indeed.

Scorsese and a cigar

It started with an evening at the Groucho Club in Soho. My great friend of 30 years plus Ray Jones (more of Ray later) and I had been invited to an auction to raise money for research into Parkinson's disease which had been put together by Sofie Mason. Sofie is a charming lady who founded and ran an innovative fringe theatre marketing enterprise called *Off West End*. Through this, she knew some very well-connected people who had donated some 'money can't buy' items for the auction and I had picked out two which really appealed to us both. The first was a half an hour slot on London's Capital Radio music station where you take over as the DJ and can invite people in to be interviewed, play records and generally have a good time on air. I really fancied that. So did Ray. The other was a 'walk on' part in a feature film (film and location TBC). I knew that 'walk on' meant basically being an 'extra' but I thought it might be fun. But again Ray was to be a rival bidder. Ray also wanted the basque that had been worn by Richard O'Brien in the stage show of his smash hit musical, The Rocky Horror Show.

We decided that it wasn't the best idea for us to try to outbid each other on those lots so we flipped a coin and Ray went for the radio slot and I went for the film. A cunning plan, we thought.

As it transpired, Ray dropped out the race when the bidding for the DJ half hour passed £1000, and indeed, it went on much further. However, it did enable him to buy the basque. The explanation that he had arrived home with a worn item of ladies lingerie as a reward for supporting Parkinson's research may have stretched it a bit in some households. However, Mrs. Jones was well used to Ray's eccentricities and it wouldn't have phased her at all. Thank goodness the basque wasn't still warm.

I couldn't understand why the filming lot wasn't so popular and was delighted when it was knocked down to me at what I thought was a bargain price. Sofie handed me an envelope containing a congratulatory letter from the "Casting Director - Background Artists", who was a lady by the name of Candy Marlowe, which I reckoned was a great name for someone in films if ever I heard one.

I phoned her the very next morning, my head full of the possibilities of being in a feature film and said, "Now that I am in the film business, shall I have my people talk to your people so that you can send a car for me to have lunch and talk about my part?"

"Sofie warned me about you" she replied.

I'd only been joking about the car of course, but she still told me I was "a cheeky bug*er". Ms Marlowe is a forthright woman but she did agree to have lunch and a date was duly agreed to meet back at the Groucho.

Now, at the time, my granddaughter Ruby was an angelic looking nine-year-old with blonde hair and she was really enjoying her Saturday mornings at a theatre school called *Stagecoach*, where she was learning all about acting, dance and singing. She had already announced to family gathering some time before that she was going to be an actress "when she growed up", so I took a photograph of her in one of her *Stagecoach* plays and, having treated Candy to several glasses of champagne and a delicious Dover sole, put it to her that it would be wonderful if my successful bid could include the chance for Papa *and* Ruby to have a bonding day on set. To help seal the deal, I also assured her that, unlike me, Ruby could actually act.

Candy laughed and told me that it would be a lot easier to cast Ruby then it would me and thus, the deal was struck.

After a couple of weeks Candy called up and said we were given the chance to be involved in a film based on a play called 'Zigger Zagger'* Apparently it was all about football violence in the 1960s (a heyday for hooliganism) and Ruby and I weren't really drawn to it so we passed.

We waited expectantly for some weeks for Candy's next call and eventually she phoned to say she thought she's got just the thing for us. "Martin Scorsese is making a film at Shepperton. It's called "Hugo" and it's set on a station in Paris in 1932".

This sounded much more like it.

"I'd like you to come over for a costume fitting this week. Details to follow. Cheerio".

I immediately called young Ruby with the news.

"We are in!" I cried, barely able to contain my excitement.
"The film is about a teenage orphan boy called Hugo who lives in
a Station in Paris in the 1930s. He invents an automaton and..."

"What's an automaton?" my granddaughter cut in. Three weeks
previously, we'd been sitting at my computer and I'd had to have
her explain to me what a spambot was.

"It's like a robot" I said "But Ben Kinsley is in it! And Sasha Baron-Cohen
and Jude Law and Johnny Depp and Christopher Lee..." I gabbled.
"Who's Ben Kingsley? And all the other people?"

Young Ruby clearly wasn't as easily impressed as I was.

"Never mind" I told her. "We'll be in costumes, make up –
the lot. It's going to be epic!"

Three days later, we were at Shepperton Studios. The studio is vast
and parking there operates on a strictly hierarchical system. Stars and
VIPs park their limos and Bentleys right at the front door, directors and
senior technical people get to park a couple of minutes' walk away, other
crew behind them...and so on until, about a mile away from the main

buildings you reach
the 'background
artistes' car park,
where the lowly likes
of Ruby and me
park our beaten-up
jalopies and make the
long hike towards
the bright lights of
stardom.

And so on arrival
we followed a long
limousine up to the
entry barrier

and saw the commissionaire salute the occupants as the barrier rose. We wondered which star of the silver screen was inside. Maybe Johnny Depp? Or Jude Law? (Ruby had been mugging up on her movie stars since our phone call). It turned out that it was Ray Winston and Christopher Lee in the limo, as they were also in 'our' film, as Ruby and I had started calling it.

We were beckoned up to the barrier and to my amazement, rather than being directed to the distant car lot, the commissioner again saluted smartly and waved me through to the VIP car park about 30 seconds walk from where we needed to be. It turns out that because I was on the Board of the Pinewood Cinema Club at the time and had my Director's car park pass on my windscreen, this magic pass was also valid for Shepperton! Nice. The best thing was Ruby was so impressed - she thought that Papa was very important!

I quickly parked and together we strolled hand-in-hand into the studio.

This was my first experience of a studios costume department and to say it was impressive would be a ludicrous understatement. A bit like saying that The Statue of Liberty is rather tall for a woman. I wasn't sure how many people were to be in this film but the frocks for it were housed in three aircraft hangar size marquees. At a guess there would have been well over 1,000 costumes, all on numbered hangers, on numbered coat rails, in numbered rows, stretching as far as the eye could see: and each one labelled with size, colour and any imperfections. And it was the same with the shoes, scarves, gloves, hats, parasols and canes.

I have mentioned before in these pages that in those days I had the build of Pavarotti, but sadly not the voice. And I feared that XXXXL might be a stretch too far – literally. But the briskly efficient costume dept. easily found me a choice of double-breasted suits to fit, along with a scarf, a trilby hat and various other accoutrements. The only thing that was a problem to this marvellous bunch were the shoes. I have a very high instep and they couldn't find matching shoes that fitted. I had some brown brogues at home and volunteered to bring those in on the filming day but I had underestimated their astonishing attention to detail. Even though we were just extras, the shoes had to be of the period! And so my feet were duly measured and I was informed that there would be shoes that had been worn in waiting for me – as indeed, on the day, there were.

If I was impressed with it all, then Ruby was in 7th heaven! Every 10-year-old girl loves dressing up BUT to have your own staff of highly trained costumiers to dress you up!! This was beyond her wildest dreams and as she stood being dressed and pampered, her beaming smile said it all.

Then, having found costumes that were right for both of us we were photographed in them and given a copy of the picture with all the reference numbers on the back so that we would have exactly the same on the day of filming.

Before we left we were taken to "hair wigs and make up" where they decided my hair was a little long and so was trimmed. Next they wanted to shave off my moustache but as I'd had the whiskers since my tennis coaching days in my late teens, I politely, but firmly, declined. But then when I was told, just as politely but firmly, "If you keep the moustache you can't be in the film", I figured a compromise was called for and the top third of my moustache immediately below my nose was removed, leaving a strip of whiskers on my top lip, which apparently was fashionable at the time. (Incidentally, I still wear my moustache that way today.)

Whilst all this was happening to me, Ruby's blond hair was being tucked neatly under a jet-black wig and we were both given our 'legends'. This was our backstory: who we were and where we were going. Although we didn't have speaking parts, the philosophy is that if you have a reason to be doing what you're doing then you'll do it better. So on screen I was to be Ruby's father – with my boyish good looks I could get away with it – and I was taking her by train from Paris down to Marseille where, I was to deposit her with her uncle and aunt for the holidays.

I was very excited. Ruby was very excited. We couldn't wait but we had to, as the date for filming was about three weeks hence. We counted them down until finally the great day dawned and I was up at the crack of, scraping the ice off my windscreen. It had been minus 3 during the night and the last time I had been up this early I was asking my Mummy if Father Christmas had been yet. We had to be at the studios by 6am so I collected Ruby at five for the drive around the M25, feeling desperately sorry for those people already on the road doing what for them was a daily commute on an already busy motorway. My luck with the parking held good, which was especially useful as the weather was still as cold as the taxman's heart and of course it was still pitch black when we arrived.

It didn't take long for us to get into our costumes and be shown onto the most miraculous set, where the attention to the finest detail was quite phenomenal. I don't know if there were to be close-ups of the news kiosk on the station but the newspapers on it and magazines were all dated 1932! It was as if a time machine had magically transported us back to the 1930s. All the costumes were impeccably of the time and there was even a station café: a perfect replica, with menus showing the day's fare (in French, naturellemént), with prices in Francs. Best of all, in this re-creation of La Gare Montparnasse stood a magnificent steam engine with smoke rising from its polished funnel and with carriages, spic and span, waiting for passengers to board. This was such fun!

Before going onto the set, we were talked though a great list of dos and don'ts (with significantly more don'ts than dos). I remember some of them; *don't* speak to any of the principal actors unless they spoke to us; *do* leave the set immediately when told to; *don't* go anywhere other than the background actors area (which was quite cramped but was the source of refreshment); *don't* bring watches, mobile phones or cameras onto the set…and so on. But the golden rule was

Do Not under any circumstances approach The Tent!

The Tent was a black canvas marquee on one side of the studio, with its solid back onto the set, open the other side to give easy access and discreet exits and this was where the power brokers were based, Martin Scorsese, his assistant, a couple of the exec producers, and the various directors of photography, special effects, sound et cetera.

Having digested this list, Ruby and I found ourselves amongst probably 200 other extras milling about on the station and we soon learnt that the unique talent necessary to be a film extra is the unlimited capacity to mill, amble, mosey, saunter, wait, linger and pause. There is an inordinate amount of hanging around on a film set and the old hands in the 'being an extra' business came prepared. The background actor's area was full of 1930's-looking characters, reading, checking phones and tapping away at laptops. A few played cards, there were two sets of fellows playing chess, and one girl even doing a jigsaw. How she was going to get it home I couldn't imagine. Just getting it all the way to the distant car park in the dark would be challenging enough. There was needlework of every kind going on, from knitting, to embroidery and I kid you not, I'm sure one lady must have be taking in repairs. She had a pile of assorted clothing all in need of some refurbishment gradually being transferred from the table to her basket following her stupendous stitching. How enterprising!

But whilst on set, milling was the order of the day and so that's what Ruby and I did while they shot some of the stars from different angles, with the sound of trains coming and going, and all the while us all in the background. We climbed into carriages; we climbed out of carriages. We had a break and as "Clear the set" boomed out, the extras left the set quickly as per instructions.

But I was curious as to what was going on in the Tent.

"Come on Ruby, let's go and have a look!"

"No Papa! We've been told we can't go to the Tent."

I needed to get Ruby on side so I explained to her that everyone else was being paid to be here, whereas I had paid *for us* to be here. The others were doing what they were told because they were professional extras and wanted to be employed again. As I said to her, "This is our day, we won't be coming back – so let's make the best of it!"

She wasn't totally convinced, but with a nervous glance and the beginnings of a smile, said,

"You are naughty Papa. OK then."

We got to the Tent expecting to find it full of big-shot power-players, chomping on cigars and barking into mobiles but instead there was just a single, rather harassed-but-friendly-looking lady on her own, pouring over her laptop. She told us her name was Martha that she was Martin's assistant and then demanded to know what on earth were we doing coming to the Tent!? She looked as if she was suffering with a cold and having just got over mine, I had some Lemsip in the car which as you know wasn't far away, so I volunteered to get it for her. It was an offer she couldn't refuse and as she gratefully sipped on it I told her what I had explained to Ruby about bidding for the day on set. She asked which charity had benefited and I told her it was for Parkinson's research. "My goodness" she said, "Marty's wife suffers with Parkinson's"

And so began a sequence of events which I could never have imagined.

My small act of kindness with the Lemsip and the connection with Parkinson's was enough for our day to be transformed. Rather than appear in the next scene, one of the assistants to the second assistant directors' assistant (or some such thing) gathered us up and took us into other studios containing more elaborate sets and showed us what else would be going on in the film: a real behind-the-scenes tour. What's more, we didn't ever go back to the *extras* holding area. Our belongings were gathered for us and we were invited to lunch with the *cast* and crew which was unbelievable luxury by comparison. And there was Johnny Depp, Ben Kingsley, Sacha Baron Cohen, Richard Griffiths and a whole heap of people we didn't recognise but felt that we should. I remember poor Emily Mortimer couldn't get warm, so I leant her my fleece and she was particularly nice to us both. And Richard Griffiths, a stout yeoman himself told me that he didn't often have to share wardrobe with other actors of "gallant magnitude!"

Ruby was completely star struck but of, course a big *don't* on the list we had been given was *don't* ask for autographs. My mobile phone was still being held hostage, and I didn't want to break any more rules and spoil the spell with a sneaky selfie or two and so I passed the time chatting with Frances de la Tour. We had met years before one evening at Leonard Rossiter's house when he was in my showbiz squash team. He and his lovely wife Gilly, also an actress, Gillian Raine, had invited me to a party. Frances sweetly said she remembered me, but I don't think she did. And why would she?

After lunch, the floor manager found us and said "Clive, Ruby I have a scene for you!" We were promoted from background to *foreground* actors. Still no speaking part, but our new friend Martha clearly was a lady of influence.

We were led to "our table" in the station café on which was a pot of hot tea and a well loaded, tiered cake stand from which we were invited to dine. The cakes were not only real, but fresh and delicious. We also signed a contract of confidentiality as foreground actors and were now being paid: £160 for me £85 for Ruby. Ruby started laughing. She told me was having the best day of her life and was now getting more that all the pocket money she had ever been given.

I couldn't believe that I was being paid to eat cake!

There were lots of background actors standing around chatting, some waiters, a few station staff, some customers, a barman, some passing travellers, and at the call to "action" all would resume their roles, as if the pause button had been lifted and brought the station back to life. A photographer had also appeared and was busily taking stills for film publicity.

The Floor Manager, who was very New York (all the really important people on set were American) came over to tell us what was going to happen. The stationmaster, played by Sacha Baron Cohen, was going to slide down a pole that was sited about 2 feet from where Ruby was sitting. He was going to hit the ground yelling "Maximillian! Here Maximillian!!" as he was chasing his Doberman who had escaped and then run out of shot. Simple!

There was a camera to my left, another on my right, one head-on and an aerial camera on some kind of boom. Just before the first take the floor manager came over to me again and said, "Hey Clive do you smoke cigars?"

"No, never" I replied.

"That's terrific", he said, handing me one of the longest cigars I'd ever seen. "I wanchya to smoke this one. Now, here's wachya godda do. Ruby, the guy's gonna hit the ground inches from where you're sitting and he's gonna be yelling loud so you've gotta look shocked." He stood in front of Ruby and said, "Gimme shocked."

Now, Ruby had four years at *Stagecoach* and she really could act! Her face immediately transformed into someone who had been truly shocked. You could see he was impressed "Hey honey," he said, "that's terrific!" Then he turned to me and said, "See if you can do as good as her, right? So, you're just having tea on the station and this asshole comes crashing through right next to your daughter. She could've been hurt! So you've godda stand up and you've godda look daggers at him. In your head you've godda think, 'What de fu*k!! Asshole!!'"

My first thought was Ruby telling this story when she got home and so I quickly told her to not mind the language and that's how everyone talks in New York. But he was off again.

"So okay, honey, gimme shocked again... even better!" He beamed at Ruby. "OK, Clive. You give me all the daggers and the 'what de fu*k'" I did my best. "Yeah not bad. Do it again. Gimme more aggression...! Yeah, I guess that'll do."

Quiet on the set! 3 – 2 – 1. **Action!**

The cameras start to swivel, Sacha Baron Stationmaster sides down the pole, hits the floor with a bang, looks like he's going to knock Ruby off her chair, and Ruby looks shocked. I'm puffing up the cigar, then jump to my feet, snarling and giving him my best WTF glare as he runs off yelling for his dog. Perfect!

Well Ruby and I were perfect. But they weren't happy with Mr Baron Cohen. The set was reset as we munched a bit more cake and a lady from makeup appeared, just making sure our faces weren't too shiny and much to Ruby's amusement, producing a teeny tiny comb which she used to comb my moustache, making sure it was just perfect! The NYC floor manager guy is back; "Okay Clive, he'll slide down, hit the floor, Ruby does shocked, you do WTF but this time, as you jump up, I wanna big puff of smoke from that cigar, yeah? Okay? That smoke's going to look great in 3D." Oh my God, I think, is this film being made in 3-D? Not too flattering for a man of my size but too late to do anything about it now. I'd signed the papers and was taking the cash. Take two!
And Ruby and I nailed it once again. But they *still* weren't happy with Baron Cohen. Five takes it took! We must've eaten the 5000 calories worth of cake between us and the cigar was little more than a stub by the time we finished. But all too soon, our scene was over. The cry went up, "Clear the set!" and it was time to go. I put my hand on Ruby's arm and said, "Look, you may have a long and fabulous career in acting but for me this will probably be my one dip into it. I'd quite like to sit here and just enjoy the moment for a few minutes and see what happens."
And as I'm talking,

I feel a presence at my side and there is Martha and with her is none other than Martin Scorsese, himself!

"Hi, Clive. Hi Ruby, thanks for being with us today."
His smile is warm and genuine.

"Well, Mr Scorsese," I manage to splutter through my amazement, "Thanks for coming to see us"

"Call me Marty" he replies, and then says to Ruby,
"How old are you honey?"
"I'm 10"

"My daughter's 10th birthday is today", he tells her. And Ruby, confident as anything, says, "What a shame you're not there with her. She'll be missing you. I know I'd miss my Dad if he wasn't there on my birthday."

And she and Mr. Scorsese chat on about the celebration he's planning when he gets home in a couple of weeks' time. Then my new friend Marty turns to me and asks, "Where do you usually act?"

"Well I'm in the events business," I told him, "so every time I've got guests with me"

"I've been watching you on the monitor,"
"You're pretty good. You should keep it up!"
And this from the man who's directed De Niro!

I began to wonder: background actor to foreground actor on one morning. Maybe now, with Marty's backing, movie stardom beckoned. This may not be my *only* day on the set after all!

However, after a moment of fleeting glory, Ruby and I went back to working with the other extras in a couple of scenes and, as we were breaking at the end of the day, for the second time Marty came over to me and I was so touched with what came next. He said, "I took the menu from the table where you sat and I'd like you to have it as a keepsake of your day with us." What a lovely gesture. I was tempted to ask him to sign it for me. I so wish I had now but it was very clear on that list that we weren't to ask for autographs. But I was very happy heading back to wardrobe to hand back our costumes. Ruby of course was exhausted. It had been a long day.

Candy then appeared. I thought she wanted to see how we'd enjoyed the day but she was bringing instruction from the Tent for us to come back to shoot more scenes a couple of days hence. Maybe I really had impressed one of the biggest directors in the film business – but of course it was Ruby they wanted! She was the chosen one, chosen to be coming back to do it all again. But I had my memories and a lovely picture of us that the studio photographer had taken of us in the café and that menu that Marty had given me. On the way back in the few minutes we had together before Ruby fell into a deep sleep I asked how many marks out of 10 she would give the day. 15 she said, before she fell asleep with a big grin on her face.

Of course I had told almost everyone I know that I was to be in Martin Scorsese's new film, and that he had told me personally that he thought I was a pretty good actor. If you've seen "Hugo", which won 5 Academy Awards, or maybe have it on DVD, you may not remember seeing me, which is hard to fathom as I am a hard man to miss in a café scene – especially with a long cigar and a WTF look on his face. But the truth is... my scene never made the final picture and ended up on the cutting room floor. Maybe Sacha Baron Cohen never did get it right? Or perhaps my WTF wasn't quite Fuc*ey enough for the Americans? I'll never know.

But what I do know is that Simon, Ruby's Dad told me he had overheard his daughter telling one of her friends about the day, saying that being saluted by the man at the barrier and parking in the VIP space at Shepperton Studios was so special, and it only happened because they recognised Papa!

Footnote:
Zigger Zagger. *Curiously, even though we had turned down being in the film, when Ruby joined the National Youth Theatre some years later, she appeared in a stage production of 'Zigger Zagger', which I discovered was a most enjoyable piece. It was staged at a delightful little theatre called Wilton's, an old and much-loved music hall theatre in Whitechapel. I would urge you to go and see something there. It is really charming, and it's important for you to know that the catering is wonderful! I thoroughly recommend the giant hot sausage roll. Have one before the performance, and if you enjoy it as much as I did, you could have another in the interval!*

INTO
Africa

Random acts
of
wildness!

Dawn over *the* Mara

One of the best things about Prestige has been the opportunities it has given me to travel. I have not just eaten and drunk my way around Europe but our *Celebration of Wildlife* safaris have allowed me to visit some of the most extraordinary places on the planet. And I want to share with you some tales of the place that has touched me most deeply.

If you get the opportunity to go on an African wildlife safari then you really must. It's a once-in-a-lifetime experience. I am lucky enough through hosting so many of our safaris over the years to now feel very much at home in Africa generally, and Kenya in particular. Which probably means that I'm running out of lifetimes. But, when the final farewell comes, then peering out of a hot air balloon, drifting over the Maasai Mara as the sun comes up, is not a bad way to begin the journey to meet your maker.

I clearly remember my very first hot air balloon ride on my planning trip to Kenya, over 20 years ago. It is a tiny bit nervy the first time you clamber into the basket and see this huge billowing expanse of fabric above you – and realising that all that's going to be keeping you aloft is hot air. A bit like being in Government, really. And I remember gripping the side of the wicker basket, clinging on like somehow this could save me from falling if anything untoward happened.

But it was a comfort – until the pilot, who seeing that I was looking decidedly edgy, thought she could take my mind off things by telling me the "fascinatingly reassuring" fact that

These wicker balloon baskets are made by blind people!

I wondered if lions looked up as we passed over, seeing the basket and thinking it was in fact a picnic basket, filled with, well, breakfast!

But before I could leap to the ground, and thereby shed most of the natural ballast, we were up, up and away.

And as we drifted upwards from the distinctive red Kenyan earth, the ever growing huge orange ball of an African sun rose with us, heralding another scorching day on the plains and I felt all my fears and apprehension fall away too. It was the most magical feeling: the closest I have ever been to feeling lighter than air... or at least under nineteen stone.

And everyone else in the basket, which held 16 of us, was hushed into a reverent silence as we gazed down on a scene that I mused probably hadn't changed very much since Biblical times. There were no towns, no roads, no factories... but there were gazelle, topi, antelope, and countless wildebeest contentedly grazing, as we flew low enough over them to see the sunlight glinting on their beards. Jackals and hyenas were roaming, and we could pick out in the distance a line of magnificent elephants in single file, just like Colonel Hathey's March in Disney's *"Jungle Book"* lumbering their way contentedly toward the silvery river snaking across the plain, and their first drink of the day.

As we drifted closer to the river we saw a pod of hippos wallowing at the bend, their ears, noses and eyes visible, and their enormous bodies submerged. At one stage we flew perilously close to the tops of the trees and were able to look down in wonderment into an eagle's nest. We collectively caught our breaths at the sight of her two unattended chicks huddled together anticipating the warmth of the first rays of the day. Mama must have been away hunting from dawn and I was sure she'd shortly return with breakfast – they did look very well nourished!

And we hung there above this scene, revelling in the silence ...

In an almost spiritual moment... until... *"Aw! Gee! Willya look at that! All the elephants and... other animals and stuff. They're all down there, walking around and stuff! And do all the big animals eat the all little animals?"*

Why it is some people need to tell us what we're all looking at. They are like life's snooker commentators. Why can't they just be quiet and look with their eyes, not their mouths?

I don't know the answer, but one of the 16 in the basket that morning was one of them. And unfortunately this lady had a voice with the volume and tone of the Staten Island Ferry foghorn.

"It's so awesome! It's like AMAZING and so peaceful! And Look! There's a tree! And there's another tree! And like, over there, there aren't any trees. It's sorta like, there are trees and then there aren't trees and, like, you know, I feel so connected with nature and..." and so she went on. And on. And on. A constant barrage of nonsense that quickly got everyone else thinking how we'd really like to connect her with nature... from the great height we were now at.

Then to her ecstatic delight she saw, as indeed we all did, a herd of grazing zebras.

"Oh!! Everyone, down there! Zeebras! Zeebras!!"

And I'm thinking ZebRas! ZebRas! Bl**dy American!!

*"Can you see the **Zeebras**, everyone. Down there! Zeebras."*

Then, New York Foghorn Lady turns to our pilot Ellie (great name for a lady working in Africa!) and says *"Are they guy Zeebras or girl Zeebras down there?"*

Ellie looks down at the herd and says "That is a small bachelor herd – they are all males"

"Awesome! How can ya tell?"

And, without missing a beat, she told her: "A male zebra is black... with white stripes... and females... are white with black stripes."

"Gee! Is that a fact!"

"Absolutely. Here, see for yourself."

And with that she handed her a pair of binoculars and got her identifying the herd. Which not only kept her busy for most of the remainder of the flight... it also kept her mercifully quiet.

A word of warning for the uninitiated: whilst a hot air balloon landing can be a gentle affair when landing upright on the base of the basket, more often than not it tips and then it's both bumpy and hairy. Because believe me, if you hit a termite mound at speed you are glad to be crouched in "the crash position" wedged and protected by your wicker compartment of the basket, as the whole contraption is dragged along the ground before slowing to an eventual halt.

But if that does happen then a glass or two of fizz and breakfast in the bush will soon set you back up and this is what follows all of our balloon rides. The team in the chase vehicles will have set up a long table for us all to enjoy a sizzling breakfast cooked over the still hot upturned burners of the balloon! It's quite something. A unique occasion in the heart of the savannah. There is always a Maasai askari (guard) carrying a spear at the breakfast site, and one of the drivers will have a rifle because it's easy to forget that there could be predators about and just because you can't always see them, it doesn't mean they aren't sometimes there.

In an unexpected confrontation, a cheetah will use its speed to avoid getting injured and will run rather than fight. But a hyena, a leopard or a lion may well use attack as his best form of defence. And let's not forget that hippos kill more people than lions ever do. But it is THEIR natural home.

I only take people on safari who respect the wildlife,

and I'm pleased to tell you that the askari would never shoot to kill. The rifle would be used to fire over the head of a charging animal which will be enough to scare it away.

The effect of the presence alone of the Maasai askari on lions is remarkable. Traditionally when young Maasai men went through their rite of passage from youth to warrior, part of the initiation was to kill a lion singlehanded. This has long since stopped but lions remain extremely wary of Maasai. Cats, whether large or small have very expressive faces, and I've been in the company of Maasais when lions have hooved into view, and even at a distance I've seen through binoculars the look of alarm on lions faces. Invariably the lions will change direction to put distance between them and the perceived danger. I don't know if it's the Maasai's red shukas (robes) their distinct aroma (no disrespect intended) or the sight of the spear, but the lion's reaction is clearly learned behaviour which appears to pass to them through the generations. And so, I can assure you that I've never had a guest eaten.

The Maasai Mara is not only one of the seven natural Wonders of Africa, it is also one of the ten Wonders of the World and an experience not to be missed.

My 50th at Pinewood

The Maasai Mara in Kenya is not only one of the most jaw-droppingly beautiful places on Earth, it is also one of the most important wildlife conservation area in Africa. I visit annually, hosting our *Celebration of Wildlife* trips during the Great Migration where they say over 2 million wildebeest and zebra cross the Mara and Talek rivers. These animals know instinctively that they have to leave the Mara, where they have eaten every blade of grass, and head back to Tanzania's Serengeti where the rains will have come, giving them fertile grazing in abundance once again. This great migration follows the rain, and it is believed that wildebeest can smell rain in the air from over 600 miles away.

During one of my first visits I was taken to a Kenyan school, the Mara Rianda Primary, and met the lovely headmaster, Laurence. We spent ages talking and I learnt from him that in Kenya, primary education is initially free but the last four years of school (from 12 to 16 years of age) had to be paid for by the student's family. He told me that many of his pupils were bright enough to complete their education but at (then) £90 a year for 4 years, most parents couldn't afford for them to do so. Laurence was a quietly spoken man but as we talked his anger and frustration at being a provincial teacher in an underfunded school in the wilds of the African savannah, unable to help his talented pupils to unlock their potential became clear to see. He desperately wanted to find a way to help these children help themselves. I was very moved by him and told him that I would sponsor a boy and a girl and also I said I would see if I could find a couple of friends to do the same.

He lent forward holding my gaze and softly said "if you can make such a difference to just one of the children it would be a miracle".

My conversation with Laurence had made a very deep impression on me, possibly because I remembered my own setback, when a Harrow School education had been so close but equally out of reach, albeit for very different reasons. I had told Laurence that I would try to get 'a couple of friends' to join me in sponsoring Mara Rianda Primary School pupils' further education and I soon started hatching a plan to see just how many I could get.

My 50th birthday was hurtling over the hills towards me and the celebration was to be held at Pinewood Studios, where I'd been on the Board of the private cinema club (Pinewood Club 7) for some years, the last three as Chairman. I thought it was time for someone else to take up the reins, so I informed the Board that I'd be stepping down at the end of April, ten days or so before my birthday and although the cinema had never been closed for a private function at the weekend, at my request the exception was made for this outgoing chairman. On the day, 120 friends and family joined Kay and I for some delicious pre-film food prepared by our friend Celia Burnett, one of the best canapé chefs I know, with an abundance of wine and even tubs of ice cream served from original but now redundant Odeon trays slung around the necks of Kay and me!

After a couple of hours of mingling and chatting which really flew by, the films began with my favourite Tom and Jerry cartoon: the one where Tom is conducting a full orchestra in evening dress, and Jerry is running around under the stage with a saw, deftly and speedily cutting out perfect circles around the chairs of each of the musicians, dropping each through a hole and out of sight. Tom has to carry on conducting and scrambling around in double quick time, trying to simultaneously play all the instruments of the orchestra! It is pure animated comic genius and I'm chuckling away to myself now and enjoying the memory all over again. I had also been in touch with Pearl and Dean, the legendary cinema advertising company, whose "Papa papa papa papa papapa!" fanfare is forever seared into the memories of generations of film-goers, and they had sent me a few of their old ads which we all much enjoyed seeing again.

We followed that with a little-known British film called simply "Sixty Six" which is funny, poignant and set in world cup winning year around Wembley in North London. This area was part of my childhood in the 1960's and the film of course featured one of my heroes Geoff Hurst who, unbeknown to me, I would later meet, interview and work with.

But before this main feature we had an interval and I took the opportunity to make a speech. Well, I had a ready-made audience and never liked to miss an opportunity!

I started with a joke or two, and then introduced my friends to the Mara Rianda Primary School in the Maasai Mara and described the conditions there: the dusty floors, holes in the breezeblock walls where windows should have been, leaking tin roofs, shared battered textbooks and at times not even enough money to top up the chalk supplies. The scene started unfolding in their minds as I described children walking to and from school, up to one and a half hours each way, some in no shoes: no fresh water, only what was collected from the roofs into huge water butts when it rained – and it didn't rain that often.

I then told our friends about that conversation with Lawrence. I read out his response to my email, in which he told me that it *truly touched his heart that a person could visit his school once, understand the challenges the children faced, want to help him to overcome, and then in a land far away would try to persuade many others who hadn't seen for themselves the needs of the people, to give their own money to help strangers they would never meet... It is fear and lack of acceptance that divides whole peoples, but it's humanitarian acts of love like this that unite us, as compassionate individuals.*

It all got very emotional in the interval and that evening our friends donated and pledged enough for us to ensure that not just two or three children benefited, but that **thirty children** who wouldn't otherwise have been be able to finish their education were able to do so. I was overwhelmed and bursting with pride that we were lucky enough to know so many generous people. I said to Kay (on reflection rather immodestly) that I thought it was a visible gesture of our friends love for me that they would support my initiative so enthusiastically.

Kay said "No Clive, you filled them full of booze, sat them in rows like a classroom, and told them a story that made them cry. That's what did it!"

She was probably right, but either way on that evening of my 50th birthday we had started something good.

I was delighted that Mum and Dad had been well enough to be with us that evening and I saw them the following weekend. If Dad ever supported what he considered to be 'a worthy cause' he did so by sending a fiver or maybe a tenner and felt he had done his bit. But before lunch that day he and I were alone and he held out his arms and hugged me for the first time I could ever remember, as he said "I'm giving you £100 for the Kenya bursaries. This is the best thing you've ever done. I'm proud of you, son."

It was the only time I can ever remember Dad telling me he was proud of me, and this meant more to me than he would ever know.

I tried not to let him see the tears in my eyes, but I needn't have worried as there were tears in his. It had been 38 years since he had scuppered my ambition for Harrow School and the relationship between us had never really fully recovered. But this was a turning point. And the day I started believing in karma.

October

The Mara Rianda School needed some money for day to day essentials – food and teachers wages. Getting a few people to give a significant amount is challenging. Getting many people to give a little is easier. So we came up with the idea of producing a wall calendar using art produced by the children, which visitors could buy as keepsakes and as gifts for those back home!

It came together brilliantly. Children who had never had an art lesson in their lives produced some lovely coloured drawings. Chris Collett put it all together for us, designing a very attractive calendar free of charge in his usual generous way, and Gary Ensor very kindly donated the printing. This meant that all of the money paid for the calendars would be able to be used directly by the school. We made it a perpetual calendar, just dates but no days. Very useful for an annual reminder of birthdays, anniversaries and insurance renewals, and more importantly it wouldn't ever be out of date. They sold them for $15 and they did make a difference.

White water - **black rungu**

That night at Pinewood marked the beginning rather than the end of my involvement with the Kenyan schools. To this day I encourage our guests to come with me on a school visit to Mara Rianda, or more recently to a small but growing community primary school called Enkereri, so they experience for themselves the differences their generosity can make to the lives to the children there. Over time our clients have sponsored shoes, sports kit, school uniforms and even the building and equipping of a kitchen for Enkereri Primary. After this opened the extreme lack of funds led to our friends, Gordon and Sarah, who had funded the kitchen to also fund the dinner lady's wages and provide the food for several months.

I'm proud to have made a difference in bringing fresh water to schools and local communities. One time my great friend Richard Long, who runs the Mara Rianda Charitable Trust, was laid up in hospital and frustrated because he needed a final £5,000 to get fresh water pumped from a spring that never dried up

in Aitong (also in the Mara) to the secondary school some four kilometres away, where some of "our" children were continuing their studies. I was co-hosting one of our "Music on the Menu" dinners with our friends at Radisson Edwardian at their luxurious hotel at Heathrow.

After a particularly uplifting set of Sinatra and Dean Martin songs brilliantly performed by my great chum Gary Williams and a delicious main course, I told the 200 or so guests that we were £5,000 short of finishing this water project and reminded people that they had been offered the choice of still or sparkling water with their meal.

I then put up on a screen a startling picture of children drinking from a muddy water hole and simply said "sadly these children don't have that choice.... but you can change that for the children who come next."

People were quick to respond, stuffing money into the envelopes we had put out on their tables, and two gentlemen came over to me (separately) both saying that if we fell short of the £5k to let them know and they'd make up the difference. The short fall was a few pounds off £1500. I told the first generous sponsor that someone else had made a similar pledge, so I would only need to ask him for £750. This dear man who has asked to remain anonymous told me "No Clive (you see it's not only Kay who tells me 'No Clive') I'll give you the full £1500. You keep me quiet and collect the £1500 from the other fellow too. There is so much to do there and I know you'll use the money wisely".

The kindness of strangers is wonderful and really can change lives.

Headmaster Lawrence said that this was the happiest day of his life.

When Richard got out of hospital he oversaw the building of a windmill to pump the water to the school, which is still going today some 13 years or so later. I'm so pleased that Richard captured this evocative image of Headmaster Lawrence and children in their traditional dress enjoying the first fresh water at the school. For some if not all of those children, this would be the first clean water they had ever seen! Another huge success for Richard and the Trust.

Richard is always amused to tell the story that about a year after our first meeting, during a telephone conversation my mind went blank and I monetarily couldn't recall his Christian name, and so called him "Lord Long", much in the way actors call each other "darling" when a name eludes them. He wrote to me shortly after addressing the note "Dear Sir C" I assumed of course that he meant Sir Clive, and it was only years later after signing myself off with that soubriquet many times, that I discovered he had anointed me Sir Cumference. I've still no idea why.

On another safari trip it had been arranged for some of our generous guests to meet some of the children that they were helping. What I didn't anticipate was that on arrival after a hot and dusty journey Kay, the guests and I were shown to a line of chairs and seated in the front row as guests of honour. Behind us were the school governors and a number of the parents, and before us literally the whole school came out to put on a show – just for us! I had been warned by Governor's Camps boss, the debonair Dominic Grammaticas who has done so much for the local communities that attending ceremonies of thanks had become an almost monthly occurrence, that this might happen. So we should have a good breakfast and take plenty of water as we may be detained for some time.

Dominic wasn't wrong. But it was a truly lovely experience. Each year group performed something for us – singing with those stirring African vibes and rhythms, tribal dancing, and other beautiful dancing, some almost balletic and yet more like street dance. It was tremendous. It was also past midday now and we were sitting in full sun, in shorts and had been for some 45 minutes or so. But it would be coming to an end soon I felt sure. Then senior boys, now out of uniform and into their traditional dress, carried on with warrior chanting and dances featuring dangerous looking spears, colourful shields and that incredible pogo jumping that it seems only Maasais can do. The sounds and the intensity of the movements, with the swirling dust created by their jumping left us amazed and speechless. We all applauded and cheered with all our might!

The new Headmaster, Peter, then surprised me by publicly thanking me for all I was doing for the school and with no warning invited me to address the whole school, children, teachers, governors (village elders) and parents. If I wasn't already sweating enough from prolonged exposure to the midday sun, I was certainly sweating now! As you'll guess, I'm not usually lost for words but on this occasion I was. With expectant faces all looking my way, I had to think on my feet and I told the children that I'd first come to Africa drawn by the opportunity to see their magnificent wildlife and to breathe in the beauty of the natural landscapes but what I took home with me was the memory of the happy smiling faces of the people, and of the children especially. That I felt a strong connection to this place – their place – and that the pleasure of helping them on their way was all mine.

I suppose it was quite a short speech (African presentations and speeches seem to drag on for what seem like days usually) so one of the teachers decided that as I was in Maasailand I should demonstrate my pogo dancing abilities. As you know I am a man of heroic proportions and jumping is not a pastime I have ever devoted any time to, nor a skill I've ever sought to develop for fear of serious injury on landing. I did my best and I'm told my elevation from ground level could be measured in inches rather than feet; in reality it was probably in *fractions* of inches. The little children sitting on the ground in the front rows of the assembled gathering probably only spoke Maa, the local language, and not even Swahili at that age let alone English, so the Headmaster's kind words and my short response would have gone right over their heads, but boy did they laugh and point at this fat *mgeni** who couldn't even jump as high as a six-year-old!

But still, there was more to come and next I found myself being presented with several rows of colourful beaded necklaces, a fly whisk (a short, beaded stick with a wildebeest tail which you wave to keep the flies off) and a colourful shawl called a shuka which looks a bit like a red and black car rug. But the main part of the presentation was my receiving a black rungu, which is a thick carved stick, a bit like an Irish shalalee with a fearsome bulbous head at one end and sharpened to a point at the other. I was told that wherever I walked carrying a black rungu I would be recognised as a Maasai elder, would be treated with the respect of an elder, and would always be welcome to sit and join anyone who had food. I quipped that I would try it back home, but that I didn't think I'd have much luck in Berkhamsted High Street despite passing at least three cafés and a bakers between my office and Waitrose.

I think my little joke unwittingly upset the headmaster. He sent someone scuttling off to his office who quickly returned with a cutting from the *Daily Nation* containing a picture of President Obama being presented

Tour guide who believes his gift to Obama made him win the poll

2006

157

with a black rungu by the Kenyan Minister of Tourism. He told me that not many white people have been honoured in this way and one of them was Prince Charles. I discovered this was absolutely true and that his presentation was made during his visit to Kenya in 2011.

Having got over the surprise of doing an impromptu speech, the embarrassment of trying to jump like a Maasai in front of about 800 Maasai and in the process proving beyond doubt that the average Englishman can't jump, this was one of the nicest things that had ever happened to me. My sunburnt knees were glowing with pride, and I thought to myself, thank goodness I hadn't had to go through the traditional circumcision as part of my induction into Maasai culture.

Usually the children hung back until they had seen you a few times but this day, perhaps because I had been willing to poke fun at myself, the children all crowded round afterwards, chattering and waving enthusiastically. Above the general babble of children's happy voices, one grinning boy asked me if I played football. Another if knew David Beckham! During a short pause in the pandemonium, a demure little girl asked me if I knew the Queen. I told her I didn't but that I had been lucky enough to have been invited to go inside Buckingham Palace. They listened almost in awe as I told them about the many rooms all filled with treasures, the beautiful thrones in huge rooms with very high ceilings hung with large paintings of past Kings and Queens of England, the lashings of gold paint and acres of red carpet, seemingly stretching for miles. I kidded that I'd almost tripped over one of the Queen's corgis. Kay had to explain that a corgi was a little dog.

Then a very serious boy probably in his early teens and stick thin as sadly they all are, boldly said "Thomas!" (this Headmaster always called me Thomas) "Thomas I have a question for you".

I asked him his name and he told me "Peter".

"I'll remember that as my brother is called Peter. Do you know what you want to do when you leave school?"

"Yes I want to train to be a doctor and it is in this regard that I have a question for you!" "How many meals a day do you eat?"

What a great question! I told him that if I was lucky I had three. He cast his eyes to the ground and in a soft voice said, "If *I am lucky* I get one".

I wanted to introduce to him the concept of exercise combined with eating so I asked him if he played football.

"Yes," he said. "I love to play football."

"Do you walk to school?" I continued.

"Yes, I walk one hour to school".

"And you walk another hour to get home. I on the other hand drive everywhere. When I go to work, I park my car within about 20 paces of the door of my office, usually only go up the stairs twice during the day and..."

He cut me off abruptly with a wave of his arm, a gesture beyond his tender years saying "Yes, yes, I'm sure all of this will be made clear to me once I get to medical school!"

Of course I've lost touch but I feel sure Peter is practising somewhere today, if not as a doctor, then maybe as a dietician advocating a few hours exercise as well as calorie counting. I do hope he remembers where he heard it first!

Lawrence, the headmaster who's conversation with me started all this, was both a respected teacher and a wise man and he once told me something that has always stayed with me; 'In Kenya there are 42 tribes, each with its own language, culture and traditions. As in the rest of the world where there are tribes or different religions, different nationalities and different political beliefs, these differences often lead to division and conflict. But we need to find the things we have in common, which can bring us together. We are all members of many different "tribes or groups" which make us stand willingly with people different to ourselves, at different times, when we share the same values or challenges'.

What wisdom!

Footnote:

mgeni: Loosely translated from Swahili, means a stranger, not from round here. It is not a disrespectful term.

African zebra *crossing*

Wake up call 6 am.

There is the faintest of pink ribbons in the sky.
I yawn, stretch and smile with the anticipation of what is to come.
It's hard to wake up in Africa in a bad mood. The dawn tickles my toes
as the new day strikes the end of my bed with sparkling golden rays.
There's no time to waste, as in the plains beyond a lion roars beckoning
me to my 6.30 game drive.

Our guests are all wearing their safari hats; I suspect it's not because they
think that they need pre-dawn protection from the rays but rather it's to
hide their bed-head hair!

I always tell our first time guests that to get the best out of any game drive
you don't go out with preconceived ideas as to what you MUST see.
You just go out, *be* in the moment and appreciate everything around you.
Going out in the Maasai Mara is like having a box of delicious chocolates,
but without the sheet telling you which ones are which. You know you're
going to get something good, but exactly what? *That* is the big surprise.

At any moment you might see
a cheetah lock onto a gazelle, or
an impala. This most graceful of
cats will stalk them with utmost
stealth, continually surveying the
area to make sure there are no
lions, hyenas or jackals around
to steal his kill. You stay silent,
barely daring to breathe, and then with a sudden burst of energy he makes
his move, and despite the cheetah's dazzling acceleration, if he has moved
just a fraction too soon the gazelles will see the movement and instinctively
be up and with the speed of... well, startled gazelles! They will be away, zig
zagging across the plain. Damn! Foiled again. The guides estimate only
one in ten chases ended in success. That's a lot of wasted energy.

We know the *big five* (so called from hunting days) are around: Lion, Cape Buffalo, Rhino, Leopard, and African Elephant. We've come up with a few categories of our own – the *shy five*, the *ugly five*, and on walking safaris the *little five*. One of our regular guests, Janet's husband Peter, said he thought the *shy five* sounded like an introverted '60s pop group. His humour gets no better with time!

Their camouflage is masterly. It is amazing how animals as large as elephants, even in herds can get lost to the naked eye once in the cover of light woodland. You can drive within a few feet of a leopard without realising that she is right there, above you laying out on the branch of a tree. They blend miraculously into the landscape.

Jacob and the other drivers are all past masters at spotting any tell-tale signs of predator activity. We'd not been out for long when he saw a gang of vultures in a tree, and with more arriving we knew that someone had a kill and we soon came across two male lions, their faces and throats stained with blood. Other members of the pride were circling around. There were four females and any number of cubs and sub-adults at varying stages of development, including a couple of very small and cute cubs, all of them waiting for their turn to get stuck in. To my amazement some sought shade in the shadow of our safari vehicle! How staggering that they had been able to turn man's intrusion into their world to their advantage - and it meant that we were less than four feet away from five hungry lions!

Jacob quietly explained to the guests that we were perfectly safe. Because everybody wants to see little cubs, so the cubs themselves get used to seeing us! From as far back as each lion can remember they have always seen safari vehicles, often quite close and are not spooked by them. Knowing that their mums were okay with that, they in turn were not alarmed. They recognise the shape, smell and sound. But if you get out of the vehicle and present yourself as human shape – well, that could be another matter entirely!

We were always amused by the warthog families. Fat little creatures with sticky up tails, curly tusks and short little legs, with tiny mini-me piglets following on behind, as if following signals from the mother's antenna-like tails! They're so fat that when it comes to eating short grass they can't bend their necks so have to bend both of their front legs and look as if they're kneeling down to eat.

Sadly for them they are also known as *lion sausages*.

There were zebra aplenty, birds of all sizes and colours, giraffe striding confidently to a destination only they knew, and a few content hippo, wallowing at the bend of the river. Out of the corner of my eye I caught sight of a serval, a handsome spotted cat, moving silently through the grass. Like leopards they can climb trees to get out of trouble, but this one wasn't in the slightest bit of trouble and was not at all bothered by our presence.

Guests on our annual *Celebration of Wildlife* migration safari have always been in the right places to see a river crossing or two. By early October, the wildebeest and zebra have eaten almost every blade of the Mara grasses and can literally smell the rains coming south in the Serengeti. They instinctively know they need to head back. But to do so they have to cross one of the rivers, the Mara or the Talek. A crossing can happen at any time, and when it does the gathering of wildebeest and zebra begin with just a few hundred on the riverbank. As time passes their numbers build to 1000, 2000, 5000 and sometimes many more animals even than that will be waiting to cross.

I was out one day with Johnny Truss, our wonderful wildlife artist, and some regular safari companions when we came across a large herd of zebra and wildebeest gathered at the bank of the river. The animals at the front were skittish – seeming to be scared of their own reflections in the water. They knew there could be snakes in the river and they could see the crocodiles, their menacing rows of teeth glinting in the sun light. Crocodiles eat only every four days or so and those about to cross will have no idea whether these predators are hungry! Then there is more potential danger to contend with, as on the other side of the river any bush or thicket provides perfect cover for a leopard or a lioness waiting to pounce on the old, the infirm or any one of them who got too close.

You could sense the agony of indecision as the herd grappled with the dilemma of *to cross or not to cross?* The rain ripened grass beyond the river must have been cruelly tantalising.

Time passed and then slowly they began moving closer and yet closer to the water's edge, bunching together without a hairs breadth between them. Crowding, pushing, then with painful slowness, a lone zebra in the front line moved ahead of the others and plunged in, slipping, lurching - then another followed by another. By now the leading animal had reached the bank opposite us, clambered up the steep muddy slope to safety and galloped on onto the plain beyond.

Behind him the commotion quickly gathering pace as the others followed, now all at once keen to get across.

For a full 20 or 25 minutes the river was bedlam.

A maelstrom of splashing, swimming, a few trampling on others; some of the younger ones, probably in a river for the first time and relying on their sixth sense to stay out of danger while struggling to stay afloat. The sound of camera motor drives whirring like helicopter blades was drowned out by

the pandemonium below us. The bank became more and more slippery with some of the animals close to the top believing they were out of trouble, losing their footing, slithering and sliding back, crashing down on those coming up from the water.

But eventually they all emerged apparently unscathed.

This time there were no lions waiting in ambush and the crocodiles weren't hungry. *Next time* maybe will be different. I turned and smiled to Mike and Judith; Andy and Lynn.

We had shared something very special together, and breathed a collective sigh of relief. Johnny reminded us that we had witnessed one of the seven wonders of the natural world.

Scenes like these have never lost their magic for me and I'm sure for thousands of others. We go on safari, because we love it! Nothing stays the same but it seems that in Africa at least it changes slowly. This remote theatre of nature's mysteries can't be imagined or bettered, and I always look forward eagerly to my front row seats for the next performance, which is why I hurry back whenever I get the chance.

I get an offer for Kay!

Of course it was the wildlife that had attracted me to Africa, but the landscapes are wonderful too and the lack of light pollution means that the night skies twinkle in a most magical and spell binding way. Out in this wilderness staring up at the heavens you can't help but wonder what life may lay beyond.

As Africa weaves it spell upon you so its people draw you to them. There are 42 tribes in Kenya, and the vast National Parks that we visit on safari are on what is traditionally Maasai land. The Oromo are the poorest tribe, with the Maasai next. But nevertheless, they have a rich culture and I always invite one of the elders to come and talk to our guests.

I've been lucky in finding people from such a different culture and background who get my ethos of being light-hearted and entertaining whilst informing our guests of their lives, culture and history. One of the most entertaining is Ben Kipeno, who is chief of his village and always a star turn. Ahead of our guests arrival at the bar tent for his talk, we put some tomato juice into a small empty water bottle which Ben secretes in the folds of his classic red and black shuka.

He looks every bit the traditional Maasai wearing leather sandals, which he had made himself, beads over the shuka and he always carries both a fly whisk and the black rungu signifying that he is an elder. What his captivated audience don't know is that he has driven to us in his Suzuki and his mobile phone is always discreetly hidden out of sight!

Ben talks about the way his people live today and how they have always lived in times past. Historically, they depended on their cattle to provide their food, clothing, and shelter. Their traditional diet relied heavily on milk and dairy products, lean beef, cattle fat, and blood. Cooking utensils and drinking bowls were traditionally made from cattle rib bones and horns. Cowhides have often been used for bedding materials and for walls or roofs of temporary shelters. As he explains it, "Maasai families try to build up large herds because owning many cattle is a way to show that we are rich. Men may have more than one wife, but only if we own enough cattle, as cows must be given to the bride's family before the wedding."

This is my cue to ask Ben if it is true that the Maasai still drink the blood of their cattle, to which he replies, "Yes we do, and it is delicious and nutritious." He then produces the bottle of red liquid and tells the guests that this is fresh blood which he's bought from his village for anyone to try. Unsurprisingly, no one is ever quick to step forward but one time, after Ben had carefully unscrewed the cap and taken a gulp one of our rookie safari guests, a lady who happened to be a farmer's wife, decided that she would try. The looks on the faces of the other guests could not hide what they were thinking about her trepidacious decision! She gingerly took a sip, and I could see by her expression that she'd caught on immediately to the prank. Without letting the cat out of the bag she agreed with Ben that it was indeed delicious and offered the bottle around. Disappointingly, but perhaps not unsurprisingly, no one plucked up the courage to follow suit.

We had become used to the terms of respect and endearment the younger Kenyans used for us older people. They referred to Kay as *Mama,* and routinely called me *Big Papa.* One time Ben had been complaining of tummy pains, so Kay gave him a Remegel, an instant stomach pain reliever which solved his problem almost immediately. He was clearly grateful for our fast acting medication and thanked 'Mama' profusely, prompting Kay to give him the rest of the tube.

I told him "medicine is just one of her fine attributes. I know you have many wives. Maybe we can do a deal on another. How many cows will you give me for Mama? 70? 80? A hundred perhaps?"

He thought for a long moment as he looked her up and down, "Nah" he said, waving a dismissive hand. "I'll give you five goats!"

I think he was half serious. Kay snatched back the tube of lozengers, muttering under her breath,

"You can keep your pain!"

Harrison is another Maasai who has done well. He attended The Mara Rianda School, and joined Governor's from school working his way up the ranks to become their first Maasai Manager. He is a charming fellow and another of our regular speakers.

We knew from Ben that for the Maasai of southern Kenya and northern Tanzania, the traditional way of life is centered around cattle. Harrison explained further, that they believe the Creator God, Enkai, sent cattle sliding down a rope from the heavens, and entrusted their safe keeping explicitly into the hands of the Maasai! So they believe they own every cow. He shares tales about how as a boy he went with his father and uncles on raids, to bring back other tribe's cattle back to their herds!

I explained to Harrison that surely this is a myth, a fable and another of Kenya's lovely tales. I went on "We would call it cattle rustling at best, and at worst, outright theft!"

But the Maasai didn't see it that way. Apparently simply *believing* that all cattle belongs to them is enough and meant that taking cows from other tribes was doing nothing wrong as they were simply claiming their birthright. I told Harrison that I truly believe that the car Creator God, Enzo Ferrari, had entrusted all the Ferraris to my tribe, the *Crafty Thomas's,* and so with that belief firmly held, I was planning to claim my birth right by liberating all the Ferraris I could find the moment I arrived back home.

"No Clive you can't do that," he told me with a serious look on this face, "it only works with cows."

Of course, the Maasai culture has changed beyond measure, and as the modern world has had more and more influence, so raids have become a thing of the past. One of the positive changes is that the women are no longer expected to take silent roles, their existence revolving solely around looking after their children. Women have become much more active participating members, both in their families and also in their communities. There are now many farsighted elders who are encouraging changes of philosophy to allow women the same rights as men, to the extent that a mother can now safely voice her opinion, especially in

matters concerning her own children, their education and marriage.

A great example of this change is personified in Jaqueline who has risen to become the Deputy Headmistress of Enkereri, the little community primary school that we help. Not surprisingly Jaqueline told me she believes that the strongest tool for this change is education. But her people are proud of their heritage and even she feels that traditions cannot be entirely forgotten in their new and developing society.

She told me "I am so proud of the many girls who have been educated beyond primary school and are being successfully employed, because from this position they can now *choose* the future they want. This is so different from the times when they were barely more than children, and were married off."

I said I couldn't imagine how frightened and powerless they must have felt, trapped by the traditions of their forebears.

Jaqueline is a great role model for the children. She teaches them how important it is to learn to live with people of different backgrounds and cultures, to be respectful to everyone, to believe they can succeed, and always be proud of where they came from. Kenya needs more great women like Jaqueline in positions of influence.

Clive's Kenya Scrapbook

The children always give us a smiling welcome. They know visitors often bring sweets!

A new classroom built by Richard's Mara Rianda Trust being swept before the desks arrive.

Hours of fun for everyone with this old parachute.

There was a very good reason that this flight was delayed.

Even the little ones are roped in to care for the animals. He loves his goat!

5Y-BSE

Celebration of Wildlife — the last night
To our delight, Governor's staff reform.
the Santana Bush Band, and the Masai
dance us a traditional final farewell.

It is wondrous to be looking
down on the carpet of nature,
detached from the stresses of life.

No need for air conditioning
in the staff room at
Enkereri Primary School.

Churchill and hippos

Africa is a land of stories: some of which are handed down through the generations as a sort of oral history and others can be created during your visit. One of my favourites concerns an elephant called Churchill.

He was an old bull elephant who over the years had become a regular and amiable visitor to Little Governor's Camp. He used to wander down the pathways stopping occasionally to nibble at tasty shoots. He was a harmless old thing who never did much damage, either to the camp or to the guests, so everyone was pleased to see him.

Little Governor's Camp is set around the edges of a huge natural water hole attracting animals and birds large and small and around the edges grow wild Marula bushes. Cultivated Marula berries are used to make a drink called Amarula. It is velvety, rich, nutty with a hint of citrus, and not unlike Bailey's.

The wild Marula fruit is also a favourite among rhinoceroses, giraffes and monkeys, but no creature is as keen and passionate about the Marula as the elephant, particularly when the berries are ripe and they ferment making the sugar turn to alcohol.

One day this old bull elephant decided to push the boat out and stripped not one but two Marula bushes of their fruit. The berries had well and truly fermented so he was a little the worse for wear when he staggered into camp, and for no apparent reason took an instant dislike to a couple of the German guests who were staying there. He fixed them with a malevolent eye, trumpeted loudly and flapping his ears, started lurching after them, chasing them past the bar tent almost to the other end of the camp.

The askari were astonished and alarmed at this unprecedented behaviour but not nearly as alarmed as the hapless couple who suddenly had an inebriated, enraged bull elephant in hot pursuit! By distracting him the askaris managed to calm the situation and the German couple escaped, somewhat shaken, but fortunately unscathed.

So the old tusker was nicknamed Churchill – because he liked a drink and had chased the Germans.

There is a wonderful picture of him in the camp album leaving against a tree resting his tusks on the roof of the bar tent apparently asleep. It is captioned *Churchill sleeping off a hangover!*

Some years later another German couple were leafing through the album and came across the picture and asked "Viy iss dis elephant calt Churchill?"

Now this is a difficult one to answer, especially if you don't want to offend the guests. Whilst the barman, who knew the truth was fumbling for an answer, George the manager and our convivial host, ever the quick thinking diplomat, told them that he had asked the same question, and was told that *Churchill* roughly translated into Swahili means *warrior/ great leader* and as this old bull elephant was a survivor of many battles the waiters had christened him Churchill! The guests accepted this as gospel, and ordered some more drinks. What a great recovery!

Africa is a wonderful place to visit for an unforgettable holiday, however it's not the ideal place if what you're looking for is peace and quiet. One night, I was staying at Little Governor's and I was kept awake by strange noises outside my tent. I was used to the cacophony made by the combination of thousands of rowdy little frogs who are very noisy, and a battalion of rambunctious crickets but *this noise* was very different to what I'd heard before. I partially unzipped the front of my tent, poked my head and torch through the flaps and saw that

I was surrounded by hippos who had emerged from the water hole and had decided to spend the night snorting and farting whilst grazing on the grass seemingly all around my tent!

Hippos are comical looking creatures but not to be tangled with.

I was relieved to know that they haven't learnt to work zips!

They move very quickly for big animals and kill more people each year in Africa than lions. I quickly retreated back into the tent; I wasn't going to go out and ask them to keep it down and let me get some shut-eye.

A Kenyan fable tells that when The Creator made all the animals, he left the hippopotamus until last and then he formed, rather than designed them, making use of the animal parts and pieces he had left. A great fat body, huge wide mouth, but with tiny ears and eyes – nothing was in proportion! It had been a long week, he was tired, and so, without too much thought, The Creator made the hippo an amphibian.

However, that night he had a terrible dream that with its big wide mouth, the hippopotamus would scoop up all the fish he had made for the humans to eat! So the following morning The Creator said to the hippopotamus "I need you to live on the land and be a grazing animal." The hippo flatly refused, saying that he liked the cool water and wallowing in the mud. So The Creator explained his reason, that he was afraid that the hippopotamus would eat all the fish.

The hippo thought for a while, and made a deal with The Creator saying "If you let us live in the water during the day when it's hot, we will not eat the fish, but rather will come onto the land at night and graze like the zebra and the wildebeest. To prove that we have kept our word, we will leave our dung on the land so that whenever you want, you can come and pick it up to see that there are no fish scales or bones in it"

The Creator thought this was a good and fair arrangement and agreed.

And so that's why the hippos wallow in the cool water during the day, and when the sun goes down come up out of the water to graze, leaving their dung every night to prove to The Creator that they haven't eaten any of the fish!

And I can personally attest to the amount of dung they leave as the next morning, the askaris and room stewards were out early with shovels and buckets clearing a path from our tents, through the steaming evidence of the hippo's nocturnal feasting.

My friends
and other animals

Our *Celebration of Wildlife* trips are travel *events,* made special by involving personalities connected with the natural world who travel with us, and share with us insights into their wonderful worlds of wildlife.

In early 2000s Jonathan Scott, Simon King and Saba Douglas-Hamilton presented an extremely popular BBC series called *Big Cat Diary,* which followed the stories of big cats in the Mara. These presenters gave the animals names which helped build bonds between them and an ever growing television audience.

So we invited Jonathan and his ace photographer wife Angie to join our first *Celebration of Wildlife* and we were able to follow in the BBC's tyre tracks when looking for *The Marsh Pride of lions, Honey* the cheetah and her sister *Kike* (pronounced "Kee-Kay"), and *Bella* the leopard and her little cub *Chui.* Finding these animals and having Jonathan telling us about his experiences with them was like having a live and very personal Big Cat commentary in our safari jeeps out on the plains. So successful was our partnership that the Scotts accompanied us on 11 trips to the Mara, and co-hosted with me in India, Zambia, and on a vessel we chartered cruising for a spectacular week around the Galapagos Islands.

In the Mara, *The Marsh Pride* invariably had any number of cubs that would entertain us with their rough and tumbles, and their favourite game of biting mum's tail. Over the years there were several pride males, the most recognisable being *Notch* with his huge and distinctive black mane, a piece missing from his ear and, despite being a fearsome lion warrior, he was very gentle with his cubs.

Cheetahs I learned are the most fragile of the big cats; their cubs are prey for lion, leopard and hyena and their kills are regularly stolen by other predators. Their own lives even as adults are always in danger from a lion or leopard attack. So being a successful cheetah mum is quite an achievement! *Honey* was a magnificent mother. Cheetahs give birth to usually four or five cubs and some say up to 90%, are lost to other predators, but *Honey* managed to raise at least five litters totalling 17 cubs to my knowledge.

Cheetahs will often hop onto a termite mound to allow them an elevated view, making it easier for them to spot any potential prey or even predators that may be lurking in the tall grass, waiting to steal their kill. Although *Honey* never did it herself, some of her cubs developed the knack of jumping on safari vehicles to scope out the surrounding area. Her sister *Kike* took it one stage further by jumping onto the roof of Jonathan's vehicle while filming and whilst up there making deposits by squatting over the open roof hatch to give Jonathan the distinction of becoming "the bloke the cheetah crapped on!"

Jonathan and Angie are the only husband and wife team to have both won the prestigious BBC Wildlife Photographer of the Year competition. Although many people come on safari with heavy long lenses, almost as tall as themselves, with the intention of getting close up shots of animals heads, I've often passed on Jonathan's wisdom of the value of taking the wider shot when photographing wildlife, giving the subject a sense of *place* out in the wild. After all, a decent head shot can be taken at most zoos and wildlife parks back home.

After a few years of running the trips, we met Jackson Looseyia, a legendary Maasai guide who joined the Big Cat presenting team and has his own camp near the Talek River – prime leopard country! Leopards are much harder to spot as they are solitary, well camouflaged and essentially nocturnal.

But Jackson, who is in tune with the daily rhythms of the bush, sees the signs and instinctively knows where these most elusive of cats are likely to be found.

One morning after the guests had departed, Kay and I were out with Jackson. It was still very early so blankets were wrapped round us. It was quiet, the sun was just waking up and I felt in need of more coffee to wake me up!
As we turned a bend, there in front of us, standing in the middle of the track was a female leopard. We stopped quickly. She didn't move nor did she seem bothered at our sudden appearance. Jackson was pretty sure this was *Olive*, Bella's daughter who they had filmed. Often all you'll catch is a glimpse of a leopard as it disappears into the forest or long grass, but here she was *out in the open* and apparently in no hurry to leave. The reason soon became apparent as silently out of the undergrowth emerged her adorable cub who Jackson immediately recognised as *Kali*, thus confirming that the Mum was definitely *Olive*. We were treated to a touching greeting between mother and son, with both cats rubbing the scent glands under their whiskers together, *Kali* nuzzling under Olive's chin while *Olive* was making low gentle awww, awww awww sounds to comfort her boy. Then they ambled off, following the edge of the road and we happily followed on behind, seeing the marks left in the dusty earth by their soft paws.

Clues for anyone coming later that they had missed two leopards!

175

Soon they veered off back into cover to spend the day doing what leopards do – keeping out of our sight! To see a leopard is always a treat, and to see two share those intimate moments was incredibly special.

The personalities on these trips are not always only human!

It's been such a pleasure to work with other wildlife experts including multi-award winning BBC cameraman Warren Samuels, who helps us get the best from whatever cameras we have, movie or still, and always brings some exciting footage from his latest assignment. On one occasion his video featured three tribesmen pulling off the staggering trick of getting some lions to stand down whilst they boldly marched to their kill and deftly cut off a leg of their impala prey, stealing it from right under their noses! The lions had quizzical looks on their faces and it looked as if they knew they had been conned but couldn't quite work out how. In case you are wondering, yes, they got away with it!

On a game drive late one afternoon Warren had the driver move on just a few feet, so that we could see the sun catching the dust on an elephant through our camera lenses, glistening as if a patissier had flung a handful of castor sugar over his back. The touch of a professional at work. Just the skill he'd need to get those wonderful wildlife images we are so used to seeing on our TV screens at home described by David Attenborough.

William Fortescue, another fine wildlife photographer had me photographing some wildebeest from a low camera angle as the early morning sun caught their beards in its watery rays. "It's always all about the light" he told me. Reinforcing what Warren had shown me and teaching me a thing or two about considering different camera angles. Johnny and Angie always talked about the light. What great teachers I've been privileged to learn from.

You see nature in different ways when you are with a photographer.

But without a camera to divert your attention you feel as if you are more than just an observer, being completely in the moment and part of the scene, immersed in nature.

Ascot Visionaries
Glasses for Africa

Eyesight is routinely not good in the poorer and more remote areas of parts of Africa, but there are mobile Eye Clinics, usually manned by volunteer opticians. We were able to provide spectacles to clinics in Kenya and Zambia with the help of Ascot Racecourse, and some of our lovely Prestige clients.

The racecourse kindly loaned me a supersize viewing box to host our "Ascot Visionaries" race day where guests were asked to bring unwanted specs. Amazingly 40 guests donated almost 1,000 pairs! Extraordinary. Our supporters roped in their offices, a choir, a school, a golf club, and even Southampton Airport Lost Property!

After collection and before bagging, the specs were all sterilised and lenses measured by a focimeter so that their individual prescription could be labelled. This enables the optician on the ground to best match the specs he has to the patient's needs. Ingenious eh? We'll do it again soon.

It was so good to see Jo, one of my best General Managers after so many years at Ascot Visionaries.

Out in Africa, some lucky people received a pair of our specs after years of blurred vision. The medics told us that people said things like "Praise God, this is like a miracle." One old man even whispered "Now my life can begin again." So humbling isn't it? I was told of a nervous young barefooted lady wearing hand-me-downs. She walked away with the lenses she needed which happened to be housed in Gucci frames! I wish we had a photo.

Cline's **Zambia** Scrapbook

The elephants have for generations been treading the same path from their forest home to reach the ripe mangos which they LOVE. That Mfuwe Lodge has been built on the path does not deter them one iota!

Sometimes the children get there first! We bought all their mangoes from the vehicle and took them back to camp.

The schools here are woefully underfunded as in Kenya.

We visited the village where the "mango children" came from. They welcomed us with a lovely dance!

The Life size Tusker!

Since the sad passing of David Shepherd, Jonathan Truss, known as JT, has been acknowledged as the UK's foremost fine art wildlife artist and is another person who always brings yet another dimension to our forays into the natural world. He loves our safaris and adds great value by giving talks over pre dinner drinks and leading an art class most afternoons, where his skills as a tutor ensure that even art no hopers like me bring home a drawing to be proud off. JT's putty rubber makes all the difference!

Doing passable impressions of Ronnie Corbett, the legendary Norman Wisdom and Alan Whicker amongst others, he is a good chap to have around, especially on one of the rare wet afternoons when the heavens open, the tracks become quagmires seemingly in minutes and we find ourselves confined to camp. My own Whicker impersonation isn't too bad but in the presence of JT I find myself always "out-Whickered!" He does have the advantage of having an actual pair of Whicker's famous horn rimmed glasses, which I'm convinced gives him an unfair advantage.

Like me, Jonathan has a few hair brained schemes and managed to get me excited about one of them with the words "I want to raise the profile of the plight of elephants being killed for their ivory and raise money for some of the teams on the ground protecting them by painting a big tusker, head on, to fine art standard. *But life size!*"

It sounded incredibly ambitious.

"But that means your canvas is going to have to be huge. A male elephant stands at least 13 or 14 feet tall Johnny" I replied.

"Yep, that's right" he said, with a horn rimmed gleam in his eye. I wondered how he would do it as he's only a little fellow. And where? His studio certainly wasn't big enough.

"Who would buy it?" I wondered.

"Someone with a big wall to fill" he enthused.

But first things were first. He asked me if I wanted to help him make it work. Of course I did!

Eager to see if we could make it happen, I made some calls, and was able to cover our costs by assembling an enthusiastic group of ten people who had been with us on safari before, and most of all who cared about elephants. They were to join JT and me on a special trip to Kenya's Tsavo East to get some photographic reference. Tsavo East is where the largest number of the few remaining big tuskers on the planet still roam.

I contacted our regular aircraft operator, Torben Rune, who fixed for one of his aircraft to fly us down from Nairobi. The kind of photos JT was hoping to get were inspired by a shot he'd seen of one of the biggest ever recorded tuskers called Satao on the cover of a book. This elephant was named after the camp near which he had been photographed, which I thought was a good omen and promptly booked some tents at Satao Camp, which I discovered has its own waterhole frequented almost daily by elephants.

I was delighted to also obtain permission from KWS (Kenya Wildlife Service) for us to go off road within a strict 48 hour period to get the best close up shots possible. I even spoke to Gyles Brandreth about the possibilities of getting JT and the finished painting on BBCs *The One Show*. We contacted Prince William in his capacity as patron of *Tusk,* a charity that does much to support Africa's elephant population, to ask if he might become involved in receiving a donation if *Tusk* were one of the elephant charities to benefit from the sale of the painting. No one had said no, so we set off excitedly with a few agreements "in principle" under our belts.

On the first afternoon the guests went off with JT in search of the tuskers, whilst I stayed behind to catch up with Torben over a beer, curiously called "Tusker!" Truly. After Torben left, camp was deserted apart from one other man who was sitting in the bar, head down editing images in his camera. I introduced myself and asked what he was doing out here in the wilderness all on his own. He told me his name was Johan, that he just wanted a few days away from the pressures, and that he enjoyed photographing the old bull elephants with the long tusks. He certainly had some impressive pictures, but I sensed he really did want to be on his own, so I said "I'll leave you to your editing – I'm here with a few friends and we're gathering for a glass or two at 7 o'clock. If you fancy joining us you'll be welcome." He warmed to me. "Thanks" he replied, "I'll come and have a beer with you before dinner."

I thought no more of it.

Later at the bar JT's pal Simon had been reading his newspaper from the flight out, and was showing some photos from it, some quite harrowing in fact, about the work of a South African vet who was having great success in saving the lives of rhinos whose horns had been cruelly hacked out of their faces by evil poachers whilst the poor hapless animals were still alive. The vet was developing never before used techniques to rebuild rhino's heads and faces! We were all both enthralled and instantly in awe of this man, pioneering new ways to save these victims who would certainly have all died from their injuries without such intervention. With that, my new friend Johan, joined us. As I was introducing him to the team, Simon was finishing the story and Johan cut in

"Hey that's me, in the story. I'm that vet!"

"No!" came back Simon, "that's just too much of a coincidence. It can't be."

Johan said "we are called *Saving the Survivors*. Does it say in your paper the name of the vet or the group?" Simon looked again, and open mouthed told us, punctuating every word "they are called... Saving... the... Survivors. Dr *Johan* Marais is their founder."

From lonely-looking-bloke-in-the-bar who I'd felt a bit sorry for, we were all immediately drawn to this good natured South African wildlife hero, as Johan seamlessly became our unofficial guest speaker for the evening, telling us about the amazing success they have had treating many wild animals left to die by poachers, and not only rhino, but elephant, cheetah, wild dogs and lion, caught in brutal traps left by these hateful individuals.

If it's injured Johan will treat it! *Saving the Survivors* is a private charity funded entirely by donations. We all made sure we had his card with the web address to make contributions of our own.

Tsavo is such a huge area, and there was no guarantee that we would find what we were looking for. But Torben had given us coordinates of where he had seen a herd not too far from camp whilst flying back the previous evening, and the following morning we headed in that direction. We'd been out for a couple of hours when in the distance our driver spotted a herd of elephants, and as we drew closer could see – yes! Several old bulls with long LONG tusks – just what JT was hoping for. How lucky! We had only passed one other car that morning, and now there wasn't another vehicle in sight, so we'd have them to ourselves. We slowly continued in their direction not wanting to startle the herd and they ignored us carrying on their walk, with our lenses fixed and KWS permission to go off road and get close, we headed towards the herd.

But then a remarkable thing happened. The other elephants surrounded the big tuskers, like guards, forming a tight pod with their elders in the centre. They continued their march, now in this new formation. It was devastating and wonderful all in the same moment. Devastating because our sight lines to the tuskers were completely obscured, we couldn't get even a half decent photo; but wonderful for the elephants because this must have been *learned* behaviour! As far as the elephants were concerned vehicles on the tracks were not a threat, but *off road,* cars coming towards them spelt trouble. This is what poachers do – and they knew what poachers were after.

Elephants are known to be highly intelligent and this was a prime example before our very eyes. Even as we drove past the herd to turn so as to be directly in front of them as they marched on, they saw our vehicle and wheeled off to the right, *deliberately* denying us a head on view, and presenting only *the sides* of non-tuskers to us.

Good luck to them, I thought. But what about JTs images needed for the preliminary sketches?

If these elephants reacted to us this way, even if we could find more, would we fare any better? We had to try. We were out all day and got a few interesting sightings of the local flora and fauna, but no more elephants.

JT knew exactly the sort of image he wanted, and as his inspirational book cover photo had come from an elephant at the water hole

near camp, we spent the next day at varying places around that popular drinking spot. Lots of elephants came and went. But no big tuskers.

Dr Johan joined us again for a couple of cold ones that evening, and whilst JT wanted to paint his masterpiece from one of his own photos, or at least taken by one of us co-conspirators on the trip, he was now beginning to think that he may just find what he needed amongst the vet's vast collection of elephant images, built up over many years. Johan was happy to collaborate and did indeed have some breath taking and glorious shots, but nothing quite fitted JT's vision.

"I wish you could explain to me precisely what it is you are looking for" said Johan, keen to help. JT remembered his phone. "I've been inspired by the cover of a book called *Great Tuskers of Africa*," he said "here it is, but I don't want to paint the elephant without permission, and even if the publisher did agree, they'd want a lot of money for the licence!" Johan started laughing heartily, "I expect they would," he said. "In fact I hope they'd ask for a fortune to use it because I took that shot. It's mine and now it can be yours too."

This was incredible. JT showed me his shot of the book. Johan's name was even on the cover, but JT hadn't made the connection between his book, and our new friend.

I was so pleased that I've never paid any attention to my parents advice not to speak to strangers in bars!

I wouldn't have believed these coincidences had I not been there. But it all fell into place, and Johan was delighted when JT volunteered to give *Saving the Survivors* a donation from the sale of the painting.

So, image in the bag, although not quite how we'd planned it, we returned home, where JT had persuaded his local Mercedes dealer in Poole to turn over part of their cavernous showroom to be his temporary studio. The 20 foot high canvas was stretched and supported on a huge wooden frame and for five weeks, working tirelessly seven days a week, mainly from a scaffold tower JT turned his vision, inch by inch, into magnificent reality. Satao, who had been cruelly murdered by poachers was now brought back to life on JT's canvas. In real life those tusks were about six and a half feet long and weighed around 200 pounds each – about the same as woolly mammoth tusks!

JT told me "I've literally lost a stone in weight doing this. I'd paint a few brush stokes, then have to descend through the hatch on the scaffolding platform I was standing on to ground level to see what it looked like from a distance, then immediately climb back up to my perch again."

"I could have done with being here and losing a stone too" I quipped.

"I don't think so," he replied, "you would have had a lot of trouble getting through the hatch!"

The grand unveiling was attended by Mercedes VIPs, those who had been on the trip, some press and local guests. Hosted by me, with JT by my side grinning from ear to ear, his smile as wide as a hippos and rightly so. This had been a mountain to climb, and the artist had made the summit in style. JT was on Meridian morning TV, the story and the painting went viral on social media, and JTs time lapse video of the painting from start to stunning finish had over 5,000 shares, and over 250,000 views! It was a truly splendid and unique piece of work admired by hundreds in the showroom and thousands more via the growing coverage in the national press.

'Tusk force Jonathan Truss, a wildlife artist in Bournemouth, has painted the world's largest elephant artwork as a lifesize tribute to a majestic African elephant that was killed by poachers. The 12ft-by-15ft oil painting of "Satao" is titled *Tusker's Last Stand.*

We offered several elephant charities the chance to benefit from the lion's share of the sale price by auctioning the piece to their supporters.

The sheer size of the canvas was its unique feature and the reason for all the attention but sadly was also its downfall. There were many who weren't frightened by the £50,000 reserve price, but even they didn't have walls big enough to display their prize.

The charities all generated a few extra donations for their efforts, but none of them were able to generate serious bids for the painting.

Of course the wider aim of the project was to further highlight the ever present plight of elephants through poaching, which it did but our efforts in selling the painting and donating most of the money to fund those in the field actually doing something about it were frustratingly not bearing fruit.

We thought getting on TV would boost our chances but *The One Show* producer, introduced to us by Gyles, told us that they wanted *new* stories and as JT had been on Meridian in *The Times, Telegraph, Guardian* and *Express* and had been so successful with his social media coverage, they didn't consider this story at all new, so we didn't get on.

We proved ourselves to be enthusiastic amateurs in terms of getting the best response from the media and from the charities. We had been delighted to get on local TV and be so well received by both traditional and social media – but our naivety had let us down. Had we kept it all quiet, offered the One Show the *first bite* and only then opened the story up to one and all, we'd have given ourselves the best chance.

It was a similar tale with the charities too. JT and I share *abundance mentalities* and had decided early on to share the proceeds of a sale amongst five very worthwhile wildlife charities but we discovered that it was this very idea of *sharing* between them that probably prevented any one of them making a real effort at securing a sale. One of their spokespeople actually told us "I was told to play this down"
Our Chairman said that if one of *our supporters* was to buy the painting then the money should *all come to us*" How sad when this kind of attitude at the top denies a decent charity the chance of income, especially when *one of theirs* would simply be a person who cares about conservation and elephants! As always, it's the wildlife itself that suffers due to politics and narrow mindedness, not to mention greed.

So disappointingly, as I write, the painting remains unsold.

More Brushes in the Bush

JT is a British artist who paints Africa but Africa has a lot of home-grown artists, who all too often don't get the opportunity to even discover they have a talent, let alone develop it. The everyday struggle for survival and feeding their families takes all of their time and energies.

However, during one visit with some guests who wanted to see a Kenyan school, a young lad in the back row caught my eye as he was at least a foot and a half taller than the rest and, being stick thin, his height was accentuated. I guessed that he had been put back a year or two, so when the teacher asked us if we'd like to sit with any of the children at their desks, I made a beeline for the back row.

The boy looked sullen and uninterested so I smiled and began with "Jambo! You know my name is Clive, what's yours?"

"My name is Eric" he replied. I asked him if he minded if I looked in his workbook and could see immediately that Eric is wired differently to most of us and I understood why, academically, he wasn't cutting the mustard. But... on the inside back cover was a fantastic pencil sketch of a rhino.

Really good. And in the inside front cover was another sketch of two
Masai jumping: perfectly in proportion with each other and the acacia tree
behind, complete with shadows and the movement of the Masai's beads.
I was very impressed and asked Eric if he had any more drawings.
He replied,

*"I did some more in my book but the teacher tore out the
pages and told me not to waste the paper."*

At the end of the visit I had a quiet word with the headmaster and asked
him about Eric. "He has a real talent for art" I told him and he agreed but
said that he didn't have the resources for an art class. I said that with his
permission, I would like to try to give Eric's talent a chance to develop
and he readily agreed.

So the following day with the backing of the ever supportive George
Murray, Manager of Little Governor's, we got one of the drivers to take
a diversion on his game drive and drop off three reams of copy paper, a
dozen pencils, three rubbers and a pencil sharpener at the school. Then,
when I got back to Nairobi I sent down some art paper, brushes, acrylic
paint and a few other bits that he would find useful.

For the next few years, my reward was seeing Eric's art come on in leaps
and bounds. He liked the style of the French Impressionists and was
already using colour in very imaginative ways and I was always telling
him to *dare to be different* and never to stop believing in the magic
of his dreams.

I missed the migration safari one year
and the next time I was at the school
Eric was no longer there and no one
knew where he was. It was fortunate
that our *Celebration of Wildlife* safari
event always takes place around the
same time of year, as later in that trip
a cardboard tube arrived in camp
addressed to me. In it was a canvas
about 2'x 3', a portrait of a very
colourful lion, painted in what Eric

called his *fancy style,* with a *message* saying *Thomas* (the headmaster calls me Thomas) *you always told me to dare to be different. Thank you. This is for you.* There was no other message and no contact details.

He wasn't asking for anything else from me.
He just wanted to thank me, and it was very touching.

On my trip the following year I went to one of my favourite restaurants in Karen (as you might guess, I have a few favourites and could take you on a *dining safari* around Nairobi and its suburbs). This particular restaurant, Tamambo, has a lovely garden set out for dining where they always have a few pieces of artwork displayed on easels for sale. As I was slowly taking in the scene whilst quenching my thirst on my first glass of cold Tusker, I thought I saw in the distance a painting in Eric's *fancy style.* I wondered if someone was selling his art. I wandered over, and to my amazement and delight spied Eric himself, gently relieving a German lady of a fist full of notes. Transaction completed we fell into a spontaneous embrace. It was so great to see him, no longer a boy but now a nicely dressed young man, and looking so well. He told me that his art was flourishing, so much so that he was now able to support his whole family.

I asked Eric why he hadn't kept in touch and he told me, "You have already done for me more than anyone could expect. I would not ask you for more." How I respected this young man for wanting to work for himself and not take the easy way out. I could see his potential still and so I suggested that we worked together – in partnership. He readily agreed and it works very well. Now on the last night of all our safari trips to Kenya each person, or couple, gets a gift of a unique piece of Eric's art which they tell me is such a lovely keepsake.

I've put on a few exhibitions of his work at places such as L'Escargot in London, Ascot Racecourse, and a stylish gallery called The Workhouse not far from where I live. I found I rather liked being an amateur art dealer and have now added to my "Kenyan roster" another hugely talented young man called Karanja and an older very skilled guy, Geoffrey (pronounced Gee-off-ray in true Kenyan style). We have launched several of our own *themed collections,* usually three linked pieces of original art, and take on commissions from people who want a relative, their pet or perhaps one of their heroes painted in colours true to life or in fancy style!

MATHENGE
Simon Karanja

A selection of artworks painted by talented
Kenyan artists Eric Mathenge and Simon Karanja

Jonathan Truss

THE TRUSSMEISTER

We always treat our guests to one of JT's outstanding pencil sketches of the magnificent animals we've been privileged to spend time with in the wild.

A Maasai *Birthday Bash*

Shortly after returning from a safari, I had a call from Jasper who was filming at Pinewood Studios not too far from where we lived and invited Kay and I to go over and watch the proceedings. At supper afterwards we were reminiscing about a weekend in Vienna we had organised a few years before for Jasper's wife Hazel's 50th birthday. On the night of her birthday a number of their family and friends had been transported through the snowy streets by horse drawn carriages to our own special celebration at a former Royal Palace, featuring a candlelit dinner at a huge rose petal strewn oak table, accompanied by music from members of the Vienna Philharmonic Orchestra. This was followed the next day by an afternoon on board the Austrian equivalent of the Orient Express accompanied by lots of Viennese cake and double cream throughout!

Jasper's 60th was approaching and he said he wanted to do *something different* to celebrate the next milestone. Having told him all about my cavorting about in Africa, swapping stories round the campfire and generally having a bit of a blast, I didn't have to work too hard to persuade him that a Kenyan safari could be perfect destination. And so almost a year later I was back at Little Governor's for *Jasper's Big Birthday Blowout*.

Camp instantly had the atmosphere of a jolly house party, made possible as everyone knew each other. But how to make an already wonderful experience even more magical is always a challenge – just where do you sprinkle the magic dust? Most of *that* happened on the big day.

Jasper told me that he thought his birthday had started in the most idyllic of ways, by being woken by the roar of a lion. But it turned out it was just the hot air balloon being inflated at the back of camp. So his day began with an outstanding hot air balloon ride over the glorious savannah, with champagne and a hot breakfast cooked on the balloon's burners and eaten out on the plains. On the game drive back we saw most of the usual suspects but with the birthday bonus of three rhino who were in no hurry to run away and best of all a leopard up a tree keeping a watchful eye on the remains of her kill, probably from the previous day. A couple of ostrich took an interest in us and ran almost alongside one of the vehicles for a while – you just never know what you are going to see from one game drive to the next!

I spent the afternoon helping set up for a special bush dinner about 15 minutes out of camp, on a majestic bend of the river surrounded by trees. A marquee roof was erected, tables were laid and set with flowers and candles, wood gathered for a campfire, with lanterns and yet more candles used to decorate the whole area. The magic dust was starting to sparkle and would do so even more when it was all topped off with a big African star strewn sky later.

Whether guests had gone off on an afternoon game drive or had stayed at camp enjoying the activity at the marsh, perhaps watching the mongooses playing by the water in the short grass, everyone was dressed up and ready for the big night out beneath the twinkling stars.

Over drinks on the riverbank as dusk was falling we were idly watching the hippos wallowing at the bend of the river, when a crowd of screaming spear-waving painted up six foot tall Maasai warriors roared out of the bushes brandishing *knobbashers** in what *only* Jasper and I knew to be a *mock* attack.

They were the embodiment of their ancestry, daubed in red ochre, their faces streaked with blue clay and lime and were very scary.

Some of the guests actually sprang to their feet and scattered! A member of Black Sabbath (not Ozzie) threw himself to the ground. Our host liked to surprise his friends and the field loos came in handy early on.

Though out in the wild and working from a very Spartan and temporary field kitchen, our wonderfully versatile Sheels and her hard working chefs who conjured up mouth-watering culinary delights from whatever the *supplies lorry** delivered had again done us proud, even offering *choices* at dinner for goodness sake! Speeches were made, toasts reaffirming family ties and friendships going back decades were drunk and then the Maasai, by now looking calm, serene and not at all fearsome, formed a line, and processed slowly between the tables with the impressive cake which Sheels of course had made. Maasai don't count birthdays, so have no equivalent of singing *Happy Birthday*. Instead they chanted rhythmically and tunefully, inserting the words *Jhaspaar, Jhaspaar* every now and again – a moving and most original happy birthday rendition in the heart of the bush.

I told Jasper that I'd heard that in Kenya when hosting a special occasion and are the one to cut the cake, it's lucky to have one foot actually *on the table* and to *cry out* loudly as you plunge the knife into its centre. He asked me if this was for real and I could only say I had it on good authority and that it was considered bad luck not to follow the tradition. It was Katrina who had told me, and her family had been in Kenya for three generations.

It must have been true. Mustn't it??

We continued round the campfire in what must be one of the most atmospheric ends of a birthday, by telling stories and with singing accompanied by Jasper and his son Jake both on guitar, with Jasper's childhood chum, drummer (famously of ELO and The Move) Bev Bevan, on bongos. It was our turn to keep the hippos and lions awake that night. And back at camp, despite signs of an approaching dawn, I had arranged that the bar was still open.

It was a hell of a grand night and of the 36 guests, four made the next day's game drive, in the *afternoon!*

A real Birthday Bash that almost everyone will always remember.

Footnote :

Knobbasher: A short stick with a knob at the top. I believe traditionally known in South Africa as a knobberry. But I think my word better sums up this implement

Supplies lorry: What had been ordered and what was actually delivered often bore little resemblance. Flexible and creative cheffing was vital!

3

Short.
Stories

The Ambassador's party

I have been blessed in my life with some wonderful friendships. Some friends have sustained me in the good times, some have helped get me through some tough patches and some, it must here be admitted, have got me into the occasional scrape. And one dear friend who has at times managed to fall into each of the above categories and thus deserves special mention in these pages, is my great mate Ray Jones.

One thing you need to know about Ray is that he befriends everyone. One of life's natural bon viveurs, whether alcohol is on board or not, he becomes something of a Pied Piper character with others following where he leads. He had a variety of jobs but ended up at the time of this story (somehow) as a Director of Time Out Magazine which, after starting out in the late sixties as a one-sheet listing of counter-culture events in London, quickly grew to become the essential guide to everything that was anything in the Capital. Consequently, my old mate Ray found his name on the invitation list for any number of first nights, gigs, receptions and restaurant and gallery openings all across town and he would often ring me to see if I fancied being his "plus one". And having always been a firm believer in the idea that *there is* such a thing as a free lunch, I would usually gratefully accept.

One evening, Ray had been invited to a reception at the Swedish Embassy just off Belgrave Square. The invitation was for two and he invited me. I have no idea now what the reception was for and I doubt that Ray did then: but if the Swedish Government thought it a good idea to break out the Ferrero Rocher chocs and ply the good folk of the UK with free food and booze, then it seemed churlish for us to complain. Much better to just go along with it we thought and thus it was we found ourselves in a magnificent room with an elegant quartet playing, liveried staff circulating to ensure the Champagne was topped up and tempting us to try Swedish canapé delicacies such as little meatballs in thin pastry baskets and beef and port pate on seeded crisp bread.

As you would imagine there were a number of amazingly easy-on-the-eye blonde blue-eyed Swedish people also circulating, men as well as women, and we fell easily into conversation with one such good-looking middle-aged lady. She was beautifully and elegantly dressed, adorned with very tasteful jewelry and, I remember, she had the most astonishingly perfect teeth: like cultured pearls behind an alluring smile. Her English was as close to perfect as makes no difference but there was no mistaking the Swedish accent and we quickly had her pegged as a visitor to our shores, keen to know more of London, a city which my friend I had adopted long ago as our own.

Ray's Pied Piper instinct for inviting newly found companions to whatever is the next place on the itinerary rose to the fore and he suggested to our new friend that she might enjoy an evening out in London with the two of us, seeing the sights and enjoying one or two of the music bars that have been responsible over the years for us missing our last trains home. "Because let's face it" he said, "these embassy dos can be pretty boring, don't you think. I mean, don't get me wrong..." he continued, perfectly reasonably I thought,

It's lovely of your compatriots to lay on the fizz and Smorgasbord and all that, but we think you'd enjoy seeing our city. What do you say?"

He gave her his most winning smile, which has been known to get him both into and out of all manner of trouble in the past. But in spite of this she seemed a little nervous and so I hastily reassured her that we weren't trying to pick her up.

"Oh that's right." Ray chimed in. "I'm a Dad, and my fat mate"
(as he affectionately refers to me in public) "he's already a grandad.
But we *do* know how to party!"

"Gentlemen" she smiled, making the most of those dazzling pearls of hers, "I would love to spend an evening with you. But I would need to ask my husband first".

"But of course" I replied. "Is he here this evening?"

"Yes" she said. "*He's the Ambassador!*"

And with that she graciously took our business cards, made her excuses, and continued round the room.

"Do you think she'll ring us?" Ray asked me.

I laughed and replied, "when she tells her husband I bet he'll say something like *if you think you're going out with a pair of chancers like that you'll need to think again.*" And that's if he's a forward thinking man.

She hasn't phoned us yet – but it was only eight or ten years ago, so there's still a good chance.

James Bond
and a faux pas

A simple truth and one that I have always believed in is that doing any major piece of business is about getting to know and trusting the people. Before you buy an experience it's good to have a chat with the person who is selling it and small, personal considerations are vital, particularly in a business like hospitality. If you have ever attended a Prestige event, no matter how large or small, you weren't there as a client, you were there as a guest.

Numbers attending my own events were usually 40 or 50 people.
The exception was Henley, where we might have had 250 people a day, fewer for the overseas trips. But I prided myself on getting to know my guests well and making them feel at home and welcome wherever we happened to be. But when we started doing the book launches, I found I was arranging events for between 200 to 300 people. We built these audiences with the help of joint marketing promotions with companies like American Express, Barclaycard and The London Evening Standard,

which meant that we had a huge number of new bookers each time who I didn't know personally. And whilst this was great for building the mailing list, it did present me with an unexpected challenge as suddenly, in all sorts of random places, apparent strangers would come over to me and say things like "It's Clive Thomas isn't it?" or "Hello Clive, very good to see you again!" like we were long-lost friends. Invariably they didn't give me their name as they expected that I would know who they were. Whereas, I wouldn't have a clue.

I'm not suggesting for a moment that I *was* getting famous, but I was being singled out for conversation by people I didn't know and not only did I feel embarrassed, I also thought I was in danger of looking unprofessional and, worst of all, rude. It was becoming a serious problem for me and wasn't at all sure how to handle it.

Most of the celebrities I had worked with were adept at interacting with their public but there were none smoother than an old friend of mine, Bob Holness, best known perhaps for his 10 years as quizmaster on television's Blockbusters, despite his long acting career in radio and on the stage. I knew Bob because I'd been a college friend of his daughter Ros and I often called on him if I needed a name to host an event. In those days Bob had a weekday morning radio show on LBC with Douglas Cameron, imaginatively called *Bob and Doug*, and was always very happy to help me.

I'd heard on the BBC's *Mastermind* that Bob had been the very first James Bond. It didn't sound right to me so I asked him about it. He confirmed that it was true and told me about making that broadcast, live in South Africa, in a tiny studio without air-conditioning from a very badly typed script. He was offered the opportunity to narrate Bond in three more stories but hadn't liked the people he was working with and also he said, "the pay was awful!"

But he did look a bit wistful as he told me, "I had no idea how big the Bond franchise would become.

I sometimes wonder whether there would have been a place for me in it as it grew."

Today we would call it one of those *Sliding Doors* moments.

Another bizarre Bob Holness 'fact' was that he played the sax solo on Jerry Rafferty's classic track, *Baker Street*. He laughed when I asked him about this and told me he wished he had but this particular 'fact' was nonsense. Apparently Rafferty didn't credit anyone on the record sleeve for performing that solo, which allowed a few people to run wild with rumours. In a segment on his show called *Would you Believe it?* radio DJ Stuart Maconie presented Bob playing that sax solo as a fact. He later told Bob that it was intended as a joke and he didn't expect anyone would take it seriously, but over the years it was repeated enough times that people began to believe it. Bob told me it had actually crept into some of the biographies of him, and as it was doing him no harm he would generally tell people when asked that he could, "neither confirm nor deny that he had been featured on that record."

Bob was such a smooth operator, making the most of his broad smile, gentlemanly manners and clean cut look, that I asked his advice about how to deal with meeting people one doesn't remember without offending them. He said to me, "Clive, I'll tell you what I do and it would probably serve you well to do the same. If it's a gentleman shake him warmly by the hand, and if it's a lady kiss her gently on the cheek. Make eye contact and say something like how lovely of you to come over. It's very nice to see you again. Remind me where we last met?"

According to Bob, this is the key question. He continued "They will tell you something like, *it was at Twickenham or the Rick Stein book launch* and if you can remember anything about that occasion then say it, because that will make the connection. With the vast majority of people that's all they want. They're not looking for a relationship!"

I thought this was brilliant advice and immediately put it to work, and to good effect.

A few months later I had just finished lunch with a client at a restaurant called Christopher's opposite The Lyceum Theatre in London. I'd settled the bill and my guest and I were walking away from the table, heading for the door when a man came over to me and said, "Excuse me, Clive Thomas?"

I immediately launched into the full Bob Holness, eye-contact-firm-handshake-beaming-smile-how-lovely-to-see-you-thank-you-so-much-for-coming-over-remind-me-where-it-was-we-last-met routine. The man looked a bit mystified as he extended his hand to present me with a piece of plastic saying, "You've dropped your credit card!"

My guest smiled, and as I gratefully took the card, he gently told the man "You must excuse my friend he thinks he's some kind of celebrity."

It certainly brought me back down to earth and gave Bob a good laugh when I told him.

The unmistakable David Vine

For many years, David Vine was one of the best known and most popular BBC sports commentators. Unlike many of today's pundits he didn't specialise in one sport but was known for fronting *Ski Sunday*, *Grandstand*, tennis from Wimbledon, snooker, rugby, show jumping and several Olympic and Winter Olympic Games. As well as this, he was the first host of *A Question of Sport* and presented the *Miss UK* and *Miss World* beauty pageants, that very weird and wonderful televisual oddity, *It's a Knock Out!* So the list goes on. I've catalogued all of these to demonstrate that in his prime David was barely off our screens. His quick smile and ready wit endeared him to the viewers and his soft West Country burr made his voice very easy to listen to.

A big part of David's charm was that he never really believed that he was a celebrity, despite his ever growing fame. But he did acknowledge to me that he was very flattered when the world snooker champion, Steve Davis, was characterised through his puppet on *Spitting Image* boasting "Don't mess with me. I'm a mate of David Vine!"

When commentating on skiing he would often talk about the skier's rhythm: A typical Vine commentary going something like... "Just watch the way Steve Podborski has the rhythm through the gates. He's really in stride, looking good, going well and... oh! He's gone! Podborski is gone."

Because much like Murray Walker's predictions that almost immediately went the other way, all David Vine had to do was to start praising a skier for his rhythm and you knew that the stretcher bearers would be readying themselves on the side lines.

I got to know him because he often appeared at Rothmans events we were asked to organise, pressing the flesh and saying a few words. I guess these days he would've been classified as a 'brand ambassador' but as a BBC commentator and presenter, such a thing would not have been allowed and so he was just a welcomed guest. But he always endeared himself to audiences at these events by telling a tale or two against himself.

My favourite story about David was when at one of our receptions he met a charming lady who asked him what he did. He politely, and with typical modesty, told her that he 'worked in television'.

"How interesting," the lady said. "And, tell me, do you work at the weekends?"

"Oh yes," he told her. "There's always a lot going on, on Saturdays and Sundays."

They talked for a little about other things and when he said he had to leave as there were other people the host wanted him to meet, she asked if she could have his card because, as she told him, "You've no idea how difficult it is to get a television repair man out at the weekends!"

MUSIC ON THE MENU

Cocktails *and* quartets

"Music on The Menu" really began as "*Opera* on The Menu" as an increasing number of my evenings were spent with opera singers at dinners we had arranged. We were developing this as new brand for the company, which came about when I was introduced to the wonderfully-named Lee Shave, who was a senior man at British Airways.

We met during a long day on our boat at Henley and Lee said he liked the way we did things. I think what he actually said, putting his arm around my shoulder to steady himself was "we musht do shome more evensh together, my new shlim friend!"

At the time BA had just adopted that evocative operatic aria *The Flower Duet* from Delibe's opera Lakme which is sung by a soprano and a mezzo soprano, which gave me an idea of exactly what I could do to entertain Lee and his BA Vips.

As you know I was involved with Pinewood Studios and they had an impressive ballroom, whose wood panelling had been salvaged from the great ship, RMS Mauritania. It had a raised stage covering the end of the room, with dressing rooms behind and a grand piano permanently in situ. It was used as a dining room for the money men and the talent involved in film making during the week but come mid-afternoon Friday until Monday morning it stood empty apart from the occasional Saturday wedding of someone connected with the film business. Just *perfect* for what I had in mind.

In those days, the catering was run by *the two Davids* as they were known, who in exchange for their own table at all our events there, gave us a wonderful inclusive deal for black-tie dinners on Friday and Saturday nights. The events we put on featured a group of singers from the Royal Opera House Covent Garden, performing 20 minutes or so of opera's best loved pieces between each serving of a delicious four course meal. These nights were very different from anything people could find elsewhere, easy for people to enjoy, became very popular and I quickly dubbed them "Opera on the Menu".

The most enthusiastic performers were the two ladies who performed the *Flower Duet*, Glenys Groves and Scilla Stewart who also booked the other singers for me, chosen from their chums at the opera house. They went under the natty title of "The Garden Party." I loved working with both of these extremely accomplished performers. They sang opera magnificently as you would expect, but were also brilliant with songs from the big musicals and I was delighted to discover, they didn't mind at all my wanting to introduce humour into the proceedings. They always took their singing seriously, but didn't take *themselves* at all seriously. They were great actresses too, always managing much convincing laughter at my often heard patter.

The various piano accompanists, tenors and baritones they brought along were mainly on our wavelength too, and we all had as much fun in our Green Room as the guests had in the dining room.

A regular baritone was Roy Gregory a fine singer with a dry sense of humour, and a withering scowl. For the first year we worked together he managed to convince me that he was a psychic. After the first set we would be back in our room tucking into whatever the guests were eating (as anyone who's ever worked on a Prestige event will know I always make sure our talent is well fed) Roy would say things like "The lady down on table two with the red dress has two sons. The eldest one is in the army and the second one is gay but she doesn't know it yet. The man on table seven. Grey hair, awful silver bow tie. He's from Vienna. He's a jeweller - no wait a minute he's just a watch salesman."

"How on earth do you know that Roy?" I would ask.

"I don't know how I know *I just do*" he would always retort.

He was so convincing, and I have been known to be susceptible to a practical joke. How the others kept a straight face I'll never know!

I told people that our *Opera on the Menu* evenings demonstrated just how much fun opera could be, and because opera was being used so much in advertising (it wasn't just BA who were doing it) even if you'd never been to an opera you would probably know most of the tunes.

In fact I would often finish my introduction to the opening set by saying to the audience,

"If you know the words, and the tunes are familiar to you, and you'd like to sing along... ... ... Please don't!"

We quickly discovered that audiences love to hear tales from behind the scenes especially about things that went wrong at such illustrious places as the Royal Opera House, the Coliseum or Glyndebourne. Like the occasion during a performance of *Madame Butterfly* when a winter bug was going through all the children who were playing Butterfly's son. They had an angelic, but unrehearsed little boy brought in at the last minute to stand in. His role was to sit next to Butterfly gazing up into her face adoringly as she sang the wonderful aria *One Fine Day*. He'd been told "all you have to do is to go out on to the stage with the nice lady, sit down at her feet and look up at her face while she sings. You don't have to say anything – and she'll take your hand to take you off stage with her at the end of her song."

However, no one had thought to warn the poor little lad that the decibels coming from the nice lady's lungs would be roughly equivalent to a fighter jet taking off next to him! He sat there for almost a whole aria aghast, with a horrified look on his face and both hands clasped firmly over his ears!

We always brought humour into our performances wherever we could. As the compère I was often asked if I sung too and had to tell people that I had the build of Pavarotti – but sadly not the voice. When our tenor came out to sing Nessun Dorma he would say he was about to sing an aria that was written for a chorus of... then pretending to count up the number of people in the room would say *68 people – what a coincidence.* He then slowly pulled from his inside jacket pocket what looked like a large white handkerchief à la Pavarotti, which he kept pulling and pulling, to reveal that it was in fact a large white tablecloth. He then conducted his impromptu chorus of 68 guests, signing the well-known melody to *laa laa laa laa laa la laaaa laaa*, out of tune of course and to great amusement.

You see, people expect opera singers to sound fantastic but be a bit prissy. Not a bit of it in our case!

One of the highlights of the show was when Scilla and Glenys mimed the cabin crew safety procedure, whilst singing the beautiful *Flower Duet* from *Lakme*. During the course of the aria the audience were treated to the position of the emergency exits being pointed out, *"here, here* and (turning their backs to the audience) *here"* the masks coming down from the overhead lockers, putting the lifejacket over their heads and tying the strings into a double bow and even pointing to the floor, highlighting the imaginary illuminated path to the exits.

So with all this already in place, all I had to do was pick up the phone and invite Lee and his partner along to one of our Pinewood evenings, having first checked with Glenys that *Lakme* (or *lick me* as we called it) was definitely on the running order that night. From the very first part of the mime, Lee was enchanted. He rocked with laughter, loving what we had done and as a result we were asked to provide a number of *Opera on the Menu* dinners as part of British Airways' 75th anniversary celebrations. No prizes for guessing what was always performed *again* for the encore!

The first was at The Great Conservatory at Syon Park, a Kew Gardens style glass house set in beautiful grounds with fountains and peacocks, an appropriate setting for a BA event as the singers had to compete all evening at regular intervals with the sound of *their aircraft* flying extremely low overhead on their final approach to Heathrow, just five miles away. I mentioned to the audience that "when I had done the reckee there hadn't been even a suggestion of low flying 747s, I suppose because on that particular day an alternative flight path was being used." Lee immediately jumped to his feet and chimed in "we changed the flight path deliberately tonight!"

But that wasn't their only peril that evening! In the staged performances of *Lakme*, the Flower Duet has a coda, (which is like a post script at the end of a letter) where the character Lakme accompanied by Malika walk *off stage* but continue singing ever more softly from the wings as if they are walking away.

Glenys and Scilla decided that by opening one of the doors of the conservatory and finishing the song from the pathway outside they could create a rather enchanting ending – and I agreed that it would be delightful. However, come the moment, right next to the open door previously hidden in the darkness stood a large male peacock blocking their path. As they were delivering the last few bars of this beautiful song, the peacock decided to turn it into a trio as he joined in squawking very loudly, as only peacocks can, with all his might.

"Well," I told the audience, "we did promise you humour as well as opera!" And I wasn't wrong.

There were even several occasions over many years when the Chairman or Chief Executive of BA were asked to speak at events or receive airline awards, Glenys and Scilla appeared to provide this most apt form of fanfare. When Lord Marshall retired his farewell was held at Banqueting House in Whitehall and we were flattered to be invited back to bid farewell to him in *our* traditional way.

I don't know if British Airways is still the world's favourite airline, but for many years they were certainly ours!

This is London's beautiful Middle Temple Hall, where Shakespeare premiered Twelfth Night over 400 years ago. A well attended Music on the Menu evening is about to begin.

Vodka!

The success with BA led to further theming ideas: adapting songs or using tunes to promote our hosts' brand or products. *The Flower Duet* of BA fame became *The **Flour** Duet* for Homepride. For Powergen who were sponsoring the weather forecast on television at the time we made *One Fine Day* their theme song for the night. But the most ingenious was saved for a Nokia hosted dinner. Mid aria Rodney our baritone who was singing *Figaro's song* from *The Barber of Seville* discreetly reached into his pocket and set off the very distinctive Nokia ring tone. Gales of laughter followed, but we weren't finished there. He took the phone out of his pocket, pretending to answer the call, and then sung the remainder of the aria as if he were on the phone call, hand gestures and all.

The best fun was when we worked with Mike Noble of drinks giant Allied Domecq (now Pernod Ricard). An accomplished event organiser himself, he loved our creativity and let us run riot. One memorable time was when we were to provide the between course's entertainment for a group of his guests in the very up market, Michelin starred Harvey's in Bristol.

The company had asked us to theme as many of the pieces as we could around drinks or drinking. So we put in *The Drinking Song* from *La Traviata; The Champagne Trio* from *Die Fledermaus*; and thought we would announce *Largo al Factotum* as *Lager al Factotum*. Also Scilla, who was a mistress of the comic song, came up with the perfect one for this occasion called *Vodka*, from a 1926 Broadway show entitled

Song of the Flame. Here is one of the four verses to give you a flavour:

"Vodka, don't give me vodka,
For when I take a little nip, I begin to slip,
And I start romancing with the man
I'm dancing with.
For vodka, makes me feel oddka!"

When singing, Scilla would stagger and sway amongst the audience with a highball glass in her hand, ice and a slice mimicking a vodka and tonic. In reality it was a glass of water and as she tottered around the room appearing to be slightly drunk, she would plunge her fingers in the glass and dramatically flick water over anyone close enough, much to the amusement of all, especially those taking a mini shower.

Mike had booked the restaurant exclusively and the singers and I arrived mid-afternoon to have a run through of the programme in the room. All venues have different acoustics and it's always good to know what you're working with. The room had been set with guests to be seated either side of two long tables. We always looked for special features that we may be able to use as props, such as a balcony to sing one or two of the arias from, perhaps stairs to walk down whilst singing, or even just a door to use to make a different entrance or exit. On this occasion we spotted a four-wheel trolley of the type that a large baron of beef could be placed upon to be easily wheeled around, and I saw a great opportunity to use it. I suggested to Scilla that she could lay on it, singing *Vodka*, holding the glass and flicking water from side to side as I pushed her between the two long tables. She loved the idea and needing no further persuasion said "I'm not sure whether I should sit or lay on it. Let's give it a go now and see if the trolley will take my weight!"

It worked best if she sat and we started working out how fast I should push her, so that her journey down the middle of the room and back would give her just the right length of time to sing the four verses.

Midway through our rehearsal using this sensational and unexpected prop, the restaurant manager appeared, and started barking at Scilla to "get off my trolley *immediately!*"

I explained to him what we wanted to do and why it would be so perfect for the host, that we weren't really hooligans and that the soprano had been on stage at Covent Garden the previous night. If I thought that would impress him and calm the situation, I was quickly disabused.

"I don't care if she was on stage at Covent Garden, Billingsgate or effing Smithfield! I absolutely forbid you from lowering the tone of Harvey's in this way!"

Whilst this was going on Mike, my client, who had arrived and watched our run-through, waited for the manager to slope off and told me, "Clive that was absolutely brilliant! I've never seen anything like that at a dinner.

*It will be the highlight of the evening.
You simply have to do it."*

I must have looked pained as I said "I'd really like to, but Mike, you heard what the manager said, so sadly I don't think we can."

Mike smiled and said "I think we have three more events booked with you this year. Think about how many times you are likely to want to drive all the way to Bristol to come here again. I'll leave it with you."

He had made his point and my loyalty, of course, was to my client and more than that, my mischievous nature always drew me to outrageous ridiculousness with not much care about the consequences. So when one of the courses had been cleared and the manager was out of the room helping in the kitchen, *we did it!* The guests had loved the introduction of the drinking songs at an evening with Allied Domecq but they absolutely revelled in Scilla's very personal rendition of *Vodka* from the trolley! I was delighted that we had delighted our client and his guests with another showstopper!

As to how often I would revisit Harvey's? I had my answer almost immediately.

*The red faced manager banned not only me, but the four performers from returning to the restaurant.
For life!*

It could **only** happen *on stage*

I am very fond of opera but, it must be said, it is stuffed full of some crazy plot turns at various levels of ridiculousness. In both *Fidelio* and *Cosi fan tutte* there is quite a bit of very obvious cross dressing, but not a single person notices. I've always wondered why. In *Cunning Little Vixen* someone ordains a woodpecker, who then goes on to conduct a marriage ceremony. And in a not so well known piece called *Lily of Killarney*, Danny, one of the main characters, meets his end when he is mistaken for a *pavarotter** and shot.

One of my favourite pieces of laughable ludicrousness is a duet called *"The Fly"* from *Orpheus in the Underworld*, written for a baritone and a soprano and performed regularly at our *Opera on the Menu* evenings by Roy and Glenys.

The story has it that Eurydice will not fall for Jupiter's charms, so Jupiter has imprisoned her. You would think that as a god, Jupiter would have the wisdom to know that this might not be best idea for attracting a maiden and would most likely be doomed to failure from the off. However, he does have an advantage; being a god he is able to change the way he appears, so he turns himself into a fly, enabling him to get through the keyhole of the bathroom door whilst Eurydice is having a bath. He attracts her attention by settling on her shoulder, and being a bejewelled fly avoids the more usually anticipated whack, in favour of being caressed and sung to.

We have to imagine that Glenys, at the front of the stage is in a bath, nicely lathered up and surrounded by bubbles, but the fly is such an integral part of the story we decided it was just too much to be *imagined*. We needed a fly!

In the absence of a remote controlled insect (these days a small drone would have done the job nicely) some improvisation was needed, and Blue Peter style cutting and sticking skills came to the fore. In order that the fly would be noticed, Glenys cleverly constructed a creature.

On the stage behind Glenys, Roy was at the other end of the stick and had mastered the art of landing the fly *gently* onto the object of his affections, as dive bombing her would have elicited an entirely different reaction! And once landed the duet is sung with Eurydice gazing ever more lovingly at the fly she has just "captured," and which she continues to hold in her cupped hands.

Obviously, Jupiter (Roy) shouldn't have been in the room in human form as he had become the fly... *Come on, keep up!*

So over his dinner suit he would don a grey *cloak of invisibility*. To make it obvious to the audience the word *invisible* had been embroidered across the front of the cloak. But the lettering was so small that unless you were on one of the front tables you couldn't read it. So it was modified into large capital letters but arranged over two lines almost covering all of the available material saying *INVIS – IBLE!*

It's a pretty tune, full of laughter, and always a popular inclusion. I didn't realise until much later when the well-travelled fly had undergone several bouts of surgery as he needed replacement limbs and wings, that the singers had christened him *Clive*.

Footnote:
__Pavarotter.__ An opera singer who bears a resemblance to an otter.

London *holds its* *breath*

West End spotlight cast members
Lori Hayley-Fox and Leo Andrew.

We had a lot of fun with *Opera on the Menu,* and when people not used to opera realised that this wasn't a highbrow evening and that they would probably know all the songs, they had fun too. The concept then morphed into *Music on the Menu* as we invited West End show cast members to take part in musical evenings of a similar format, but with musical content from London, Broadway and beyond.

But there was another idea too. Working with *Simpsons in the Strand* on Friday and Saturday nights, we put on *Curtain Call at Simpsons.* Invited cast members who had been in shows that night joined us to perform again in a decent size first floor room at Simpsons, which we would transform by theming with theatrical backdrops and atmospheric lighting. Our guests would enjoy a delicious after theatre supper and a glorious live cabaret from spotlight performers that some of the guests would have seen on stage an hour or two earlier.

I was convinced that we would be onto a winner with this and so was Simpsons' very supportive and encouraging General Manager, Brian Clivaz. He is a fellow gent also of somewhat heroic proportions, and a great ambassador for the hospitality industry.

My lifelong *flawsome** friend and confidante Ray Jones was never far from any of my events which may produce some good entertainment and a chilled glass or two. And in case you were wondering we still haven't had the call from the wife of the Swedish Ambassador!

Ray had blazed a cabaret trail in London already doing something similar called *Centre Stage,* which he put on in the basement of the Mountbatten Hotel at Seven Dials, just off of Shaftsbury Avenue.

His venue was a lot smaller than ours and he could get away with one singer and a pianist, although I was there on one charity evening when it looked as if he had the whole cast of Les Misérables on stage! There were more performers than guests at tables.

One evening I saw A. A. Gill, the then Times restaurant critic enjoying the entertainment. I remember thinking, I hope he's come in for the fun and not to write about the food, because the thing about Centre Stage was you wouldn't go there just for the food. Don't get me wrong; the food was good but it was the atmosphere, created by a combination of the basement "speakeasy" type venue, the friendly service and most of all the entertainment that made it a great place to be. Gill wrote in his column the following weekend that his first dish at the newly opened Centre Stage contained what were described as *wild mushrooms*. He said, "These mushrooms wouldn't have been wild if you'd soaked them in ecstasy and given them guns!" followed by other amusing but disparaging comments about the cuisine.

I rang Ray to commiserate, but he was delighted. He didn't care, saying "Cliveski, people come in for the music not the food. Isn't it great that we're in the Times before we've been open a month!" Which was typical of Ray's glass always full to overflowing philosophy, let alone half empty!

Ray was always very encouraging of any of my enterprises, and rather than see Curtain Call as competition, he was delighted that someone else was also flying the flag for after theatre London.

We had both been in cabaret clubs in New York that had been successful for many years, such as *The Algonquin, Manny's,* and *Copacabana*. At one stage, they became so popular that it wasn't just chorus members from Broadway shows wanting to earn an extra few dollars on the way home that performed there. Back in the day, some of the greats – Sammy Davis Junior, Dean Martin, Tony Bennett and even Frank Sinatra and Ella Fitzgerald used to go and sing after their show.

The places were hugely successful because no one ever knew when one of these legends might drop in. So the more often you went the more chance there was of you being there on the right night. We wanted to somehow try to rekindle that lost era and had lofty ambitions – or was it fantasies? - of who might just drop in on us. But Ray and I both quickly discovered that there is one BIG difference between New York and London, which was to make ALL the difference. In New York, the transportation ran all night, so getting into one of their venues at say 10:30 to have a leisurely supper and a couple of 45 minute Cabaret sets was no problem, as getting a train out to the 'burbs' at 2 or even 3am was easy. But with some of our guests having to be away to get a last train from *Charing Cross* back to *Little Dripping* at some ridiculously early time like 11.21 meant we didn't really have a chance with the mass market. But people who lived in or close to London or who were staying at one of the hotels in the capital came to Curtain Call and enjoyed *our* show after the show.

These were golden years for entertainment in London: Michael Crawford had been in Phantom, and Colm Wilkinson in Les Misérables, ensuring that their box offices were sold out for months if not years ahead. Over at the Royal Albert Hall, the likes of Eric Clapton were doing Rock, Blues and Orchestral gigs - and for me, best of all, was Frank Sinatra, a man who could sell out The Hall for several evenings on his own, was appearing with two other greats in a show modestly called *The Ultimate Event*. Sinatra was so cool and relaxed treating us to hit after hit, inspiring Liza Minnelli to be at the top of her game and almost literally on fire, and when I recall

Sammy Davies Junior's complete charisma making London draw its breath with his opening bars of Mr Bojangles, my spine tingles again at the memory.

We had some great performers too, who I'm delighted to thank again on these pages. Lindsay Hamilton when she was playing Fantine in *Les Misérables*, Glyn Kerslake who was **the** *Phantom*, Lisa Hull who played Christine in the same show, Jacinta Whyte the original Ellen in *Miss Saigon*, Sharon D. Clark the Killer Queen in Queen's *We Will Rock You*,

Shona Lindsey, Alison Jiear, Mark O'Malley, Gary Williams and Charles Shervill - the list could go on for pages. The performers could always be sure of two things. I'd feed them well, and if they brought other cast members with them, I'd also stand them a drink or two and make them welcome.

Gary Williams in full swing.

Their solo pieces, such as *Bring Him Home* from Les Misérables, *Memory* from Cats, and Lindsay's wonderful rendition of the song she always drew standing applause with on the stage of the Palace Theatre, *I Dreamed a Dream*, were always a feast for the ears, and being so up close and personal to these electric performers was truly sensational. But guests also loved the duets from Jesus Christ Superstar, Evita, Sunset Boulevard, and of course *All I ask of You*, sung by Glyn and Lisa, which was always a favourite and hard to follow. Invariably performed by them with passion and a discernible intimacy that was palpable and moving. And when a pianist like Stephen Hill or Nathan Martin were in a mood to mix it up with some jazz, or a bit of ragtime à la Scott Joplin, the place started jumping. From *Sweet Georgia Brown* one minute, to Dave Brubeck's *Take Five* the next.

Performers have entertainment running through their veins, like seaside rock has the name of the town, and they could *never resist* joining in. The lure of a spotlight and a spare mic was just too much to resist. These impromptu busking nights when a dozen or so singers who had just popped in for a drink ended up on stage too were the best!

"When you Hear The People Sing" smashed out by a well bevvied chorus, all singing their hearts out as the final encore in our cosy cabaret room made for some great memories.

I make no pretentions. We were low brow. But we gave the people what they wanted to hear, tunes they knew, and encouragement (sometimes) to join in if they wanted to. Always with some humour, I encouraged our Curtain Call Cast to share their backstage stories with us from the stage.

I discovered that it's something of a tradition in the theatre in London, I'm not sure whether the rest of the world has adopted this, that on the last night before a major cast change, the outgoing cast will expect to get up to some pranking. If you've seen Les Misérables you will be familiar with the biggest prop in London. The *helicopter* in Miss Saigon is probably the most spectacular, but the *barricade* in Les Mis is huge and very impressive. It looks as if it has been constructed with beer barrels, cart wheels, huge pieces of wood, old furniture, delivery pallets and anything that the revolutionaries could lay their hands on. Its construction is solid as several of their number have to clamber over it on their way to the top, to take pot shots at the soldiers the other side.

We the audience first see the barricade from the back where the protestors are. It is on a revolving platform, and at one point the whole barricade turns through 180° to reveal the other side, strewn with the bodies of the revolutionaries who didn't make it to the safety of the barricade. A serious and moving moment.

Lindsay used to tell of a particular night at the Palace Theatre when she was playing Fantine. The outgoing chorus had collected up various bits of the performers own clothing from their dressing rooms, and with clothes pegs had attached them to a long piece of rope which they had fixed high on the front of the barricade, stretching it from one side to the other, whilst it was still hidden from view. This was a great jape, the idea being that the washing line full of *modern day clothes* would be exposed to the audience when the barricade turned! Depending on how you look at it, fortunately or unfortunately, one of the stagehands saw it, grabbed a couple of his mates who climbed up to tear the washing line down and drag it out of sight, literally a minute or so before the computerised revolve was programmed to make the turn. Anyone in the front stalls quick with a camera might have earned a few hundred pounds from one of the Sundays for a great front page picture the following day.

Another story that always made me laugh, was told by Lisa Hull who had played Christine in *Phantom of the Opera*, opposite Dave Willetts. It was Dave's last night and the cast were determined to find a way to make Dave corpse (laugh mid aria when he shouldn't). They saw their opportunity for a prank during a scene set on the lake in the basement of the Opera House, where the Phantom and Christine are on a boat. The Phantom, taking Christine to his lair, is standing with a punting pole propelling the boat towards the front of the stage through swirling mist (created by dry ice) singing the very powerful theme song of the show which is *the* Phantom of the Opera song. All very atmospheric and dramatic. Christine is sitting and at one point her back is to the audience as the boat turns.

There had been a recent infestation of rodents in the basement dressing rooms, which inspired Lisa to bring in a little furry toy mouse. She had attached a long tape to either side of it. Off stage, Lisa had nestled the mouse in her cleavage and with the aid of her dresser the tapes were passed across her chest and down each arm so that with her hands pulling on them, the mouse would pop-up from its hiding place in her costume to appear between her breasts!

Lisa tells that the first time she did it Dave's eyes visibly widened and fairly popped out of his head with the shock, but he managed somehow to carry on singing. When mousey retreated but then immediately and repeatedly popped up he tried his hardest to suppress his laughter, but this only made him snort, and he had to quickly give into it, feigning a coughing fit mid aria! Mission accomplished. Thank goodness neither of the show's producers, Andrew-Lloyd Webber or Cameron Mackintosh were in the audience that evening! Lisa never did tell us whether Dave ever saw the funny side of it or not.

Unlike the New York venues we never had any of the huge stars who appeared in London like Barry Manilow, Tony Bennett or Madonna drop in. That would have been flattering, but we didn't need them!

Our good old London cast members were our megastars and we loved them all.

Sadly though, for all the fun and brilliant performers, we couldn't make it pay. We put it on almost every weekend for about a year.

Some nights we were packed, with people standing at the back, and on others we had bookings for 6 and no walk ups. Despite our lobbying, with no signs of the London's underground or British Rail's timetables being extended through the night, I was very sad to have to let it go. But I'm so proud we did it, and I'm still in touch with

those great musicians today. We got away with never having any *lobsters** in our audiences!

Brian has moved on to greater things and still welcomes our occasional *Music on the Menu* nights at L'Escargot, the much acclaimed London restaurant which he now proudly owns.

Our guests were always up close and personal.

Footnote:

*Flawsome. Acknowledges his flaws and knows he is awesome nonetheless.

*Lobsters. People who throw or lob things in the direction of the stage.

Singing for our *supper*

The singers always claimed that the more they *ate* the better they *sang*. It was always my contention that the more the *rest of us* drank the better they *sounded*.

From the very start of my working with professional performers I heard horror stories of there being no parking spaces reserved for them, having a cold toilet in which to change and hang clothes, nowhere private to rest when not performing and, worst of all, having cold and unappetising food thrown their way whilst the guests were often enjoying the finest cuisine known to man. So I made sure that on all of my jobs, these things were always taken care of.

With this in mind, I generously made it easy for the various chefs and caterers because rather than have them divert their attention from giving guests exquisite food and having to buy us sliced bread and corned beef for sandwiches and perhaps give over a part of an oven to warming through frozen sausage rolls (or heaven forbid 'deal of the week 3 for 2 pizza'). I made it effortless for them by saying "*Make it easy on yourselves* and just give us whatever the guests having. That'll be fine with us". Do you know, it worked every time!

We found ourselves singing in the palatial homes of Chairmen and owners of household name companies; five star hotels; discreet private rooms in top restaurants and clubs; museums and galleries; stately homes and castles, and two others which I want to tell you about, as they became firm favourites.

It's very flattering when people remember your name, and from the very start two who always did were Anton Mosimann and his son Mark who runs Mosimann's Private Dining Club with skill and foresight.

It always felt special going to Mosimann's in Belgravia

for the beautifully decorated and themed surroundings, the dedication and reliability of the staff we worked with, and of course experiencing the wonderful culinary magic worked by the chefs, using the freshest of ingredients combined with a profusion of inspirational and sometimes unique recipes. Always under the watchful eye of their 2 Michelin star proprietor.

During the pre dinner drinks there one evening, one of our lovely Scottish guests, (in order to save embarrassment I'll just call her Hilary), downed several glasses of champagne on what she later claimed was an empty stomach.

Anton himself popped up to see us as agreed, sharing gossip with some of the guests and chatting briefly about his time presenting cookery on television both here and in this native Switzerland.

Having enjoyed many delicious meals from Hilary's own kitchen, I particularly wanted her to meet Anton and having told him of *her* culinary skills, had persuaded him to share with her one of his unpublished recipes. She knew nothing of this of course. I guided her towards him, making the introduction at a suitable gap in conversation. Anton was always charming, having said to me earlier "Ah Clive, I think you have lost a little weight since last we met." (I hadn't). He greeted Hilary with "It is such a pleasure to entertain a fellow cook here at my Club" to which she slurred "sshhouldn't you be away to the kitchen keepin' a wee eye on the pots an' pans?!"

Even before the laughter from the rest of us subsided, Anton had backed away saying "You are right of course, I'll go and attend to that now" Hilary immediately realised her faux pas and was blurting out an apology. But too late! Anton had flown, taking the secret recipe with him.

Mosimann's food presentation was and is always noteworthy.

In fact I've seen more attractive designs on Mosimann's plates than on the walls of some of the more avant-garde art galleries.

I remember during one night there with the opera singers, the colourful desert was collage of exquisitely arranged finely sliced and layered selection of fruit and Roy actually commented "I'd like to hang this on my wall." He actually gazed at it adoringly for several seconds before destroying this particular work of art with *gutso**.

The Mosimann's signature, pre-main course risotto bowl and the pre-dessert, light as a feather bread-and-butter pudding had been added to the three course menu, for us as well as the guests. Naturally!

Scilla and Glenys always used to bring billowing suiter bags containing a sufficient number of ball gowns to allow them to appear in a different costume for each new set. Glenys often relates the story about this evening, when alarm bells should've rung as she and Scilla changed into their finale outfits.

She remembers it this way: "We both ignored the warning signs of the struggle to do up our zips and buttons" They began that final set with a cheery duet called *Mira o Norma* sung between the High Priestess Norma and her handmaiden Adalgisa. Given that this story concerns over indulgence at the dining table I thought it amusing that name of one of the characters in this song, **Adalgisa** sounded like remedy for indigestion.

Glenys continues "I thought Scilla sounded a little laboured but didn't realise the extent of the problem until it was my turn to answer with the second verse." she recalls "It was horrendous! My dress was so tight I couldn't take a decent breath and it was an enormous effort to make any sound at all. I felt as if every mouthful of the dinner was hanging on my larynx! As the duet progressed it got more and more difficult and we both had to work harder and harder to keep going. At last it was over and with a sigh of relief we waddled off, relieved that the tenor's solo, Nessun Dorma, was the next item."

As they passed Roy at the piano he said unsympathetically, "Well that will teach you two not to eat so much before you sing that duet next time."

"Not at all!" they shot back. "It's taught us not to put *that* duet so late in the programme."

Footnote:
gutso. Eating with speed and voracity.

The Royal Yacht!

As well as Mosimann's my other very favourite venue is The Royal Yacht Britannia, now permanently moored off the east coast of Scotland at Leith. This was always an opportunity for me to revel in my love of *touching history* once again. Putting on events that I had devised and created in the actual dining room where the Queen had entertained Heads of State and leading lights from every walk of life, including her first Prime Minister Winston Churchill, was especially significant for me.

I was given an introduction by my friend Gerry King, the man then in charge of private boxes at Ascot. His appointment at the Queen's racecourse had come from The Duke of Edinburgh who knew and trusted him from his many years' service as Signals Officer aboard The Royal Yacht.

Gerry told me that when Prince Charles and Princess Anne were children they were often aboard and loved the freedom to run around safely. Britannia was one of the few ships whose crew still slept in hammocks and some of the sailors decided to play a prank on an old salt on his last tour with Britannia. They had put the inexperienced young Charles up to tipping this somewhat cantankerous and feisty old Scotsman out of his hammock whilst he was still snoring, telling HRH that he loved being woken up that way! The old seafarer hit the deck with a thump and was no sooner awake than was on his feet with fists clenched ready to attack the misguided perpetrator. In an instant he took in the scene, by now a somewhat bewildered looking son of the Queen before him, and filling the room a bunch of his shipmates all in hysterics. He then floored everyone by saying quietly to the boy Prince, *"If yee want to grow up tae be King, laddie, I wouldnae do that again!"*

With no intentions of tipping anyone out of their hammocks, I knew I was in safe hands on the build up to any event on Britannia as their Head of Operations, Diane McRae never left anything to chance. Diane is a leading exponent of the *"7 P's of organisation"** . Then on the night, if I were met by the immaculately attired Bruce MacBride as I stepped on board I knew I could begin to relax. Bruce, for me, is one of the finest Maître d's in Britain. He always greeted me with a perfectly mixed Bombay Sapphire and tonic with slices of lemon *and* lime presented on a silver tray, remembered everyone's names, and ran the room of white gloved waiting staff with deft military style meticulousness.

I've often seen Bruce clutching a ruler, making sure the long banqueting table was laid with inch-perfect precision. Place settings exactly equidistant, a forest of gleaming crystal, and a small arsenal of cutlery flanking the porcelain plates, each monogrammed with the distinctive Britannia livery, and all perfectly placed.

Fresh blooms, beautifully arranged, gave off a heady aroma and silver candelabra, each supporting six long flickering candles, set the scene for the next extraordinary occasion to come.

Guests couldn't fail to feel that they were for that evening at least, sharing a fantasy world usually out of reach without a Royal invitation.

The rest of Britannia looks much the same today as she did during her many years of service for the Royal family. The drawing room is still set out as the Queen liked it and the original piano that Noel Coward used to play remains in situ. I've been privileged to begin many of our musical evenings by greeting our guests in the drawing room, before a guided tour of the ship, followed by dinner and entertainment in the state dining room, always keeping our format of light hearted compeering and songs between courses. These included many of our festive *Carols by Candlelight*, pre-Christmas dinners. Others with a 24 piece big band, with charismatic crooner Gary Williams and with members of the London cast of *The Rat Pack Live from Las Vegas*, featuring three incredible performers, Neil Gordon, Glenn Macnamara and Jim Whitely; playing Frank, Dean and Sammy of course. Jim is an ex Manchester City footballer, so we shouldn't have been surprised at his dazzling footwork when enthralling us with his *Mr Bojangles!*

As I became increasingly fascinated about Britannia's past and the historic events that she had hosted, senior execs Angela Stewart and Bridgeen Mullen kindly gave me access to Britannia's archives and I was able to leaf through the records of all sorts of interesting ceremonies and celebrations that had taken place over the years. These were so detailed that in some cases, in addition to guest lists, the menus, wines and even the cocktails offered on arrival were recorded.

MENU

Amuse-bouche

Poached Maine lobster

Roasted English beef
Jersey Royal potatoes
carrots and butter beans

Key Lime Pie
vanilla ice cream and lime zest

Chardonnay Wente Morning Fog (California) 1981
Chateau Tour St. Joseph Haut Medoc, Bordeaux 1974

Friday 4th March 1983   Long Beach, California

The Royal occasion in 1983 on which our first *Historic Moments* dinner was based.

Neil, Jim and Glenn. *Our* Rat Pack!

I decided to try and recreate some of these events and came up with the title *Historic Moments aboard The Royal Yacht Britannia*. Our first was based upon an event which took place in Long Beach California in 1983 when Britannia had taken Her Majesty and the Duke of Edinburgh on an official visit to the United States. The Queen had offered to host a dinner on board to celebrate President and Nancy Reagan's 31st wedding anniversary. Appearing on the President's guest list were some stars of stage and screen including Frank Sinatra, Dean Martin, Sammy Davis Junior and Dionne Warwick. Frank Sinatra had the idea that after the main course he, Dean (and in the absence of Sammy through illness) Dionne could perform a set of Rat Pack songs for a bit of fun. He took some sheet music with him, and approached the piano accompanist ahead of the dinner who of course was flattered to be asked and delighted to join in with Sinatra's plan.

What Sinatra wasn't to know was that the Queen *hated* surprises, *especially* on home turf. Much to the delight of the *other* people in the dining room and to the extreme irritation of Her Majesty, the trio launched into this seemingly impromptu performance of hits that the guests would all be familiar with. By the time Sinatra was singing *I Get a Kick Out of You* he'd picked up on the distinct vibe that the Queen was *not* amused. She was sitting stony faced, avoiding eye contact and most definitely not applauding.

So when he got to the line *I know that you adore me* he changed the lyric, and looking directly at her sang *I know you **do not** adore me*. The story goes that the Queen smiled faintly and nodded twice in acknowledgement.

So our first *Historic Moments* evening on board recreated that very night. Guests were piped aboard and were offered the cocktails originally served Reagan's party, which were Manhattans and Champagne Cocktails. The very talented Britannia Executive Chef Mark Alston told me that he would put "a modern twist" on the original menu items of poached Maine lobster, and roast English beef. In fact it was very much "a Scottish twist" from Mark, with Organic Shetland Salmon with a saffron and shellfish dressing, and roast fillet of Inverurie beef! I am always amazed and delighted at the culinary delights Mark and his brigade produce from within the confines of Britannia's very cramped galley.

We served the same wines where we could, later vintages of course and even reprinted the original 1983 menu card within our souvenir menu leaflet, complete with photos from the state occasion. After the main course I told that Sinatra story, and to the delight of the guests, Neil, Glenn and Jim bounced in singing *Strangers in the Night* followed by all the songs that Sinatra and his pals had delighted *their* audience with 31 years before. Our guests had the bonus of a second set of singing after desert. Although there were at least two old queens at the table, Her Majesty herself sadly couldn't be with us that evening.

I was recently checking some of the facts with Glenn and he reminded me that I had given each of the performers a personalised plaque to commemorate our performance that night. He told me that his still stands on his mantelpiece. It is always a talking point for his visitors, and that performances and achievements come and go on his musical CV, but his appearances on Britannia are a constant.

As they are on mine.

Glen told a lovely story about Dean Martin telling Sinatra (who famously owned a Lamborghini) that he was very excited about taking delivery of his first Ferrari. He told his friend, "I really feel I've arrived!" "Thays great kid," said Sinatra. He went on, "If you wanna be someone – get a Ferrari. If you are someone, get a Lamborghini!"

Any great team needs an inspirational leader, and Britannia has Bob Downie. I was amused to see a recent post of Bob's on LinkedIn where he wrote in reply to a comment I had made: 'Clive you are a legend up here' How nice. I wondered if it were for bringing some amazing musicians on board, or perhaps because of all the money we had raised on Britannia for charities over the years. I was so flattered when he told me it was because when I had been their guest on board some years before I had spontaneously said a few words of thanks on behalf of the guests following a brilliant after dinner speech by their Chairman, Admiral Rankin.

I had no idea that what had stuck in their minds were my opening remarks when introducing myself. I'd said "Like John Lewis is never knowingly under-sold my name (clutching my stomach) is Clive Thomas and I'm never knowingly under-nourished" following on with "Since I was last here I've been voted a sex symbol - for women who no longer care!"

Oh well, I suppose we all have to be remembered for something.

Footnote:
*the 7 P's of organisation.
Proper Planning and Preparation Prevents Pi~s Poor Performance!

On my
TRAVELS
Again

PREST GE
SAFAR CLUB

LA DOLCE VITA
THE RALLY TO VENICE

MONTE CARLO or

Celebration
of
African
Wildlife & Tribal Life

HIGHLAND Fling

THE PRESTIGE
ROAD RALLY CLUB

Celebration of
Zambian
Wildlife

SNOWBALL RALLY

IL LAVORO ITALIANO
-The Italian Job

Celebration of
INDIAN
Wildlife

Whale
Watching
Baja
California

The Grape Escape

ESPAÑA to LA FRANCE

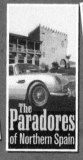

The Paradores
of Northern Spain

Celebration
of
Wildlife
in the
Galapagos

The **Fringe**, the **Tattoo** and *Gyles Brandreth*

When not on stage with 'my' singers, I've enjoyed spending time year on year watching others tread the boards up in Edinburgh at the Fringe Festival. Ray and I always made a point of going on the first weekend before some of the more fierce critics have chance to savage a performer's best endeavours and potentially influence any choices we might make. Also, to get the word of mouth going, many shows do two-for-the-price-of-one ticket offers over the first few days!

During the Fringe the population of Edinburgh explodes and the streets are awash with people going from one show to another, and down Princes Street and along The Royal Mile there are merrymakers of all kinds clapping and cheering at street musicians, jugglers and mime artists; and any number of costumed actors and actresses performing snippets of their shows, hoping that passers-by will like

them enough to take a promotional leaflet and then *buy a ticket!*

The Fringe is on over the same four weeks as The Edinburgh International Festival (the posh bit), the Film Festival, the Book Festival *and* the incredibly popular Military Tattoo.

Ray and I have a mutual friend, Major Brian Leishman, who for many years was the top man at the Tattoo. Run literally with military precision under Brian's control, this spectacular event takes place at Edinburgh Castle throughout August and features displays of choreographed military music from around the world.

Brian had invited us to be there one evening as his guests and we were surprised and delighted to find that he had seated us in the front row of the VIP Box overlooking the display arena and the dramatically illuminated castle beyond. I was sat at the row end with Ray next to me and, as usual, it didn't take him long to get into conversation with the smartly dressed lady sat next to him. She asked him what else we were planning to see during our visit, and Ray mentioned a couple of bonkers things that we had picked out from the programme, including some general buffoonery featuring synchronised swimming on dry land, a contortionist and 10 men on bicycles; and a late night comedy show entitled "Whoops Vicar, is that your Dick?" (With hindsight, this title proved to be by far the funniest thing about the show). She didn't look that impressed with our choices and said "Don't forget that the Kirov Ballet are here this weekend as well as the Hungarian Symphony Orchestra who are really terribly special."

Ray enthusiastically told her that we were really here for, "The madness of The Fridge" and, "we don't much bother about the serious festival bol**cks." Continuing with, "and what about you, what are you planning to see?" The lady replied

*"I expect I'm probably going to be too busy to see very much as I am the person in charge of the serious festival bol****ks!"*

Never one to be phased or embarrassed, Ray shot back, "here's my card. If you want to escape for a couple of hours and come to something *that's fun*, please give us a ring!" Like the Swedish Ambassadors wife, we are still waiting for the call.

Another friend, Mervyn Stutter, a founder of *The Flying Pickets* and a very talented songwriter/satirist and performer, has for almost 30 years hosted a lunchtime *Pick of the Fringe* show where he invites acts to come on and do a ten minute trailer to an audience of around 300 people. This gives him a wonderful variety show to host every day and hopefully the acts may well generate a few dozen extra ticket sales. It's a mutually beneficial arrangement and Ray and I have regular seats as it's a great way to get a curated collection of some of the best performances in town.

Edinburgh has introduced me to some fine exponents of musical comedy who, after a glass or two of cleansing ale I managed to persuade to work with me at *Music on the Menu*. My top three are still; virtuoso *Rebecca Carrington* and her cello which mimicks other instruments; *String Fever* with ingenious use of their amazing electronic classical strings, and *Kev Orkian* with his wicked sense of humour and inventiveness at the grand piano, which he plays with the originality of a modern day Victor Borge.

You need all the help you can get finding the best things to see as each day over 300 venues across the city promote over 3,000 shows from ten in the morning until 4.30 the following morning, covering every type of performing art you can think of; children's shows, drama, comedy drama, serious music, comedy music, tribute music, modern dance, ballet, stand-up and sketch comedy and some completely outrageous things.

I remember attending a play for five people only. We sat in the back of an MPV whilst driving round Edinburgh as the plot unfolded. They sold out every night. Very clever! Then there was the low ceilinged, dimly lit basement venue where we were left standing, to be yelled at and pushed around as if we were heading for the gas in Nazi Germany. It was a unique theatre experience. Incredibly disturbing, moving and thought provoking. So it's certainly not all comedy and having a laugh – but *much* of it is!

It was at Edinburgh that I met Gyles Brandreth when he and the cast of the comedy he was in appeared on Mervyn's *Pick of the Fringe.* Gyles is one of quickest-witted men I have ever met and was very funny that day, beginning by telling the audience that *"photography is strictly encouraged as all of us on the stage needed all the publicity we can get!"*

He went on to tell us that... *"mobile phones can be left on. Anyone taking a call will be joined by me and this microphone and I will share your conversation with everyone in the auditorium!"*

He went down a storm and I met him in the bar afterwards where we shared a pot of tea. The Fringe is that kind of a place. He was not only funny but incredible amiable and I thought it would be fun to do some events with him.

The opportunity came some months later when I was offered the chance to buy all the tickets for the last guided tour of the afternoon at The Houses of Parliament, meaning that we could turn it into a private event as it would be only our guests taking part. The timing of it was perfect for lunch followed by a speaker at a venue close enough to The Palace of Westminster to be there for 3.30. I thought that Gyles, who had been a Member of Parliament and was in the Whips office during John Major's Government, would be the perfect speaker.

However, the thing you have to know about Gyles is that

He has an irresistible sense of mischief and revels in saying the most outrageous thing that comes into his head.

Which is probably why when he took the lectern he first of all thanked me for inviting him to be there and then referred to my colleague Becky Knight by saying "I must also thank Becky, *Clive's love child* for looking after me today!"

Gyles was Conservative Member of Parliament for Chester from 1992 for five years and rose to become the Lord Commissioner to

 The Treasury and told us about his time in Government saying "It's very different now, so at last I can speak the truth. I can tell you the one thing I really really couldn't bear when I was an MP was having to spend any time at all with my constituents! Let's face it, the people have contempt for the politicians but I can assure you, it is *nothing* to the contempt *we* have for *you!*".

He went on humorously telling us about changes in Parliament since his time there, including that the role of the Backbencher had been severely diminished, saying "No one even knows who they are now, unless they turn up on the front page of a newspaper because the taxpayer has been unwittingly footing the bill, forking out for their moat or duck house."

When asked by one of our guests about Prime Minister John Major's four year affair with fellow politician Edwina Currie, which no one knew about until she shocked the nation by revealing it in her memoirs, Gyles told us that Lord Archer's wife Mary had been quoted as saying "I am shocked, not by Mrs. Currie's indiscretion in publishing the fact, but at Mr Major's lapse of good taste!" Gyles commented, "It was known that John Major always dressed very well, and at times very quickly!"

The story that I really liked was about Gyles's maiden speech in the House of Commons, where tradition has it that the House gives a new MP making his or her maiden speech a day off from the usual heckling and jeering that is often thrown at Members whilst on their feet. Gyles explained to us that John Prescott was Deputy Leader of the Labour Party at the time and was sat opposite him in the front row of the opposition benches as he made his maiden speech.

"It's true that I had a reputation for wearing colourful knitwear during my appearances on breakfast television," he told us, "but of course I wore a smart suit for Parliament. As I started speaking, Prescott called out *"woolly jumper ha ha ha!"* and continued doing this regular intervals and with ever increasing volume. So eventually I paused and addressed him directly saying *"the joy of having a woolly jumper is that you can discard at will, but the blight of having a woolly mind, is that you are lumbered with it for life!"* It was a good line and on the day won me loud applause and laughter from both sides of the House. However, I fear that John may have the last laugh, for he has been elevated to *Lord* Prescott, and taken his seat in the Upper House, whereas I am *here*, today, talking to *you!"*

Indeed he was and we were all very happy about it as I can't honestly think of another former politician who is as funny, honest and refreshingly self-deprecating as Gyles. If you ever get the chance to see him in the theatre or hear him do an after-dinner on any subject.

I urge you not to miss out. You'll be in for a treat.

India: Tigers, Trains and *Trumpets*

It's been well documented that arriving in India for the first time is an all out assault on the senses.

The streets thronged with bicycle rickshaws, tuk tuks and thousands of people packed into the spaces between the buildings, some just ambling along, others scurrying hither and thither, the ladies resplendent in vibrant colours, men in kurtas and matching baggy pyjama style trousers, and children, eyes everywhere, shouting and running to their friends, their mothers anxious about them getting lost in the crowds. The noise, the smells and the heat all create a sensation that so many Europeans before me have attempted to capture on the page, so all I am going to say is if you want to know what India is like, you must go there and experience it for yourself.

For my India will be different from yours. I guarantee it will be a shock to the senses but you will be richer for it.

I first went to Delhi on a recce for tiger watching trips I wanted to bring into our *"Celebration of Wildlife"* hosted safaris. I was overnighting in New Delhi which is spick and span India for the tourists. I was drawn to the old part of the city and was instantly aware of how the atmosphere and the buildings of Old Delhi are very different. Few are in good repair, most seemingly held up by the ones on either side, and all are hung with miles of telephone cables adorning every wall from the first floor up, some even stretching tangled across the streets. On the roads getting there the traffic is overwhelming, with everyone jostling for an extra inch of road space, while all the time blasting their horns to create the *City Centre Symphony*, a great cacophony of noise in three movements, all of them slow.

People are everywhere. Even on the busy main road from the hotel there were always people walking day *and* night, and my car taking me to meet Manoj, my local contact, moved slowly following a truck with half a dozen or so labourers slouched in the back amongst bags of cement and the mixer. Coming towards us was a motorbike ridden by papa, with mamma at the back, two children squashed between them and a toddler perched between the handlebars. Behind them a cow looked about to totter onto our side of the road and was causing traffic to veer around it. The driver explained that you don't dare risk hitting it because if you did you'd probably find yourself in prison. Cows are holy beasts in India. You don't eat them and you certainly don't run into them!

The scariest thing was that there wasn't only cows coming towards us on *our* side of the road. Trucks and coaches did it too! Maybe it was to skirt around a pothole the size of a crater hollow, or perhaps to give a wide berth to a truck overloaded to three times its capacity carrying old tyres to be recycled, or maybe a harvest of corn not only piled extremely high but *extremely wide*, making the vehicle take up three times its width in the road.

My new friend Manoj, a fellow travel professional who had lived in London and understood what I was trying to achieve, became my local fixer and knew all the right places to take me. One of them was the fabulous Oberoi Hotel at Ranthambhore, close to the tiger reserve where we were to spend the most time.

Tupin the General Manager, an obliging sort of fellow, greeted us on the first morning when I emerged from my room bleary eyed at 5.30 with a bowl of porridge to warm us ahead of our game drive. The temperature would rise to 35 degrees by 11 o'clock, but before dawn it was just a little above zero. Tupin suggested that adding a shot of whisky to the porridge would fortify me yet further! It amused me that we always think of India as being a hot and humid country, and here I was wearing three layers, tucking into a good old British winter staple with *the milk of Scotland* thrown in for further insulation.

The Oberoi hotels are truly incredible. They have their own training academy and every single one of the staff are fantastic ambassadors for their hotel; from the bellboys to the GM, you couldn't imagine any better. My brilliantly designed detached room had the brick walls of a building, but the ceiling of a safari tent, giving a real feel of being in the wilderness. The attention to detail and comfort was such that we had *two* air-conditioning units in case one failed, his and hers basins, a shower *and* a roll top marble bathtub and more charging points than even Bill Gates would need. There were also wonderful touches like silver stars and golden tigers embroidered into the marquee roof lining, which caught the light and twinkled above me and on the first night, and when I returned to my room, I discovered that the room steward had tidied every one of my many charging leads with Velcro cable strips. Even the little containers of shampoo, conditioner, face cream and sun cream were special. Made especially and exclusively for Oberoi in France, I felt sure that otherwise honest guests would scoop as many of them up as they could for onward journeying, not only because they were freely available in the rooms, but because they smelled so delicious!

The bed was extraordinarily comfortable and my pillow sommelier (I can think of no other way to describe him) offered me a choice of *eleven* different pillows, ranging from very soft to very firm and with a variety of fillings, taking into account any possible allergy that a guest may have. I felt sure that if I'd asked him for a *pillow made from hand plucked peacock feathers, in a case of a cotton, silk and satin mix depicting a scene from the Bayeux Tapestry, then a matching pair, monogrammed with my initials, would have been on my bed by nightfall the following day.*

I was used to game drives in Kenya's Maasai Mara where within minutes of leaving Governor's camp you could be with a whole pride of lions, and on that same drive see cheetahs and even a leopard. Tigers on the other hand are extremely shy and like to stay hidden. However, the Gods were with me because it was on that very first planning trip that I saw my first tiger, majestically resting on a ledge by a stream.

To see this magnificent mature female was a most unexpected treat. She was used to the vehicles, of which there were only two others on this occasion, and she wasn't going anywhere fast, so there was plenty of time to grab my camera and bang off a couple of shots in the excitement of the moment, then carefully chose the right lens, the right exposure and shutter speed, and wriggle myself into the best position to get the composition right. Then, having better tiger photos than I ever thought possible, I sat back and relaxed, enjoying the magical moment of just being in the company of this most majestic of the big cats. By now there were several jeeps in attendance, full of people revelling in their good luck, and like me, very quietly, even respectfully basking in the moment, not wanting to spook the tiger with any loud noises or sudden movements.

However, during my excursions to see wildlife in wild places, loud American women seem to be attracted to me like aging rockers to a Rolling Stones tribute gig, as once again the mood was broken by a lady from the United States in one of the other vehicles. She was trying to get a shot of the tiger on her phone. Rather than ask her driver if he could move her to a better position, she stood up recklessly waving her arms about and yelling "Here kitty kitty, here kitty kitty!" An older, and I later learned, much respected guide in another of the vehicles hissed at her "Madam! This is *not* a domestic cat. This is the pride of India. *Have some respect!!*" Quite right too.

When I returned some months later with my group, some of whom were veterans of Africa trips with me and now looking forward eagerly to see the biggest of the big cats, I thought it would be a good idea for them to have a couple of days in Delhi to acclimatise to the weather. I'd been in a quandary about the timing of the trip. The best chance of seeing tigers is when the weather gets *really* hot and water evaporates from the shallower watering holes, meaning they are forced to come out into the open in their search for water in the larger ponds and lakes. April, when it's about 45°, is best month but I had to balance this with how my largely older audience would cope with the heat. I decided that leaving the end of an English winter in March to be plunged into a humid 34 or 35° was quite enough for them to cope with. Also I didn't want our people to miss the experience of *Old* Delhi. On my trips I never want guests to see only the aspects of the country that the tourist board would like us to know about – the sanitised version of the reality – which in this case is New Delhi, designed by English architect Sir Edward Lutyens, the seat of Government, with its wide tree lined and largely beggar-free streets, and impressive white mansions mostly behind high walls and electric gates, where the diplomats and only the very wealthy have their residences.

However, as you know I had found Old Delhi to be fascinating. This part of the city is basically a huge market, or bazaar. And to our eyes it appears as a bizarre bazaar with people selling stuff from every shop, vacant piece of pavement, grass verge, barrow and cart.

There are whole streets and alleyways set aside to specific businesses; in one street people selling rice, nuts, seeds and grains displayed in varying sizes of pots and baskets, some the size of small ponds; in another textiles on great rolls; and then more set aside with hundreds of little businesses working with leather and dying, artisans making and repairing things in wood, straw leather, silver; then fruit and vegetables some familiar to us and some not; and so on for street after street. There are rickshaws and bicycles everywhere, so you can get a bit barged and knocked, and every now and again someone is likely to thrust the stump of a disfigured arm to within inches of your face, holding out their other hand hopefully.

So I thought a neat way to introduce our guests to the real India of old Delhi would be to put everyone in cycle rickshaws so that they could see, hear and smell the streets, be truly in amongst it all, yet still slightly detached.

Manoj organised it brilliantly and even gave nicely printed *Celebration of Indian Wildlife* tee shirts to each of the rickshaw drivers so that they could be easily identified, and off we went, 15 rickshaws in convoy! Most people had bought some pretty snazzy cameras with the hope of getting a few good shots of tigers, but now they were getting through a good few megs of their memory cards without even leaving the city.

I wanted to make the journey to Ranthambore a memorable event too. Roads are very potholed and I didn't want guests to have to go through an airport again so soon after their arrival, so I figured the train was by far the best option. Indian trains are probably the most crowded form of transport in the world. Not only do people cram into the carriages but they hang onto the sides and sit on top of the roof. If an Indian phones you from India and says "I'm on the train," he could be talking quite literally.

Manoj said he'd get our guests into first class air-conditioned carriages, which I remembered from my recce were extremely comfortable. There was even a toilet cubical at each end of the carriage. But there was a problem. I'd discovered from personal experience that the toilets were horrifically disgusting. And I don't mean just the smell, worse was the foul state in which some people had left them beggared belief. The journey was six hours long, the chai-wallah (person who pushed the tea trolley) came through regularly and our guests were, at some stage going to need to use the toilets. And so Manoj, ever the resourceful, came up with a cunning plan and suggested that we hire a person whose sole job it would be to keep the toilet compartment sanitised from ceiling to floor, finishing each cleaning bout with a squirt or two of air freshener.

Manoj told me that Ramesh, the young fellow who had agreed to undertake the task and be our dedicated *poo-wallah*, was unemployed and had said he would do anything to earn some money. I liked his spirit, and made a point of thanking him. He responded by putting his hands together as if in prayer, bowing his head slightly toward me and saying "No, thankee you Sahib. I am very pleasee for today to have a big jobee."

And he did so well that Mr Jobee, as he was by now affectionately referred to on the equally potentially hazardous *return* train journey, earned probably the biggest tip of the trip. And rightly so! Bringing food to our table, or driving the coach was not nearly so dicey a service to provide, as overcoming the perils faced by the bold Ramesh.

And if he wasn't an Untouchable before he started, he certainly was by the time he'd finished. At least until he'd had a hot bath!

As the train pulled in to Ranthambore Station there was a band playing and about 300 people gathered round, some of them dancing and clapping in time and it was only when they saw the big *Celebration of Indian Wildlife* banner that our delighted guests realised that the band were playing to welcome *them* to Ranthambore! Admittedly the 'band' weren't the best tuned of musicians but they were extremely enthusiastic and the volume, especially from the overconfident trumpet section, went a long way to making up for the lack of musical ability.

They were a bit like a cross between Mexican mariachi band, and children tuning their recorders. But it didn't matter a jot. The great thing was it was **fun**. The guests felt like arriving Royalty and we had also entertained some local people, who added to the spectacle by encouraging our initially somewhat bewildered group to jiggle and wiggle with them. It was a very happy time at the station.

The welcome at the hotel was regal too. Two porters sat astride decorated elephants who raised their trunks to us as by way of a salute as we approached – the elephants not the porters – and when I stepped into the fantasy existence of my room I smiled to myself, as my clothes had been unpacked and hung neatly in the wardrobe, my razor and bathroom accoutrement were laid out on the marble basin surround, and once again I stopped to admire the beautiful, embroidered ceiling twinkling above me.

But within minutes my phone was ringing. It wasn't unusual for guests to think they must have the very item that had been overlooked, despite our meticulous planning. But this time it was an Indian gentleman who said in a most cultured voice "Good evening Mr Thomas this is Vikram Oberoi. I understand this is the first group you've bought to my hotels." Not quite *Good evening Mr Bond, we've been expecting you* – but close!

Vikram is the grandson of PJ Oberoi, the founder of the Oberoi hotel dynasty, and is their Chief Executive. I had never before been afforded this level of professional welcome by so senior a man.

"Well Mr Oberoi how very kind of you," I said.
He countered with "No no, the pleasure is mine, and you must call me Viki."

"I want you as the host to be relaxed while you are with us. All of my general managers are handpicked by me and should exceed your expectations. But let me give you my phone number, and if there's anything I can do to help you while you are here please be in touch."

"Thank you Viki," I said, "will that number get me through to you personally?"

He laughed and said "No not quite. It will get you through to one of my secretaries, but I will know about it."

During dinner that night I was telling Naheed, one of our guests who has since become a firm friend, about the call, and asked her if she thought it could have really been Mr Oberoi, a man who is worth many millions of pounds, and employing almost as many people.

"You aren't serious?" She asked with some incredulity "on a Sunday night? Let's face it Clive you're not the biggest of tour operators are you. It was probably a good PR man just doing his job." Naheed had been a senior figure at the Foreign Office and had attended meetings with Cabinet ministers and even at The White House. I knew, with that background she could spot a scam at 30 paces, and was worth listening to!

I thought no more about it until the following morning. I'd told a few of the guests about my amusement at finding porridge and whisky in India, and was much looking forward to shortly becoming reacquainted with it. To my dismay I saw that there was none on display, and an array of fruit skewers and pastries was resting where I had last seen the porridge tureen. Tupin had risen from his bed early once again, and was making sure everyone had settled in alright. I sidled over to him and whispered in his ear, "You'd best hurry up with the porridge and whisky as we need to be leaving in 10 minutes or so don't we?"

He told me "We're not doing that anymore. We found that the croissants and fruit were so much more popular."

"But Tupin," I responded, "I've been telling my guests all about porridge and whisky and the idea of it appeals to them just as much as it did to me!"

He must have seen the look of disappointment on my face but continued anyway with "Well Clive like I said we're not doing that anymore."

I hate to pull rank and try only to do it on very rare occasions but this was definitely one of them. I *wanted* my porridge!

"Tupin, I had a lovely conversation last night with my new friend Viki Oberoi." I began.

Before I could continue, his expression had changed in an instant as he clapped both hands to either side of his head saying "Oh my God! I wish the boss would stop making these calls! If you really want porridge tomorrow, then you will have porridge."

"Thank you Tupin" was what I said. *Thank you Viki* was what I thought.

Before going on a tiger safari, you should know that lions, who are the apex predator in Africa, will lay about in the open and let you pass at incredibly close range but the tiger is essentially nocturnal, shy, and has honed his skills in avoiding people. Maybe they have long memories from the times past when shooting parties had hunted them in this very park almost to extinction. So who could blame them? Our guide told us that you can live your whole entire life in the jungle without ever seeing a tiger, which is why I'd taken Manoj's advice and booked us in for 4 nights, giving us the chance of seven outings into the reserve.

Ranthambore is a former Royal hunting ground but it looks more like something from *The Jungle Book*, with its ruined temples in which tigers can sometimes be seen, lakes shimmering under a sun that quickly gets fierce, and even a crumbly palace on an island in a large lake which is a magnet for thirsty animals. I've seen tiger there, leopard, and chital deer which are spotted like our fallow deer. But never all at the same time.

There is a large flat area with an impressive archway near the entrance, which is a meeting place for people and for scampering, leaping and chattering langur monkeys. Amusing to watch in action, they can steal any food not well protected, and take hats which they sit in and throw to each other. But for much of the time they sit like old men in a European town square, watching the day go by and unlike old men, seem happy to pose for the many eager photographers passing through.

We had also shortened the odds on a sighting for our guests by inviting Vijay an experienced local naturalist to join us, together with Jonathan and Angie Scott from the BBC's Big Cat Diary, who as you know had been regular co-hosts of mine in Africa, and knew a thing or two about big cats. As well as doing fascinating talks just for our guests, Johnny and Vijay were two more pairs of experienced eyes to help the drivers spot the pug marks in the dust or mud, and read the signals from the other animals. Angie, whose amazing images illustrated Johnny's talks was the best spotter of all.

Whenever a tiger is on the prowl it's not only birds that will squawk a warning; alarm calls will also include the chital barking and of course loud screeching from the omnipresent monkeys. The timing of the drives is a great help too, taking place very early in the morning and during late afternoon only, as in the heat of the day tigers lie up in the relative cool of the forest, well out of the glare of the sun.

During the drives in Ranthambore, you experience currents of excited anticipation and eagerness as you screw up your eyes to peer through the shadows in the woodland trying to get your first glimpse, mixed with periods of calm as you contrast the stresses, pollution and humidity of Delhi with the liberating feeling of being in the fresh air and at one with nature. As the reserve covers well over 500 square miles it's easy to find your own space. Some of our guests have told me, that sometimes years later still the most surreal and memorable moment they'd had in their lifetime which they can relive in an instant is their first tiger sighting.

If fortune is smiling on you and you round a bend and see the biggest cat on the planet there before you in full view ambling purposefully towards the lake's edge, the sense of euphoria is indescribable.
You catch your breath, you can't believe your luck, and you are in total astonishment of his size, inherent power, and smouldering strength.

You tingle with glee as you sit transfixed by nature's most finely tuned predator. Kay told me later that she felt humbled in the tiger's presence, and I agreed.

Clive's India Scrapbook

Celebration of INDIAN Wildlife

We presented our guests with traditional costumes for the last night gala dinner. The ladies all needed help tying their beautiful silk saris, and wore them well. The gentlemen looked resplendent in their colourful turbans, but were reluctant to wear them for the camera. What wimps!

Just a glimpse of what you will see in incredible India: the colourful hues, people, places, and if luck is with you, stripes!

Relieved that all our guests had seen stripes in the wild, I could begin to relax and enjoy their company on our escorted trips still to come. Jaipur must be the handicraft capital of India, its back streets and

markets full of talented artisans. Manoj told me that the city was estimated to house 1,000 bangle makers, over 4,000 sari makers, and around 35,000 marble workers, many being descendants of those who laboured long on building the Taj Mahal. The Amer Fort, back then reached up a steep incline on elephant back but now only by jeep, was worth the visit for the views from up there alone. And being in Rajasthan there were no shortages of very impressive moustaches everywhere!

By now in Agra, visiting the Taj Mahal at dawn when fewer people were about, we were helped to create our own mementoes by Jonathan and Angie showing us some different angles from which to shoot this much photographed intricate white mausoleum, glowing in the early morning sunlight. It took huge teams of skilled craftsmen 17 years to construct this white marble marvel of architecture. Built by Mughal Emperor Shah Jahan as an everlasting memorial to his favourite wife Mumtaz who tragically died giving birth to their 14th child. Poor woman. It crossed my mind that I hoped The Emperor really *had* cherished her in life, having paid her such a great tribute in death.

The final part of our Indian Odyssey involved the guests taking part in elephant polo!

Yes, that's right. Four elephants per team, goals the size of football goals, with the ball to match and mallets long enough to reach the ball when sat astride the elephants back. The mahout sits on the elephant's neck to guide him, and unlike traditional polo which is played with agility on ponies which are fleet of foot, elephant polo is conducted in spurts of relaxed indolence.

We had decided that the competitive spirit would be best kept alive if we divided the guests into *The Gentlemen* vs *The Ladies*.

The relaxed pace was to be livened up by a commentator, who on this occasion had failed to turn up. So inspired by memories of my chum Murray Walker I volunteered to take up the microphone, only to be told that the commentator is always mounted on an elephant of his own. I was quite happy on the side line, bring fed samosas and tasty pieces of chicken tikka, but I was told the rules were very specific on this point and *demand* that the commentator is mounted, and I felt I should agree before hearing the rules demanded that he be stuffed as well.

I know little about polo, so reverted to humour, saying things like "Get a move on Sarah. Give it a whack!" and as one lady was bending down low to try to hit the ball with her extended mallet, buttocks pointing skyward I posed the question "does my bum look big in this? Yes I rather think it does!" And "Steve's elephant isn't moving very fast, probably because Steve is nearly as big as his mount!" Looking back, I'm surprised I had any clients left!

Sarah's husband Gordon ever the Mr Competitive was particularly pleased when he scored the opening goal for *The Gentlemen*. I described him as having "the poise of a victorious Centurion returning to Rome, his weapon held proudly aloft," as he had raised his mallet above his head, whether in celebration or astonishment at having scored I'm not too sure. I continued now in the high octane style of Murray "and now Gordon is looking as if he is urging his steed to attempt a gallop back to his own half! His elephant is unique, except it's identical to the other seven elephants on the field!" This one and only experience for all ended in an honourable draw, but only because one of the *Ladies* elephants kicked the ball to score a last minute own goal, which the referee counted, denying the surprisingly ambitious sportswomen what could so easily have been a satisfying victory.

Great fun though the extra experiences were, the *one reason* we had come to India was to see tigers in their natural habitat, which is why it depresses me that the main heart breaking reason these most majestic of cats are hard to spot is that their numbers have been in steady decline for many years, not only in India but across all of Asia, and this is due to human greed. Of all the cats, tigers are closest to extinction, and three of only nine sub species, the Javan (from Java), Caspian and Bali tiger, are already extinct. No more. *Gone forever.*

The rest are all currently classed as critically endangered due to a combination of loss of habitat and human encroachment, which also leads to depletion of prey species. However, most depressingly, poaching to satisfy the seemingly relentless and utterly appalling demand for their body parts which are used in traditional Chinese "medicine" remains prevalent. Whiskers, eyeballs, brains and bone are illegally harvested and the ghastly trade in wildlife parts is apparently the third most profitable international black market, after drugs and weapons. Resources for guarding protected areas where tigers live are usually limited. The intention is there, but lack of funds limits what can be achieved. There is some good news from Nepal, which has been best at protecting their tigers and recovery of their numbers is ahead of its target.

The Nepalese revere the tiger and believe that no one should live in a world without wild tigers. It's a sentiment that anyone who has been privileged to see one of these overwhelmingly beautiful creatures, noble to the point of majesty, understands.

Because the eventual emotion of seeing one is an intense feeling of happiness; your special moment with the wild tiger stays with you in a way as mysterious as the tiger himself.

Clive's Bhutan Scrapbook

Paro is the place of entry stamped into your passport when you fly into Bhutan. One of my talks is about my travels and is called *"Paro in my Passport,"* as to reach this mountain kingdom sandwiched in the mountains between India and China is another feather in a traveller's cap, a real adventurer's achievement. Like Easter Island in the Southern Pacific, and the Antarctic at the bottom of the world. Paro Airport has been squeezed onto one of the few flat pieces of land in Bhutan, being wedged between two Himalayan mountains. So difficult is the approach down a valley between 18,000 feet peaks, that pilots receive special instruction for this daylight and manual only approach.

But phew - we made it!

Having flown close to Mount Everest on the way up from Delhi we were aware of the cool pure air of the Himalayan Mountains, and we breathed deeply. This delightful little country is sandwiched in the mountains between India and China, and to get the country's proportions into perspective, it is about the size of Switzerland. But its population is similar to the size of *Suffolk* at around 750,000 compared to Switzerland's 8.4 million! Tourism is still in its infancy. Around 300,000 people visited Bhutan in 2019, which is pretty much the number that visit London every five days, so it's really not very many!

Our guide Boddhidharma, *"Just call me Bod!"* quickly got us up to speed, telling us that they

have just one set of traffic lights in the country, but they do have some roundabouts, and we discovered these are all very creatively adorned. Smoking and all tobacco products are illegal, and we were told it is forbidden to climb to the high peaks as this is where spirits dwell. As if we were planning to!

But our guests did climb the 700 steps to the Tigers Nest Monastery, passing many prayer wheels and hundreds of prayer flags along the well-trodden way. On conquering the 700 steps back again, those smug and smiling fit guests were rewarded with a hearty late lunch.

The Bhutanese believe a meal is unworthy without chili peppers. If you are on the same wavelength, you'll be in paradise! The country's national dish, *ema datse*, is a simple, fiery curry of chillies and cheese, always paired with a generous helping of nutty red rice. In case it's not quite hot enough, it can be topped off with *ezay,* a sauce made from (what else?) dried chillies!

Imposing Monasteries abound, often perched on hillsides with commanding views. Monks spend much of their time in meditation and prayer, but can found sharing stories and playing board games, often watched by old men waiting their turn and clutching their prayer wheels. We were invited to join an ancient tea ceremony at one of the monasteries, and it felt as if we were time travelling sitting shoeless and cross legged on the floor, listening to the celestial chanting taking part in a ceremony dating back to the 15th century.

The Paro Festival was a highlight of our itinerary - an extraordinary explosion of colour with all the local people in their traditional national costumes and attended by the King and Queen. With so few visitors from outside we in our western clothes were much in the minority. Our guides there Tashi (translated as Luck) and Chime (Immortality) were very excited

when they spotted the King, and were keen to let us know that he does an enormous amount to improve the lives of his people, resulting in his citizens in turn truly loving their Royal Family. I believed them. It is well known that the King believes that *Gross National Happiness* is more important than *GDP,* and this, with the positive Buddhist philosophies and the inspiring teachings of the Dalai Lama who resides in nearby Tibet, I am sure must have a great bearing on the general feeling of wellbeing, which we all found to be infectious!

We had some very high level help in Bhutan, including finishing the trip with a *Diplomats Departure.* Not only private room hospitality, immigration officials coming to us and bags being whisked away not to be seen again until landing, but guests were each presented with an envelope containing a dozen Bhutanese stamps *containing their own portrait.* Extraordinary! Some of us hastily wrote a couple of postcards back home to see if the stamps worked. They did. I never doubted that they would!

Floating your boat *in* Thailand *on our* Tour de Tuk Tuk

I've realised that I'm starting to reach the end of this book but I have so much more I'd like to share with you. On the other hand seeing as how I'm not going to expect you to wade through Clive Thomas' personal *War and Peace* I'm going to have to start to round things off.

I have told you about our European rallies which were great fun but I always wanted to expand the concept and introduce new motoring events to provide fresh ideas and destinations for our regular drivers. Despite people telling me that no one would want to do a driving holiday in *Scotland* in *February* our *Snowball Rally* on empty roads edged with snow-covered fields and mountains, with the promise of a log fire and a warming whisky by nightfall have proved to be very popular.

I'd read about an English chap called Bruce who had moved to Northern Thailand, bought 12 Tuk Tuks which he'd refurbished to a very high standard and was hiring them to people who wanted to explore the real heart of the country and truly be in touch with its people.

Now you know that I can't resist a Tuk Tuk, so I got in touch with Bruce to see if he would work out a route for a rally and hire all or at least most of his fleet to me, so that we could announce that as well as *Monte Carlo or Bust - The Elegant One; The Snowball Rally - The Cold One*, we now offer *Tour de Tuk Tuk - The Bonkers One!*

A week driving a Tuk Tuk. Would anyone want to join me? Not 'alf they did!

Now in Northern Thailand, having had just 24 hours to acclimatise *we were off!* After a morning of serious tuition where guests learn how to get the best from driving these little machines, Bruce had a Buddhist monk bless the trip and each one of us before we set off, I wondered if this was a precaution on his part! I hoped we wouldn't become dependent on divine intervention, but it was good to know that some good karma was already in motion!

En route, time for a little conservation at the MaeVang Elephant Home where their simple philosophy is just to care for elephants who need looking after. We had the time of our lives, swimming in the river with them and hosing them and ourselves down.

Whilst there are many great benefits in driving Tuk Tuks on mountain roads, especially Bruce's with their brightly coloured and well padded leather seats, higher canopies and better suspension; maintaining a fast pace is not one of them! I always tell guests on the other rallies when they bring their Ferraris, Aston Martins and Porsches to *never drive faster than their guardian angels can fly*, and I felt confident, especially with our private blessing on the trip that even a *clodhopping* rather than a *cloud hopping* angel would be able to comfortably outpace us.

The joy of *The Bonkers One* is all about being out in the fresh mountain air on good and invariably deserted tarmac roads, the rustic lunchtime street food, the incredible views and a refreshing wallow in the swimming pool once at that day's final destination.

Looking back at the wonders, it's the colours that have burned longest in my memory. Muted greens and browns of the forests giving way to the iridescent green glow of rice paddies. Hazy grey morning mists being scorched off by the increasing heat leading to cloudless deep blue afternoon skies. Then at sundowner time, after a satisfying day on the road, the burning orange sun dropping below the horizon leaving a magnificent sunset and finally, with little light pollution, the twinkling of thousands of stars to faintly illuminate the black landscape.

This is *real* travel. Culture jumping out at you from every angle, incredible scenery everywhere you turn, beautiful Temples that bring on a feeling of calm and serenity and people who are genuinely pleased to see you. In fact when we turn up in their villages like a wagon train in convoy there is a look of surprise on people's faces which turns to astonishment and finally to curiosity when they discover that all of the occupants are *farangs!** Their *inquiosity** gets the better of them and as our friendliness becomes apparent, we enjoy close encounters with people we shall almost certainly never see again. They are very happy to share stories as they stand or sit with us and chat, as interested in where we come from as we are about their lives, community, and their culture. I discovered that these simple things stay with us as forever.

As in Africa, it is the people as well as the landscape that make this a truly beautiful part of the world.

Our Tour de Tuk Tuk takes us to the far north, up close to the border with Burma (now Myanmar) between Mae Hong Son and Pai, giving us experience of places that that few international travellers reach.

Simply stunning is the only way to describe this hidden gem of a province. Steep mountains, narrow valleys, Hill Tribe communities, National Parks and more *Wow!* moments in a day than you'd get in a month of beach life. We avoid international hotel brands on this

trip and include cool, laid back *local* places that are full of character and charm. There are no crowds and we have time to enjoy nature at its finest.

Being in the mountains and forests in our open sided Tuk Tuks on good roads, with an absence of crowds is incredibly rewarding. Our days are spent surrounded by fresh air, waterfalls, and towering trees. We are even able to appreciate the chatter of birds that must be all around us, but with little flapping, fluttering or hovering to be seen, they mainly stay out of sight as if in an avian game of hide and seek!

After Pai we turn for home: with more mountains, a huge amount of forest cover, awesome winding roads, superb food, and even more fascinating hill communities comprising some of the most welcoming people anywhere in the country.

So often we keep the best 'til last, as our Tuk Tuk Rallies take place in November when its not humid and when the whole country celebrates what many say is the most beautiful Thai festival of them all: *Loy Krathong* which translates literally as *floating banana trunk* but actually means *Festival of Light*.

Wherever there is a body of water, people cast off little tastefully decorated boats, often handmade of banana leaves or half coconut shells into which stubby lit candles or tea lights and a coin are placed before being launched. To take part with the local people you just need to *loy* (float) your *krathong* (banana trunk) and as you do you are letting go of your sins and misfortunes as the water carries them downstream and away for good.

I told Kay about this lovely tradition and she asked if I had a battleship made to carry my sins away? How very dare she?!

Each candle represents the person's prayer, memory, or wish for the future attached to it, as the krathongs are also symbolic of new beginnings. It is an amazing and moving sight watching thousands of lighted banana-leaf boats floating away!

Then on the banks, having prayed to the water goddess Mae Khongkha, giving her thanks for providing water, people join in with the bright and bustling celebrations featuring live music, and visiting brightly lit street bars and hawker stalls full of delicious hot freshly fried and barbequed finger food. Later people send up lanterns too, lifting their hopes for the year to come skywards. And as they hug us and each other farewell, fireworks fill the sky bringing it all to an exuberant close.

I am delighted to have Bruce and his dedicated team of locals as my Thai partners, making everything happen for us seamlessly. He takes us to where the real heart of Thailand surely lies and our guests all agree that through these unique road trips we are privileged to catch a special glimpse of it.

Footnote:

*inquiosity. *An inquisitive curiosity.*

*farangs. *This is actually a real word. Thai meaning for a foreigner.*

Clive's Thailand **Scrapbook**

Tour de *Tuk Tuk* Thailand

PRRC

Map labels:

Burma / Myanmar

Lod Cave

Huai Nam Dang Park

Doi Luang
2205m 7234ft

Lisu Hill Tribe Village

Doi Mae Yan
2205m 7234ft

Pai
Night 6

Mae Hong Son
Nights 4&5

Wat Mae Yen

Nam Tok Mae Surin Park

Wat Chan

Chiang Mai Province
North West
Thailand

Karen Hill Tribe Village

Doi Suthep-Pui Park

Chiang M
Nights 1,2

Khun Yuam

Airport

To Phae

Doi Inthanon
2590m 8497ft

Phra Mahat Napametanidon

Mae W
Start

Doi Inthanon Park

Lamphu

Mae La Noi Cave

Op Luang Park

Mae La Noi

Hai Luang Cave

From smooth country roads to mountain tracks we travelled some 430 miles to places most visitors never lay eyes on, meeting people few travellers would come across.

The scenery was invariably breathtaking, and the locals gasped too when they saw and heard our convoy hove into their usually quiet backwater.

The Thai culture is full of colour, from clothes and footwear, to mythological dragons and even their Gods. We loved seeing the way the people at The Mae Vang Elephant Home care for their rescued residents!

Celine's Thailand Scrapbook

I'd been thinking about whether our next "Celebration of Wildlife" would centre on whales or polar bears when I chanced upon some serendipitous footage on You Tube. People in a small boat who had come across a struggling humpback whale tangled up in fishing nets. Armed with only a small Stanley knife, one of the men jumped off the boat, calmed the whale and set to work. It took him a whole hour before he freed the whale who then proceeded to do the whale equivalent of jumping for joy at being free, by repeatedly breaching and doing flipper slaps and surface rolls!

The post was by *The Great Whale Conservancy* of California. I rung and spoke to their Director, Michael Fishbach. (Great name for a marine biologist!). I wanted to express my respect for the whale's saviour and also tell him of my interest in setting up a trip. To my astonishment Michael declared that it was he who had freed the whale! It had happened on Valentine's Day and that they had named the young female humpback *Valentina*.

I knew the name Fishbach. There was a world top 50 tennis pro by that name, and in the late 1970s at Wimbledon, I had been in the packed interview room with him. How astonishing that our paths should cross again, although of course he would have no reason to remember a cub reporter from 35 years before! It was soon agreed that our whale watching trip to Baja and the Sea of Cortez would be hosted by Michael, and our guests would spend much of the trip out in the ocean on Michael's research boat.

The Sea of Cortez is where many of the whales on the planet take their first breath, and every winter something incredible happens there. Almost the entire world's population of grey whales, humpbacks and over two thousand blue whales migrate to its calm waters rich in nutrients and plankton, to socialise, mate and give birth in its shallow and protected lagoons.

Michael and Alberto, his local boat captain, instinctively knew the just right areas to head out for and we saw them all. Daily! I loved the curious and gentle grey whales, which will often approach small boats in the lagoons to be *stroked by us humans.* They stay alongside for ages and our guests tired of it long before they and their calves did! I marvelled with childlike excitement at actually *touching a whale!*

The Mexican landscape was a revelation, rugged in part just like the old Spaghetti Westerns with huge cacti growing wild at the roadside, most taller and some wider than our mini coach. We welcomed the guests with a burst of Herb Alpert's *Tijuana Taxi* when we collected them at Loreto Airport!

Our breath was taken away when we saw manta rays skirting the sea and flapping their wings as if in brief flight, and just as in Galapagos, baby sea lions who were playful and inquisitive. We chanced across a super-pod of bottlenose dolphins which Michael estimated was between 1,000 and 1,500 strong! Even with the help of my co-host, photographer Dave Newton our pictures couldn't begin to capture the enormity of this electrifying scene.

As we were there on February 14th we chilled down a magnum of fizz so that when Alberto navigated us to where Michael had freed that whale in distress, we could all raise a glass in a toast *"To Michael, and to Valentina!"*

long may she stay free
and roam the oceans!

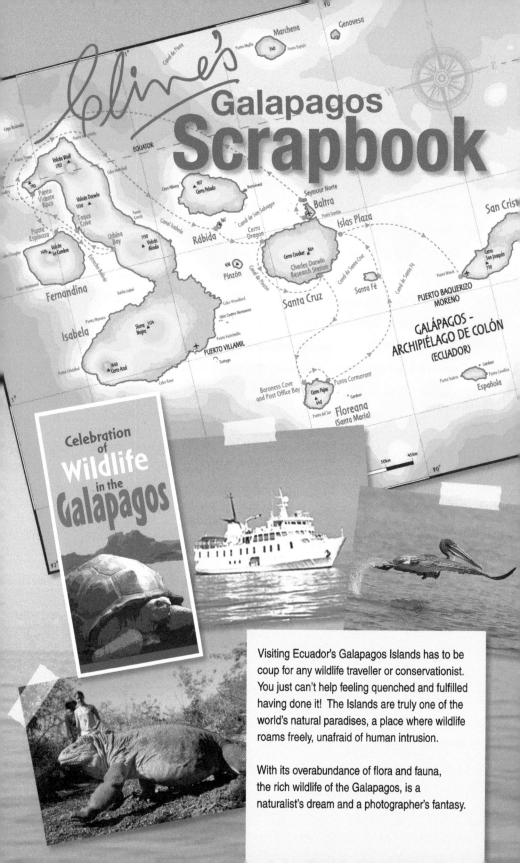

Eline's Galapagos **Scrapbook**

Celebration of **Wildlife** in the **Galapagos**

Visiting Ecuador's Galapagos Islands has to be coup for any wildlife traveller or conservationist. You just can't help feeling quenched and fulfilled having done it! The Islands are truly one of the world's natural paradises, a place where wildlife roams freely, unafraid of human intrusion.

With its overabundance of flora and fauna, the rich wildlife of the Galapagos, is a naturalist's dream and a photographer's fantasy.

Having explored Quito on the mainland en route and discovering that I rather liked Ecuadorian cuisine, especially *Locro de Papa*, a thick gloopy cheese and potato soup that comes bubbling in a good size black metal cauldron,

it was just as well we had to leave for unique animal encounters before my arteries completely clogged up.

I chartered a very comfortable 24 berth ship called La Pinta which was small enough to get us into some of the little bays which would be denied to the bigger vessels. In a week you can't visit all of the islands, but we landed in a different place twice a day and were up close and personal with much of the local wildlife.

The most colourful were the red, yellow and blue Sally Lightfoot crabs, scavaging in gangs at the shoreline; and the frigate birds with their huge red inflatable chests which they puffed up to attract a mate. The best at camouflage were the marine iguana, often seen languishing on the volcanic rocks, heating themselves back up after diving to cold depths for up to twenty minutes to find seaweed, which makes up almost all of their diet. They are fearsome looking, especially when they are spitting salt from their nostrils, but being strictly vegetarian pose no threat to us.

The most entertaining were the blue and red footed boobies, with their wonderful mating ritual dancing hopping to their own rhythm from foot to foot. The biggest were the giant tortoise, the oldest living creature on earth, visible on all four of the inhabited islands, and able to move more quickly than you'd imagine.

We all swum in the warm sea (we were there in May) and some of our guests snorkelled amongst the manta rays, sea lions, fur seals, turtles (mainly green and leatherback) together with a plethora of octopus, cuttlefish, squid and an abundance of colourful fish.

Our three local naturalist guides, Arturo, Juan and Isabella (like the island) each had their own speciality and had *so much* they wanted to tell us about what makes these islands unique: Firstly the *Ring of Fire* on which Galapagos sits where the tectonic plates clashed, the earth's crust broke and lava flows formed the islands; then the three currants coming together, the Humboldt bringing cold water, the Panama bringing warm, and the Cromwell driving nutrients from the deep all of which allows many species to flourish there. They could write a lengthy tome between them on Darwin, but all I'll say is that he discovered the islands and his theory of evolution is already well known.

Santa Cruz Island and *San Cristobal* where we landed are the main inhabited islands. Next to the harbour they have fish markets where the fresh fish is gutted and filleted on open air concrete slabs. Sea lions and pelicans jockey for position to grab the discarded chunks of unwanted fish amongst the local shoppers, for whom this is quite normal!

With a number of keen and very proficient photographers on board we organised a competition for the last night. Our judging panel comprised our own Jonathan Scott and Johnny Truss, who were joined by the ship's Captain. Tom Littlejohns won with this image of a gannet diving, as it was judged to be the hardest of all images to capture. Fellow guest Jarle Tatt rewarded him with a lovely prize of 200 personalised greetings cards featuring the winning photograph.

Always loving anything quirky I was delighted to discover on Florentina Island what must surely be the world's strangest post box. It is at the aptly named *Post Office Bay*, thought to date from the late 1800s and is a barrel mounted on a post into which visitors both take and deposit postcards without stamps. They are franked from time to time and the tradition is that you take a couple or three addressed to somewhere in your own country to post when you get home, leaving yours for others to collect when franked. We sent two, to our nephew Flynn in Wimbledon which arrived by Royal Mail, and to our niece Momo in Paris which was *hand delivered* by two American ladies who told Kay's brother Robin "We are passing through on our way back home from Galapagos!" Such is the thoughtfulness of those who care about the natural world, and who travel thousands of miles to be immersed in it.

It is considered cheating to add a postage stamp and the postal authorities around the world seem happy to keep up the tradition,

which in today's avaricious and often unforgiving world I find utterly charming.

A TASTE *of* PORTUGAL
plate *by* plate

Sardines

Thailand is world famous for its street food, but it's not the only place where cooks stand at the roadside rustling up delightful plates of local goodness. Discovering new places to enjoy such culinary delights is always a joy, particularly when accompanied by joyful people, like my dear friend Clive Travers, with whom I share my initials, a love of tennis and the desire to do a deal on a handshake and mean it. But our most important and deepest bond is that we are brothers in gastronomy.

We decided we were 'gastronauts' and started using the term to describe ourselves long before it found its way into the English language. As an astronaut travels far to seek out and explore new worlds, so a gastronaut does the same to seek out new tastes and flavours, always questing for exquisite food, well made wine, local beer and occasionally wicked local spirits too!

In the early 1980s Spain was already a popular destination with Brits, but its neighbour Portugal was much less visited. A property developer friend went there with the intention of purchasing most of the Algarve and whilst he had failed spectacularly in making any land purchases he had succeeded, so he told us in finding some great places to eat, mainly through the local knowledge of an estate agent he happened upon in Lagos called Fernando.

The temptation to seek out new platters, to boldly go where few British stomachs had gone before, was too great to resist.

So we forewarned Fernando of our arrival for a few days in the winter sun with the intention of him acquainting us with some culinary delights away from the usual tourist trail. Then together with the other Clive's father, Oliver, who was the only other man I know who enjoyed a good snack, lunch or dinner almost as much as we did, we set off for Faro, armed with a phrasebook and a good supply of Gaviscon and aspirins.

We three were as one on our philosophy of the joys of the table; whilst dishes that have been deconstructed, reconstructed and reinvented have a place in the culinary world, all too often this type of cuisine is used to justify eye watering prices at pretentious restaurants. We all agreed that part of the joy of travelling was finding places that either don't make it into the guidebooks or deliberately choose not to be seen there. The places where the farmers, the fishermen and the locals in the know go to relax. They are often family owned and run and they offer simple dishes, made with local ingredients that are fresh and probably from recipes handed down through the generations. I like simple, not messed about with food.

However, I do like to fly in style and I knew someone at TAP, the Portuguese airline and managed to get the three of us upgraded to Business Class, which was very nice. And a great start. But as the aircraft was coming into land, for some reason best known to himself, Clive inflated and burst a sick bag. I think even *he* was surprised at the volume of the explosion as an extremely loud and alarming "BANG!" rang out from our seats in the front row just as the wheels touched the runway. One of the stewardesses, who had been very friendly to us during the flight, leapt from her seat facing us and standing over Clive remonstrated fiercely with him for being so irresponsible and reminding him that there are always nervous passengers on an aircraft who could easily be sent into a state of panic at the thought of a tyre blowing out on the landing.

Not such a great start.

Clive's childish behaviour at the start of the trip had been far from his finest hour and he took his Iberian bollocking, humbly apologised and we were allowed sheepishly off the plane under the disapproving gaze of the crew and fellow passengers. But we quickly decided that we weren't going to allow this to spoil our trip and were soon being warmly welcomed by our new friend and guide, Fernando. He told us his plan was to go to lunch at one of those very places on the way to our Lagos hotel which then was about an hour and a half's drive from Faro Airport. It all sounded more than fine to us.

On the way to lunch Fernando suggested stopping for cooling drink on a café terrace with the most magnificent views overlooking the gorgeous bay of Praia da Rocha. Age old sandstone rocks, azure blue shimmering sea, wonderful sandy beach with swirling patterns left by the outgoing tide and best of all warm sunshine in the middle of January. This is what Clive and I call a welcome *snacksident**.

In Portugal in those days they were a good many stray dogs and cats who did their best to eke out a living as best they could. They were no trouble to anyone and naturally, restaurants and cafés provided good pickings for them and waiters invariably spent much of their time shooing them away. As we took our seats I noticed a little tabby cat: skinny and with a gammy back leg and fur that had seen better days. She was eying me with that heart-tugging look peculiar to any hungry animal. The poor thing sat patiently by my chair for a good 10 minutes until I broke my resolve and couldn't resist any longer. Fernando had ordered a plate of mixed cold meats on which to nibble with our drinks, so I put a piece of presunto ham, which is like Spanish jamon, down to her level and before I'd let it go she had put a steading paw (not a claw) on my hand and had taken it from my fingers.

In that moment we had bonded and I decided that when we left I would leave a few bits on a plate and take it away from where everyone was sitting for her to enjoy. But the little cat's hunger got the better of her and she jumped up onto the table. And disastrously for her, this was just at the moment the burly owner was passing. He saw her on his table and with a sweep of his arm scooped her up and like a basketball player throwing the ball over his shoulder to score in spectacular style, this bully of a man turned and hurled the poor creature over his shoulder and over the balcony of the restaurant! I was incensed! I jumped up ready to flatten this loathsome individual.

As I rose, yelling Anglo Saxon invective at him and launching my six foot twenty something stone self in his direction, Oliver swiftly rose, caught my punching arm before the blow could be landed, probably saving me from being arrested and spending the rest of the trip in a Portuguese police cell. I have a temper, but do come down as quickly as I go up and so now, under control and with my face inches from this cat killer, I looked him directly in both eyes, said forcefully through clenched teeth.

"I like cats, and I don't like people who don't."

He seemed instinctively to know better than to retort and scuttled off at speed in the direction of the kitchen – whether to hide or to get reinforcements I didn't know or, at that moment, didn't care. I went and looked over the balcony at the drop below which although a good 15–20 feet was fortunately on to flat ground. I had expected to see my new feline friend crumpled and motionless far below but to my surprise and delight she was nowhere to be seen. One thing was for sure; to have survived that ordeal one of her nine lives had been well and truly used.

My friends knew that particular party was over and we left without asking for or receiving a bill and of course never went back. I don't think Fernando did either.

"I reckon you should have decked him Tommo", said Clive, never minding a bit of controversy, provided he *wasn't caught up in it* of course!

If Fernando was wondering who on earth he'd got himself caught up with he was far too polite to say so and carried on with his role as our unofficial food guide by telling us that we were heading for "the best sardines in Portugal" Under the old bridge at Portimao was a café that consisted of three enormous charcoal barbecues and a mass of plastic garden furniture of different designs and colours, topped with sun umbrellas which had definitely seen better days supplied by various local brewing companies and the ever present Pepsi Cola sprawled out across the paved waterfront. It really wasn't much to look at and Fernando, seeing our less-then-impressed faces, smiled and told us that we "Portuguese eat with our stomachs but you English eat with your eyes." Even as we approached the tantalising smell of the barbeques hit our hungry noses! As we settled down, I reckoned people could smell the sardines cooking along the waterfront from a few hundred yards away, and we certainly needed to make sure we weren't downwind of the clouds of smoke as they cooked!

When we Brits think of sardines, images of old tins being brought out from the back of dusty cupboards spring to mind. I can remember opening these tins with the key provided (why do sardine tins open with a key?) and being rewarded with something that looked and smelt like oily cat food. As you are probably gathering, I'm not a big fan of tinned sardines. But in the Algarve, where they know their sardines and more importantly, in Portimao, where they know how to cook the fresh ones to perfection, this humble little fish is transformed into a gastronaut's delight.

We told Fernando that we were keen to order but he just smiled again and told us that wasn't necessary as this was a restaurant without a menu. People came here specifically to eat sardines grilled expertly over wood and *so there was no need for a menu.* There was *no* something else. Fernando told us that we could have new potatoes and salad if we wanted, but the local people pile their plates high with sardines and enjoy them the Portuguese way by forking each fish onto a single piece of bread, scraping off the skins and once all the fish are finished, enjoy the sardine soaked bread to complete the meal.

A waiter did appear but only to ask us what we would like to drink with our sardines. We selected a bottle of the chilled local rosé wine (with was delicious) and when he returned with it I asked him were all these sardines were coming from. He pointed across the cobbles to the moorings where half a dozen fishing boats were tethered and their crew were selling their catch, directly to the waiters from various restaurants, who were lining up with orders.

Was it only sardines they sold, I asked. The waiter shrugged and said it was normally, but it depended on what else they had happened to catch that day. "For example" he told me, "I know that boat there has a big catch of sola today."

My ears pricked up because, as delicious as the sardines clearly were, when it comes to fish, my absolute favourite is grilled sole. And the idea of sole fresh from the sea was irresistible. The waiter volunteered to skip across the cobbles to the fishing boat for me and a minute or two later he jogged past our table, arm outstretched proudly holding a massive sole aloft, just for me.

You could call fish the underdog of the barbeque. People get excited about racks of ribs, new season lamb chops and charred rib-eyes and as undoubtedly wonderful as they all are, in my humble opinion, grilled fish doesn't always get the love it deserves. And here, in this modest pavement cafe, we couldn't help but get worked up anticipating how wonderful these plump sardines, and the freshest sole imaginable would taste with a bit of char on them.

While we sipped our wine Fernando told us: "Mackerel and sardines are so implanted in our food culture; they are part of any person from here. We've been eating this almost from birth! I remember the first time I ate sardines, I did get quite a few bones stuck my throat, but that didn't stop me falling in love with them from being a child".

He went on "I live in a block of apartments, we have a few wood barbeques on the roof and some of the residents go up there to cook. You can see the sea from there and it's very sociable. I was about to cook some sardines early one evening before anyone else had begun. I left the sardines outside on the tray while I went back inside to fetch the salt. In that moment of my absence, seagulls swooped down and started chomping them! When they see food appear, they sit around and wait for a nitwit like me to go back inside. They stole my sardines! Their game plan paid off".

We were complementing Fernando on his impressive grasp of English, particularly the use of the word *nitwit!* He told us he had learnt it at school, but was able to polish it up when he was an hotel manager in Portuguese Angola.

We had some fun testing him on several uses of English phrases, and much to our annoyance couldn't catch him out at once. He even knew a bit of slang, although Cockney rhyming slang was a step too far. He did find it fascinating though, especially 'boat race' for 'face.' "How on earth could you ever work it out?" He asked. Noting his natural use of the phrase *on earth,* I sad "You can't work it out. You have to know it – that's the whole point".

Then, as if to show off his mastery of English, he said to us "When you are speaking between yourselves, if you were talking about someone who speaks many languages you would say they are *multilingual* yes?"

"Yes!" we replied in unison. He continued,

"And someone who speaks two languages is *bilingual.*"

Impressed with his knowledge of the distinction between the two, we had to agree, and he continued,

"And it's true isn't it, that a person who speaks one language is *English!*" he said, laughing heartily. We asked him if he knew any American English, and started him off with the term "wise guy".

The plates of food arrived and did not disappoint. The wood grilling makes all the difference, as does the local knowhow, and the freshness of the fish. I don't think I've tasted a sole that delicious and that fresh before or since.

It was only Day 1 and already we'd survived being deported at the airport and getting into a fist fight in a restaurant. But it was all worth it for this taste of the real Portugal!

Other Clive is a very handy barbeque chef and as the customers were drifting away, and with Fernando translating, he asked one of the chefs the secret of great tasting sardines. We were told "You always want to salt them really heavily. When the salted fish hits the grill it creates a beautiful steam that draws the moisture from the fish and also creates a barrier so the meat doesn't stick to the grill. In Portugal, we use sea salt.

"I salt them a little bit before and then put them on a really hot grill. Make sure you find the hot spot on the grill to give them a hard sear. Once they're marked and not going to stick, transfer them to a cooler part of the grill let them cook gently for a couple of minutes and then take them off. Don't overcook! They cook so quickly, and you want to have a little bit of tension when you bite into the meat, so you definitely don't want to overcook them. I do recommend you scale them first. I think a lot of people in Portugal don't scale them, but I do".

So now you know.

And if you are ever barbequing sardines on wood or charcoal, do invite me – I'll bring my own sole!

Footnote:
snacksident. Stopping for a snack "accidentally" – often on the way to a pre-booked lunch or dinner.

Oliver's *Breakfast*

Back at the hotel we agreed to have some time to ourselves and meet again at 8 o'clock for supper. Fernando had decided to take us to a favourite locals place inland at Bensafrim, which he has asked me not to name because he doesn't want it to become touristy. Fair enough.

I sat out in the sun by the pool and after a while dozed off into an alcohol induced slumber. I've always believed that sleeping off a lunch is a sight easier than walking it off. I woke with a start when it begun to get chilly, to discover it was getting dark as well. There was just time for a quick wash and brush up and a phone call to home saying, "Yes, yes we've all been behaving ourselves... Nothing really to report yet... apart from some great fish at lunchtime..." I could almost feel my nose growing like Pinocchio's. "Yes I expect we'll have an early night given that Oliver is with us and we don't want to tire him out too much on the first day."

To my surprise, the three of us managed to meet in reception as planned at 8pm sharp. Other Clive was looking dishevelled and I was glowing like a red beacon having fallen asleep in full sun, but Oliver had shaved, showered and looked as if he was ready for anything. Oliver had been in the RAF during the war: one of the brave young man who signed up to defend our country and after minimal training took to the skies. I tried to tease some stories out of him but like many veterans he really didn't want to talk about it.

He said as we were leaving "Is this one of the strange countries that gets light at weird times?" Clive and I didn't know what to make of this rather odd comment and so smiled vaguely and ignored it as we climbed into Fernando's car. He drove us inland on unlit roads to Bensafrim, which wasn't a village, or even a hamlet. It consisted of a dark street with some houses, a bar on one side of the road and what could be a restaurant next to where he parked up. I looked in past the plate glass floor-to-roof window, through which we could see a very uninspiring room, brightly lit by bare fluorescent tubes. It had rough wooden tables with uncomfortable-looking little wooden chairs, the sort that I had last seen at my old primary school. There was also an antique black and white television in the corner.

"Why are we stopping here?" I asked Fernando.

"Because the food is extremely good," he replied, sternly reminding me about *not eating with my eyes!*

Once inside, Oliver ordered an orange juice, which I thought was very wise after what we had put away at lunchtime. However, I wasn't there to be wise and so I ordered a large gin and tonic. Other Clive, who was still rather hung over from lunchtime, obviously agreed that this would be the ideal livener and joined me. Oliver gave us a look that could only be described as 'old fashioned' and when Fernando's friend, Estevo, who was both the waiter and the owner, brought us the menus, Oliver didn't afford them even a glance. "Can you do me bacon and eggs?" he asked.

"No problem señor" Estevo said politely. "And for you gentlemen?"

Fernando told us that we were in luck as Estevo's wife was cooking that night and so it was the night to order the *porco de casa*. He translated this as "pork meat".

"Pieces of pork," Estevo explained, "cook-ed in homemade creams sauces of peppers. Is very flavour. With vegetable and many poco segmentos of batatas frittaded."

"She does the potatoes in the frying pan, I don't know what with," said Fernando "but as you English say *they are bloody lovely!*"

"For me please", said Clive. "And me." I rejoined.
Oliver couldn't contain himself any longer and burst out with,

"This is ridiculous! I know we're on a foodie weekend but large gin & tonics and pork in pepper sauce for breakfast is outrageous!"

It dawned on the three of us simultaneously what had happened and our laughter was uncontrollable.

Oliver had decided to get some quality rest and put himself to bed. Proper bed – in between the sheets. He had wisely set his alarm for 7.30.

Of course it was dark when he woke and he thought it was morning, whereas in reality he had a 2 hour siesta. Once he realised this, he promptly ordered a large gin to go in the orange juice, said he'd have the bacon and eggs as a starter and joined us in the pork meat and segmentos frittated under the fluorescents with the old TV grinding away in the corner.

And, despite the unprepossessing surrounding, it turned out to be our second spectacular meal of the day.

Local dried meats to begin, a mug of piquant homemade soup, the exquisite tender pork meat in the pepper sauce, which I think contained some grain mustard, and when I asked about other ingredients I was told by Carla, the cook, that they were *mucho secreto*. The little segmentos were fried to a crispy perfection, and we hadn't ordered it but the homemade chocolate mousse was light, fluffy and simply lush!

The other item we didn't need to order was the wine. Chilled white port to begin then a choice of much too quaffable local red or white throughout the meal and a bottle of ruby port on the table at the end to accompany the cheese, which magically appeared. The much needed gaps between courses allowed time for digestion, more wine to go down than was necessary, and best of all good conversation.

Fernando thought that as we three were so at home at the dining table, that we should learn a bit of restaurant Portuguese. He started us off with simple things like *"voce tem?* for *do you have?* Usually to be followed by a strange mime of some sort! *E fresco?* for is it *fresh?* And *uma grande porcao para mim, por favour,* meaning *a large portion for me, please.*

As we leaned back, savouring another culinary triumph, I looked across to Fernando and said, "OK Fernando, tonight we've had the table groaning under the weight of the food, the wine has been more than generously poured all evening, and there's a bottle of good port on the table. So, how would I say to Estevo and pointing at you, *my friend will pay?"*

Quick as a flash Fernando came back, "I'm sorry Clive, but in Portuguese we don't have this. It's just not allowed!"

I later discovered my new friend wasn't being completely truthful and *meu amigo paga* has been the foundation of my 15 word Portuguese vocabulary ever since and put to good use countless times.

Unappetising *Artist*

The next day was spent exploring Lagos *(Pronounced La-gosh)*. It is quite a big town with paved streets filled with artisan shops and cafés with tables on the street supporting a vibrant café culture. The new basic, concrete whitewashed uniformly square buildings showed signs of recent investment in the area but were sadly built for practicality not for style. They were juxtaposed against the more impressive red roofed three and four storey buildings lining the cobbled passageways and wider thoroughfares that looked as if they had been there for a few generations and extolled a much greater degree of architectural style and charm.

The town has its own waterfront with colourful fishing boats docked alongside close to the fish market, where people gathered daily to buy their fresh fish. It's always struck me that so many places where fishing boats land, just send the catch off to other cities and often other countries. It surprises me how few of them serve their local communities. But in Lagos the fish market, resplendent in age old blue and white tiles and with the omnipresent fluorescent lighting, is a bustling hive of activity, where people don't just come to buy fish – they came to moan about the weather, grumble even more about politics, and lament how there was never enough hours in the day to do everything that needed to be done. The peoples of the world may speak different languages, but we share many of the same worries and burdens.

The cafés all around were buzzing and even early in the morning there were a few old boys sitting out with their newspapers, cigarettes, black coffee and a shot of what in France would've been cognac but here was macieria. It was a rather rough brandy but most palatable whilst sitting out by the moorings next to the fish market in the morning sunshine. But trust me, from experience, it's one of those things that doesn't travel at all well.

After a morning of exploring and trying to resist buying more tasteless tat as Kay disapprovingly calls my travel keep-sakes, we decided that lunch should be a modest affair, so settled for a couple of beers accompanied by a *prego* each. A *prego* is the Algarvian lunch staple. It's their equivalent of a burger but much better. A reasonable size piece of spice-rubbed veal fried or grilled and put into a buttered roll that would have been delivered by the baker only hours before – nutritious, delicious and filling. We just couldn't resist strolling along to the bakers along the street to finish with

Pasteis de Nata, little custard tarts as symbolic of our host country as the Portuguese Rooster. These delicious eggy, custardy puff pastry cinnamon topped treats beckon from almost every bakery window, and as the queue of locals at this one was out into the street we reckoned that theirs would be good. We weren't disappointed!

The afternoon was lazy. I made sure I had remembered my hat thus avoiding further sunburnt skin where hair had once grown. We walked a while on a deserted beach enjoying the sound of the crashing Atlantic waves and the call of the gulls, then rested before the next promised epicurean adventure.

Fernando couldn't make it that evening and had passed us on to a friend of his, a local architect called Costa who, luckily for us, was as charming and gracious and also spoke excellent English. He collected us and drove us even deeper into the interior than we had gone the previous night. It was real farmer's country and Costa was very excited to be introducing us to a place we would never have found on our own. We later discovered that when Fernando was persuading him to be our escort for the evening, that he had told Costa that *meo amigo* would definitely *paga,* which might have contributed to his enthusiasm.

Costa told us that evening's restaurant was owned by his friend, an artist called Jorge who spoke no English. He sold a few paintings but needed more of a regular income so opened up to visitors just three time a week, Friday and Saturday night and Sunday lunchtime. We pulled up outside what looked like a dilapidated, ramshackle farm, where a few other cars were parked up outside one of the barns. Inside was a long wooden table down the middle that would seat probably 30 people and there were maybe 20 there already, all seated together like a "club" table. This level of local patronage looked promising! At the end was a smaller table set for four.

As we walked in the conversation abruptly stopped and all eyes looking towards the strangers. This truly WAS a real locals place. Costa broke the silence with a cheery "boa tarde amigos", and a friendly wave which was enough to set conversation buzzing again.

Many of Jorge's paintings were hanging on the sturdy wooden supports of this rustic building and is was clear that he was obviously an abstract artist: what I call the school of 'splash it and see'. I know that art is subjective, but I hoped that Jorge's cooking was better than his painting. Costa explained that like the first restaurant we'd visited, there was no menu. But this wasn't because Jorge only served one dish, like sardines, but because he cooked and served whatever he fancied on the day, which was normally dictated by what was fresh in the market.

I was discovering more and more how the rural Portuguese still bought fresh every day from the butcher, the baker the fish market and the fruit and veg market, which also sold local honey and home-made jams and marmalade. People only ventured to a supermarket to buy pet food, packet cereal, washing up liquid, and the like. But not food. Of course as we all know a supermarket gives you the convenience of a one-stop shop. But if you are able to make time in your day to walk a bit, and buy from specialists, then this becomes less important. If you have time for a coffee or a beer too, then all the better.

I asked Costa if he would tell us what today's menu consisted of and he said he didn't know, but Jorge would announce each dish just prior to arrival. We sat at the table for four and to begin with, a little burner with a live flame was brought to our table with a small frying pan on top and in it a fat blackened sausage, curled around and ready to cut up and share, by way of an a*muse bouche*. Oliver thought it was a bit dubious looking and enquired hopefully "is this a sausage of pork?"

"No" said Costa "it's a sausage of blood."

Oliver had a little taste and declared "I'll sit this out." We polished it off. It was of course what we would call black pudding and wasn't at all bad.

Jorge's next announcement was translated as "soup of fish" and had Oliver rubbing his hands in anticipation was thinking yes! *Like a bouillabaisse - wonderful.* Then a witches style cauldron came up and poking out of a somewhat suspect looking liquid, was a massive fish head and lurking beneath the surface some tails and a few bones. It didn't look very appetising: in fact, it looked like the sort of thing that most restaurants would boil down to make fish stock. It tasted only marginally better than it looked. Costa tucked in with gusto, whilst Other Clive and I did little more than sample. A single mouthful was enough to convince Oliver that this was another course to sit out. Jorge looked a little perturbed.

Costa's next translation found him telling us that we were to have "stew of ... ..." He hesitated, then proceeded with a mime: folding his arms up by his sides, flapping them like wings and making a clucking sound!

"Oh" I said "stew of chicken. Chicken casserole perhaps?"

"Yes," Costa agreed, "but not chicken, *mother* of chicken."

Well, this poor hen had probably been boiling away for hours in an attempt to get the tough old mother clucker into an edible state. And in our view, the effort had only been partially successfully. It seemed that in his attempt to breath some flavour into it, Jorge had chucked in every herb and spice he could think of. A bit like his painting, really. There was certainly plenty of garlic, but also, I distinctly remember tasting aniseed, cloves and lots of pepper.

It was all a bit of an overwhelming clash of flavours and not very pleasant or satisfying to our taste buds.

Glancing over at the other table they were all tucking in heartily chewing on the meat and mopping up the greasy looking liquid with great wedges of the bread. We agreed it certainly wasn't the epicurean delight we had been hoping for and Oliver, desperate to eat, did try it, but once again decided to sit it out. I could see he was hungry, but this was all a bit too much. Jorge was beginning to look quite crestfallen.

"Was that the main course?" I asked Costa. "No, the main course is coming next."

"And what is it." I ventured, praying that it would be our saviour and that Oliver might yet forgive me for bringing him to this place.

Costa asked Jorge and translated his reply as "cow and dog." For goodness sake! I'd been in far more far-flung places than Portugal and hadn't been required to eat labrador or poodle yet!

This had become just too ridiculous and I knew we'd have to leave. But not wanting to offend either Costa or Jorge, who were both doing their best to please us, I thought we'd best be sure.

So following Costa's lead of explaining through mime, I thought animal noises would work just as well in cutting through the language barrier. So I said "Cow - moo mooo?"

"Yes!" said Jorge and scampered off to fetch it from the kitchen.

"And dog - rough rough rough?" I called after him anxiously as he left. Costa started shaking his head, rocking and laughing. "No, Mister Clive. Not dog. *Dough!*"

At that moment it arrived, we saw the bowl and Other Clive said, "Of course! By dough he meant pasta."

What a relief! It was beef tagliatelle. Not quite as we know it and, having clearly used up all the contents of spice rack on the previous dish, this main course had gone completely the other way and tasted of... really very little. It was a bit like eating a plateful of beige. Not totally horrible but weirdly not very pleasant either. Poor old Oliver was tempted, but by now was very wary and his first forkful didn't tempt him to go further. All he had eaten was the bread, and he was getting very fed up.

"Is there any desert?" he asked expectantly. Jorge told us there was cake. Now for Oliver any kind of cake is more than acceptable under normal circumstances. But these were far from normal circumstances.
He asked suspiciously "what's in it?"

"Oh", translated Costa, "flour, sugar, eggs, and some lemon zest."

Oliver perked up and said, "It sounds a bit like a Madeira cake to me. I can't think how they could mess it up."

"That's right," said Costa, "it's a special cake that we usually only have at Easter." *If you've ever had Portuguese Easter cake, you'll be ahead of me here.*

The cake came in slices, and each slice looked like a Grosvenor Pie that you see in delicatessens: pork pies which have hard-boiled eggs within the body of the pie. And Jorge had indeed put eggs in his cake, but they were raw eggs... *still in their shells!* During the baking, the eggs had become hard-boiled, or in this case hard-baked, so that you could plainly see a cross-section of egg still with the *shell* around it within each slice.

"How the **** are we supposed to eat that without getting a mouthful of shell?" I exclaimed.

Even Oliver, starving as he was, saw the funny side of it. And as we were laughing heartily, Jorge felt able to laugh too. We declined coffee and after dinner drinks, as we had a plan in mind.

As far as the food was concerned, the night had been an unmitigated disaster! So much for me forever going on about eating where the farmers the fishermen go. The theory of finding good food there had always stood me in good stead, until then. The art had been colourful, it was a friendly enough place, and no one could say that we hadn't had an authentic experience.

As we were waved off by the locals on their club table, tucking into their boiled egg cake, we were calculating the length of the drive back to Lagos, whilst trying to remember what time room service finished at our hotel.

Perfection

The next day dawned bright and over breakfast on the pavement watching the fishing boats come in, we three intrepid gastronauts decided we weren't going to let one bad meal put us off and today we would finish our trip with a hunt for that jewel in the crown of Portuguese cooking: the perfect chicken piri-piri! There are plenty places on the Algarve serving this famous dish, known locally as *frango assado* and the coastal town of Albuferia not far from where we were even hosts an annual festival devoted to it. Some say the best place is O Teodosio in Guia, but Fernando assured us "it's an industrial size chicken factory on two floors and very commercial." Others say *Ramires* in the same town is the best – and being the oldest it does appear in many of the guidebooks and web reviews, which probably gives it a favourable bias. Basically, everyone in Portugal has an opinion on who cooks the best piri-piri and it is rare that two opinions are ever the same.

Obviously Fernando, who was back on guiding duty with us, had his own thoughts on the matter. He shepherded us into his car and we headed off for the town Monchique, about 40 minutes' drive up into the hills. He told us it was home to a *churrasqueira* (barbeque) restaurant called the Paraiso de Montanha (Paradise of the Mountain) where – in his opinion – we would find the best chicken piri-piri on the Algarve.

It is certainly off the beaten track, high on the Mountain of Foia and we found ourselves driving up winding roads lined with cork, eucalyptus and pine trees. The higher we drove, the more the enticing the aroma of the eucalyptus hanging in the air and the more spectacular the views behind us of the coastline below became. I was pleased we had decided to come during daylight.

Our confidence in local knowledge, which had been shaken the night before was fully restored now we were back in the safe hands of Fernando, who shared his knowledge of this famous local dish with us as we drove. We discovered that for what seems to be a very simple dish of grilled chicken, much is needed to come together to make the perfect chicken piri piri.

Fernando explained that the dish has its origins in the Portuguese colonies of Mozambique and Angola. The Portuguese brought chilli seeds from South America to Africa on spice ships, planted them, and the people there began mixing the chillies with other ingredients to create a distinctive hot sauce. The dish evolved and developed through the generations, with different regions making slight changes and families handing down recipes until it became the popular piri-piri chicken dish we know today.

Had I been driving I would have sailed past the restaurant, with nothing to suggest it would be worth stopping for. Although you could see the top of its tall whitewashed chimney, blackened with decades of wood smoke from the *churrasqueira* below the building itself was bland and unimpressive. My expression must have given away my thought as Fernando laughed.

"How many times must I tell you about not eating with your eyes Clive?"

As we moved through the equally uninspiring white walled restaurant towards the terrace, we couldn't help but notice that the place was full of local people at wooden tables, laughing and gossiping about nothing in particular. I was pleased not to hear one English or American accent! We took a table outside looking down the mountain over the trees towards the coast shimmering in the haze. Fernando's friend Maria, mother and grandmother, certainly the lady of the House, joined us and shared a glass of our Lancers Rose from a stone bottle, as Papa expertly marinated the next batch of chicken while watching, turning and basting the pieces already browning over the huge wood grill and giving off a deliciously tempting, picante aroma that encouraged the gastric juices to flow in anticipation. The terrace was as lovely as the inside was dull, a fig tree casting its shadow to give a perfectly shaded spot in which to relax.

We asked Maria if the skill lay in the cooking, and would any chicken be ok to use. "No! Any chicken will NOT do!" she told us.

"It must have lived outside and eaten vegetables and cereals. And in Portugal size matters. My husband knows whether the chicken is right just by holding it in his hands." She went on, "The chicken should have a *happy ending** at 25 days, not 45, and weigh no more than 750 grams.

For the cooking, using an oven is not the best. Is best when cooked over fire - charcoal or wood."

We wouldn't learn more until later because as plates started to arrive at our table Maria graciously withdrew, going back to her other guests and her overworked till.

The chicken came out gleaming with crispiness. A whole small chicken cut into 8 pieces on a platter. We picked up a piece each and I took my first bite.

And **what** a bite!

After the crunch of the delicate, oh so skilfully seasoned golden brown skin, came the moist mouth-watering meat. Chicken is such a great carrier of other flavours and those flavours immediately started tantalising my taste buds.

"Good place eh?" asked Fernando.

"Good." said Oliver. "Better than good. Exceptional!"

This was food you could get your fingers into! Picking up the pieces and nibbling the bones, leaving greasy marks on our glasses, the chilled Lancers rosé dampening the chilli-buzz and working its magic on an already enchanted afternoon.

The precision charring and that special sauce – quite spicy, but with a little bit of sweetness, more than slightly salty, infused to deliver an explosion of flavour – ensured that it tasted like no barbequed chicken I'd tasted before. A second platter – another whole chicken arrived and we tucked in eagerly. Oliver especially had some making up to do after the previous night!

The chips were superb too. Crispy but soft and yielding in the middle.

I often talk about food being simple and good and this was one of the finest examples of good simplicity that any of us had enjoyed for a long time.

Perfection on a plate!

"Keep them coming" said Other Clive, and neither Oliver nor I contradicted him. How we envied Fernando having this piri piri palace on a mountain so close to where he lived.

"What a shame that we can't reproduce this in England" I said, thinking of hosting merry piri-piri barbeques at home in Hertfordshire.

"Well we might be able to," said Clive, "if we could find out the secret of this sauce. Would you have the recipe Fernando?"

Fernando explained that every family had their own version of a piri piri recipe, passed down from grandma and before.

"You want to have THIS recipe don't you – from this place. I don't think they'll tell you, but we can ask."

We invited Senora back to our table. *Senor* was still busy with making sure there was enough to feed the steady stream of arrivals, on foot and by bicycle and motorbike. More locals. A tribute to their consistently fine fare.

"So Maria," I began, flashing her my most ingratiating and widest smile, "this was the best food we've eaten in our whole trip! We love your piri piri so much, we can't possibly leave your beautiful country without the recipe for the sauce,"

Maria was happy to talk about it, but was giving nothing away when she told us, "the blend of chillies gives the sauce it's flavourful heat." She went to explain that Papa, her husband, adds several herbs and spices, some garlic, vinegar, olive oil, bay leaves, and lemon juice. Clive was furiously jotting all this down.

"And the quantities", he asked, "and which chillies and spices exactly? When to marinade, and do you leave the chicken in overnight?"

"Well," she replied, "ours is authentic, much the same as the sauces created by the early conquistadors."

And that was it. No more was forthcoming. Maria slowly sipped her wine.

"Is it better I ask your husband?" enquired Clive.

Maria smiled, "Ah, you want to know *everything* that was passed from my husband's family. This is our most precious jewel. I cannot give you the secretos because I don't know them. He knows but will not reveal to you or anybody the secretos."

The recipe was most definitely NOT for sharing.

"But there is a way," said Maria, "that you can enjoy our special tasting chicken piri piri whenever you like."

"Yes?" shot back Clive expectantly.

"I invite you to return as often as you like! Remember we are closed on Wednesday afternoons". And with a broad, mischievous smile she was away to entice some other keen guests to have 'just one more platter'.

All too quickly it was time for our wonderful food guide Fernando to take us back to the airport. His local knowledge had been worth so much more than his fee. I'd really enjoyed his banter and wasn't ready to say goodbye to him. Because of him, in this short trip we had seen some of the Algarve, enjoyed a few hours of surprisingly hot winter sun, and most of all had tasted just a bit of the real Portuguese culture through its fine cuisine. We knew we would be back.

"When you come back next," asked Fernando, "if you only had the chance to return to one of the places I've shown you, which would it be?"
"Sardines under the bridge for me" said Other Clive.

"Piri piri in the mountains would be my choice," I replied.

"It would be the *pork meat* place for me" said Oliver. "I was so pleased to be told I hadn't missed a dinner!"

Fernando smiled broadly at us and said, "For me, I would like to have been at the place that served *cow and dog* – Costa told me it was out of this world."

"I think something has been lost translation there," said Oliver, *"I'd say it was like nothing on Earth!"*

Footnote.
happy ending. *A strange choice of words describing the despatch of a chicken!*

Estevo's idea of a bit of fun!

When we asked for brandies to accompany our port Oliver had told him to "Please make them large."

A real happy ending for us as well.

I wrote this book to entertain and amuse.
I hope you've gathered that by now?
So I was very much in two minds as to whether
to even write the following chapter.

It is serious and dark, about being defrauded by
a trusted colleague and the subsequent strain
of the investigation and anguish of the trial,
which the fraudster attempted to sabotage.

In writing this it was hard to maintain the book's
whimsical style, but I've told it anyway to give
balance, and to demonstrate that even my luck
doesn't always hold!

almost
done &
dusted

Court
&*Covid*

Having read this far, I reckon you'll have the general idea that, by and large, I've had a pretty good life. I created a company, *Prestige*, that allowed me to do things, go places and meet an extraordinary range of people that young Clive Thomas, growing up in the 1960s North London suburbs could have only dreamed of. And it's true. *Prestige Promotions* has given me a fabulous life.

I've achieved my ambition of doing a lot of Alan Whicker type things.

I am proud of it all. But, when all is said and done, *Prestige* is a business. It is my living and the thing that I count on to provide for Kay and I when we finally get too old and doddery to jet off around the world and want to find somewhere to put our feet up. And although Prestige is my baby, it isn't just me. Over the years I have built up a team of good, trusted people to help and support me and the business. These are people who I have worked hard to never let down, and will never *let* me down.

Or so I thought.

Early in 2018 I was becoming increasingly worried that although we were doing good business, there was always a lack of cash in the company and I couldn't fathom out why. I hadn't changed my car for years, Kay will tell you that I'm not really a follower of fashion. I don't gamble. I do eat out and I do travel – but blimey, not to *that* extent!

It is the nature of the business that on occasion we would go deeply into overdraft when having paid suppliers, we would wait for client's funds to arrive and so I was used to seeing negative balances. But they weren't coming back into the black like they used to. I was putting more and more money back *into* the business and my gut feel was that something was wrong.

Jack Katz, my tax accountant of some 40 years and close friend, checked some payments, including some I had made to Amex and he told me that what had left my account didn't tie up with what was on the Amex statement. With the somewhat reluctant help of HSBC, we found that two payments that appeared to go to Amex on our bank statement, had actually gone to an account in the name of my internal bookkeeper. We started digging and went back over five years and with an ever increasing sense of incredulity established theft of in excess of £140k. This bookkeeper, who I have known and trusted for years, had systematically stolen money via online bank transfers, taking advantage of a loophole in the bank's system, which allowed the payee reference which appears on the bank statement to be different from the account into which it was being paid.

It was laughably simple: a fraudsters paradise (now partially corrected I understand, but too late to help me), which only needed his clever use of my credit cards coupled with *my trust in him* and was all very neatly covered up. But eventually we discovered he had stolen from the business account, my personal account, my joint account with Kay containing money we'd made on the sale of our house and, even more despicably, from my charity account, which exists largely to help educate and feed children in some of the poorest regions of the world.

I am not going to sully the pages of my book with the fraudster's name, but will refer to him only by initials, *TTB**. He was a trusted senior member of my team. I felt totally betrayed. Was I angry? Yes of course. But it was more than that. All through my life, in business and in pleasure, I have believed that a person's word is their bond and I have closed deals, sometimes for large sums of money, on a handshake. Until now, I had never crossed or been (seriously) crossed by anyone. So not only was I bitterly disappointed, I was shaken, as if something I had always lived my life by had been sullied. And, I must also admit,

I felt like a fool to have *so* misplaced my trust.

I confronted him and unbelievably his reaction was to threaten me! And when that didn't work he signed a letter pledging to pay money back. Both were attempts to stop me going to the police. Without serious financial support from my brother Peter who is always in my corner, my 40 year old business almost certainly would have been at an end. HSBC, who I had banked with for all of that time, were as disgracefully unhelpful and uncaring as you could imagine.

Around this time at my annual check-up at the surgery with my lovely Dr Jeannie she diagnosed PTS, just from the changes in the way I was and from what I was saying. I said that I thought Post Traumatic Stress was what soldiers suffered after armed combat but she told me it can happen to anyone who suffers a major and unexpected trauma, and the brain struggles to make sense of it all. That was certainly the case.

I really didn't want to relive it all, but on the other hand, just accepting it, doing nothing and letting him get away with it would have made me feel even more wretched. I gathered as much evidence as I could, dates, amounts, requested copy cheques from the banks showing the names of some of the accounts he had cleared cheques through, and armed with these, I went to the police and made a long and detailed statement. The officers were *very* interested and told me that on the evidence I'd given them alone, *if* they could get the case to trial he would most likely be facing a custodial sentence, but that while they would try to trace my money and get back what they could, that I should not hold out any realistic hope.

In the following months progress seemed to be painfully slow, but in the end there were two dawn raids on TTB's flat, each followed by a three hour long interview with the police, during which I understand he said, "no comment" to every single question put to him – including at one stage "would you like sugar in your tea?"

The second of those police interviews was led by an extremely tenacious officer who I felt had some sympathy with me from the beginning. This interview led to TTB being held overnight and on the basis of what they knew from me, backed up with a myriad of documents they seized from his property on the first raid, the Criminal Prosecution Service charged him with five separate offences of fraud, and two of theft. It was looking like justice may be done after all.

The trial begins:

After a two year investigation by Thames Valley Police, in early 2021, right in the height of the covid pandemic, the trial finally came to the Crown Court. Press releases to national and social media were subsequently issued by Thames Valley but for this book I've changed the names of all concerned to be discreet, and to maintain an air of humour, even though this was one of my life's darkest periods. I'm also assuming that you won't be overly familiar with how things work in a Crown Court, so I'll explain as we go.

The court room itself is a soulless and sombre place and my first experience of it was being told to report for 10:30 and not being called until 3.45. This is quite typical. I hadn't realised just how ponderous the process is, with the barristers asking questions very slowly and deliberately and then everything coming to a halt when both barristers type the replies into their laptops. So a conversation that might take you and I half an hour can literally take three hours, with long, very long pauses between each exchange.

Then there were the jurors who, to say look bored would be an understatement, like saying Diego Maradona was an OK footballer, or that Donald Trump was a bit peeved when he wasn't re-elected. I knew I needed to get them on my side but I had been counselled by friends not to try and entertain the jury and to simply answer the questions put to me. Any embellishment could give the defence a bit of extra ammunition and I certainly was not going to risk self-sabotaging a trial that we had waited two very long years for.

My part began with the court standing for the arrival of *Judge Jeffries* (of the Hanging persuasion I hoped) and my swearing the oath. Then the prosecution barrister, a high-flying lady I christened *Buffy (The Fraudster Slayer)*, started by asking me questions about what Prestige did – I tried to remember that this wasn't an opportunity for a sales pitch and from what I could tell it didn't look likely that any of the members of the jury could be up for a Wildlife Safari or for blasting their Ferraris around Europe in the near future. But hearing about what we do could have been the most interesting thing they had heard for several hours. I smiled and made eye contact where I could and tried to be at my most endearing.

Later on in the questioning I was asked why I needed a separate charity account, which gave me the opportunity to talk about the support we give to two primary schools in the Masai Mara, how we had sponsored 30 children through their primary school years in terms of dormitory fees and feeding. Of course she asked these question deliberately. She wanted to portray me as a big man with a big heart and she was doing well. My initial nerves were starting to disappear and whilst the environment still felt intimidating, I was starting to feel more comfortable in the witness box. After all I really was only needed to be telling the truth. I didn't have to remember what I had *said*, I only had to remember what *had happened.*

And then all too quickly, after just 30 minutes it all came to a halt. I had forgotten that Judges pioneered the principle of working "Gentleman's hours." Court hearings don't begin until 10.30am, they break on the dot of 1pm for lunch for a full hour, and afternoon court routinely adjourns at 4.00pm, and certainly no later than 4.20. It was 4.15, there was a natural break in questioning and so His Honour announced that court was adjourned for the day.

As the jury filed out it gave me a chance to look more closely at the court scene. The Judge and barristers were wearing wigs that would look quite at home in the props room of any decent theatre. And the colours of their fancy dress - sorry court attire – caught my eye, especially the scarlet and purple robes worn by the Judge. Very colourful and so camp! I thought it best not to mention any of this. A *"Yes Your Honour, and if things go a bit quiet on the legal front you'd make a great Widow Twankey in that get up of yours,"* might amuse the jury but would also probably get our case thrown out.

I was in Portsmouth, in the pandemic lockdown of a cold and wet January and everything was closed. At my hotel the pool was closed, the restaurant

and bar were closed, but room service was operational. This consisted of dinner in a box. Literally. Not even on a plate in a box, but in this leak proof box. With plastic cutlery. The evenings would be long. But to be made so more bearable by the incredibly welcoming staff, Becky, Maz and Olivia on reception and Rachel in the breakfast room, who after the first day gave me warm plates and some metal cutlery –
but *shhh* - don't tell anybody.

The arresting officer, who I shall call *Hercule* and I had agreed to meet for a glass or two and although we couldn't discuss the case, we were both over 100 miles from home and were glad of the company. We bought ice and a few bottles of the South coast brewery's best, and turned the basin of my bathroom into a nice ice bucket for our nest of beers. As the 'Irving's Invincible' worked its magic, I started to feel a lot calmer about the prospect of interrogation from the defence barrister, (who I refer to as *Morgana the Merciless*), the following day.

I was up with the lark and up for the fight! I think the Irving's had taken me a step closer to feeling invincible! After a leisurely morning and getting some good fresh sea air in my lungs, I was again heading up to the court in Winston Churchill Avenue. It felt like an omen because I've always been a huge admirer of Winston, a man who against the odds, never lost his self-belief and whose maxim was "Never ever EVER give up!" I resolved to be inspired by his example.

Back on the witness stand, the Judge sat to my right and straight in front of me at a distance because of covid regulations, were the 12 jurors who were clearly starting the day they meant to go on and were already looking fed up. By now they knew what the next few hours would bring. I suppose for them it was a bit like doing a speed awareness course that lasted for days and days. The two barristers were to my left, Detective Hercule sitting behind them and in the middle at the back, in the dock the accused, TTB.

I was wearing a grey suit and tie, TTB was clad in a white crewneck T-shirt, a green sleeveless gilet and beneath his shaved head, sported a pair of large dark sunglasses. If I had been a juror I would've picked him out as being dodgy before I had heard a word of evidence. I know that's not fair, but human nature being what it is I hoped that has gone into their subconscious. Hercule thought he looked like a Mexican drug dealer!

Buffy the Fraudster Slayer gently took me through more questions. She was on my side but it was pretty daunting, remembering and raking over in detail what I had been trying to bury in my mind, and through it all staying calm and in control. When His Honour decided he was getting peckish, he announced the break from 1 until 2pm and for one of the few times in my life I had no appetite for lunch.

The afternoon brought Morgana The Merciless' turn to have her go at cross-examination. I really wasn't looking forward to that at all and knew it was going to be arduous to say the least. But luckily she put to me a number of scenarios that I could categorically deny. They were so far removed from the truth as to be laughable. And at one stage when she put to me that a document TTB had signed to try to persuade me from going to the police saying he would return £50k of the money he had stolen, by way of monthly payments was in fact *an attempt by me to force him to give back undocumented overtime money which was legitimately owed to him,* I just said "is that the best you can do – really?" At this His Honour, looking more like a Hanging Judge by the hour, admonished me saying that I should refrain from making comments like that - but he didn't disagree with me!

I got into my stride for the battle with Morgana!! She was making a very good fist of casting doubt on what I and the prosecution had laid out, aided by a series of fake invoices for "over time and expenses" which had appeared as if by magic. They say you can't polish a turd – a deliberate comparison – but she was doing very well in sprinkling some glitter on him! Hercule told me later he thought we had won every one of the exchanges, and that he was looking at members of the jury who were nodding their heads during my replies. At least they were still awake for the afternoon session! Both he and Buffy thought it had gone well. My evidence over, I was feeling relieved and was able to begin to relax for the first time in days.

The mental energy expended in Court is immense. The build-up is stressy and then the relief after answering dozens and dozens of questions under oath is huge. But even though I was free to go, I'd decided I would like to see the rest of the trial and be there when the jury gave their verdict. It wasn't through any sense of personal vindictiveness towards TTB, but it was more a case of having been enmeshed in this nightmare I needed some sense of closure. I knew I'd get an idea of timings from Hercule when we met for our evening beer fest... I mean *briefing*, and was feeling that this marathon was now coming to a close. We had come round Tattenham Corner for the last time, were on the home straight and although of course the verdict couldn't be predicted, I prayed that we were heading for the winning post!

An unexpected hurdle

But the next day didn't quite go to plan.

TTB had phoned the court first thing, claiming he and his partner had *covid symptoms*. They both were to be tested and we would have to wait over the weekend until Monday for the results, so the Judge could do no more that adjourn for the day. Thankfully, His Honour was seeking independent verification of the result. I was in complete despair as I was convinced this was yet another of his scams, this one to scupper the trial. But there was nothing I or anyone else could do.

It was likely that with a positive test and the need to self isolate for 10 days that the Jury could be dismissed and the trial **would collapse**. There would be a retrial, starting from scratch and, given the backlog of cases, this could be over a year or two hence. I plunged in seconds to despair.

I needed this over. So I could get the daily reminders of him and his betrayal OUT of my life!

After a long weekend of uncertainty, and the real fear of the trial being abandoned, Monday came and to no one's surprise his (verified) result was negative... BUT his partners (unverified) result was POSITIVE. Could we have her result independently verified? Apparently not. She wasn't facing any charges and it would *infringe her human rights.* I have been told many times that "the law is not based in common sense" and here was another glaring example, where a simple verification of her covid test could have had TTB back in the Dock, and the case wrapped up in 48 hours. For surely if she had been *truely* tested positive she would have had no issue in the court verifying her test result.

I'm sure that TTB thought he had succeeded in getting the trial scuppered. He was certainly looking smug. But the Judge announced that he was using his power to PAUSE proceedings while TTB isolated and ordered that he and THE SAME jury were back in court 14 days later, for the trial now three quarters done, to be completed. I learned later that pausing a trial usually only happens for a day or two, perhaps to get evidence further verified, or to await the arrival of a delayed key witness. I reckon the Judge could see as clearly as the rest of us that TTB was trying to scam the court, and he wasn't having any of it!

Trial resumed

Two weeks later, we were all back in court. Detective Hercule was in the Witness Box and was cross examined by both barristers. His evidence was factual, concise and robustly backed up the evidence.

Then TTB was given his chance and was questioned first by his own barrister, Morgana (The Merciless). He was under oath - but the lies he told and the things he made up beggared belief and any tiny vestiges of compassion I once had for him (and remember I had thought of him as a friend for years) quickly went up in smoke. He was disgraceful and shameless. He had smartened himself up, spoke softly, was not antagonistic and was quite convincing. As far as I could see it may be hard for some of the jurors to tell the difference between the facts and what I knew to be the complete and utter bollocks he was saying. I was thankful that there was such a wealth of undeniable evidence, gathered by Hercule backing up the charges.

Buffy (The Fraudster Slayer) asked him about the letter he signed acknowledging indebtedness to me of £50k. He said I had made him sign it under duress that I had threatened his family and often talked about my connections with the Russians and the Albanians! Buffy put it to him that if that were true, it's likely that he wouldn't be *standing* in the Witness Box, or indeed standing anywhere at all after all he had done to me.

TTB also said that I was well connected with the police and because of that he didn't trust them. He told the court what a slave driver I was. If it hadn't been so personal and painful it would've been laughable being in a Crown Court and hearing me described as some kind of Mafiosi "Mr. Big!"

I mused at how much more fun life would be if liars pants really did catch fire.

The next day seemed like Day 53, but in reality it was only Day 7 and was the day that Buffy proved that she really was a fraudster slayer. Apart from the money he claimed was overtime, TTB's sole defence on the other 6 charges was to simply deny everything, including stealing the cheques, one of which was cleared through an account in his family surname! Everything else was through aliases, (one of which was Clive Thomas!) and every single one was traced back to him and mailboxes he controlled.

Finally Buffy had him seriously riled and he yelled "It's all ridiculous. There is some big fraud going on here and I'm being stitched up for it by him (pointing to me) and the police. How would I know the answers to all these stupid questions, I wasn't involved" I think that was the moment when, after all the years I *thought* I had known him, I finally saw him for what he was: a thoroughly nasty, untrustworthy thief and liar and after what he had done to me personally, I couldn't feel sorry for him in the slightest.

Hercule and I reviewed the day's proceedings in our by now traditional manner. We were by now developing quite an affection for Whitstable Pale Ale. He explained that the next day we'd hear the closing statements from both barristers and the judge – and this may take most of the day. The jury would then be invited to retire to consider their verdict – and could come back within the hour, but more likely would go into the following day. It was looking good, but another night in limbo was to follow. I was keeping everything crossed and hoped I was praying to the right God.

The Judge started by going through each of the seven charges individually and outlining the five criteria that must be satisfied in *each case* to convict. He told the jury "if you have any doubt on any one of the five then you must acquit". Buffy then gave a lengthy summing up pretty much slaying the fraudster. Finishing with,

"If it looks like a duck, walks like a duck and quacks like a duck – then it IS a duck!"

I must confess that when leaving the courtroom at the 1 o'clock break, I was a few paces behind TTB and did my best Donald Duck impersonation. Loudly! Childish I know, but satisfying.

But it was that afternoon that the defence barrister Morgana revealed her merciless side. She cast doubt on just about everything the prosecution had said. I have to say she was brilliant!! Even with regard to the stolen cheques she planted confusion in the juries mind by saying that "it may not have been TTB who stole them and it may not be TTB who was the eventual beneficiary of the money, because after the cheque going into an account in a family member's name we can't follow the money any further". That was patently a smokescreen but I could see the members of the jury paying close attention to her. She was such a persuasive manipulator of words – and constantly reminded them of the Judge's comment about not having any doubt if they were to convict. And not to base decisions on assumptions, however strong.

This was turning into a real cliff hanger, and was a roller coaster of emotions for me, especially as, with only 45 minutes to go until the end of the court day, the jury were finally told to withdraw to consider their verdict. It was certain I was in for another restless night before hearing the result. What was less certain was the following day's outcome. Even with the strength of evidence we had, it was impossible to foretell what conclusions the jury may come to. After Morgana cast her final spell, I felt it was now looking little better than 50/50. But Hercule, a good man to share a Whitstable with at a time like this told me he was still absolutely certain the jury would give us the right result! But the restless night duly followed.

The Verdict

It took until the afternoon of the final day before the jury delivered their verdict. We had been in court from 10 o'clock. It had been a long day of waiting, the tension had been building, my nervousness increasing all the time, despite being reassured by Hercule that the longer the jury were out the more likely the outcome we had worked so hard to achieve would become the reality.

He had been charged on seven separate counts of fraud. The waiting was over. The jury filed back into the court room – their faces impassive giving nothing away. But the wait was over. On the first count (the one where TTB had produced fake invoices) they found him "*Not* Guilty!"

Oh no, if they were fooled by that, we may be sunk. The words caused a physical reaction and wished I'd brought my Stugeron sea sickness pills with me!

But then, good news all the way. The jury convicted him on each and every one of the following 6 charges! Six out of seven! I was ecstatic. This was a major major result!

The sentencing was set for five weeks hence but the Judge, having been told via Hercules' continuing investigation that TTB had been caught committing further fraudulent activity even *during the pause in the trial,* denied him bail and remanded him in custody immediately. That meant that he would be going *directly* to prison. The secure van that I'd seen on my way in may even have been his transport that day and so there was no chance of him slipping onto one of the many ferries leaving Portsmouth and disappearing.

For the first time in two years I felt the weight lifting from my shoulders. This had been a long, hard and testing road and it felt wonderful to be close to the end of it.

The Sentence

In the five weeks until sentencing I read up on recent court outcomes and learned that financial crimes were sometimes punished by a *suspended* sentence. I have to admit I thought he richly deserved a custodial sentence, given that he had stolen such a large amount of money and over so many years. I couldn't help thinking that a suspended sentence would feel like a hollow victory, but was facing up to the fact that there was a chance it might be.

On the day of sentencing at Portsmouth Crown Court the Judge described TTB as a disgraceful fraudster without morals who carried out a campaign of despicable crimes against me, the person who had appointed him custodian of our company finances which he then systematically destroyed entirely for his own benefit. He also used the words, loathsome, repugnant, vile and detestable, and odious. My mood lightened as the possibility of a *suspended* sentence fast receded!

We then heard His Honour say that judges had been instructed to consider discounting sentences in an attempt to have fewer people residing in our prisons during the pandemic.

My heart missed a beat. I swear it did. I thought "No more roller coaster – PLEASE no more!" The Judge continued, "I have fully considered this, and in your case... ... ... I see absolutely no merit in affording you, a scheming and evil fraudster, any kind of concession."

He then followed with the solemn words "You will be taken from this place and hung by the neck until you are dead!" No, no, that was in my dream the night before.

What the Judge actually told TTB was.

"You will go to prison for 5 years"

This was a very gratifying result for me, extremely satisfying for Buffy, and especially so for Hercule, of whom I could have asked no more, and who I shall be able to call my friend from now on.

Everyone in this story knows who they are and apart from one of them, should feel a glow of pride for a job very well done. Even Morgana, a good woman who should always carry more glitter than she thinks she'll need to sprinkle when acting for turds. And to the Judge and jury who made sure justice was done – a simple heartfelt Thank You.

Footnote:
TTB. Are not the fraudster's initials, but an acronym for "That Thieving Bastard." *The thought crossed my mind that with all the time on his hands whilst in prison, if TTB might also be writing a book, and whether it would be entitled "I thought* **I had** *got away with it!"*

A Queen, *a* Baroness *and a* ginger cat

MV Zambezi Queen

Okay. That was a true story but on reflection, isn't the one I want to end this book on. I've had a great time writing it and sincerely hope that you've enjoyed reading it. So, let's spend a little more time in each other's company as I share my final tale.

I'm not great on boats. I get seasick and it feels horrid. So I was in two minds when Kay and I were invited to spend a couple of nights on the Zambezi Queen, a very ritzy cruiser on The Chobe, the river that marks the boundaries of Zambia on one side and Botswana on the other. My hesitation prompted our would-be hosts to say, "But look – this is a river, there are no waves to make you feel ill and the boat is sturdy with seven big cabins down each side, so you always have a view. And have you ever seen the animals coming to for a drink at the river's edge *from the water?*" No I hadn't. And I was hooked!

As we were taken out to the Zambezi Queen on small boats, we started chatting with the others who were to be our ship mates for the next 48 hours. The group naturally separated with those of us who spoke English teaming up; there was another couple from England, Tim and Emma, from the Chalfont's (I jokingly told the others "we aspire to live there – they probably have a moat and at least three servants!") and two couples from South Africa, Sharon and Colin, Nicki and Jonathan. By the time we boarded, the bonds of fellowship between nations were struck, as most of the crew lined up on either side of our walkway and sung to welcome us aboard. Happy singing; clapping, smiling, laughing and swaying from side to side, hopping from foot to foot as the Africans with their natural rhythm do so uniquely well. Even Moses our barman, managed to sashay across the deck while carrying a loaded tray balanced on one hand, and four large wine glasses carefully arranged between the fingers of the other.

As we relaxed on board, wildlife slid past while cruising, but my favourite experiences came from our twice daily excursions in smaller boats, quiet and calm, getting close into the riverbanks which were wonderful for birding and, as promised, for seeing the animals from a completely different perspective as they come down to drink. Elephants and hippo have no need of visas and yellow fever jabs and are no respecters of man's made-up boundaries. Seeing them cross the river close up from a boat that has you sitting at water level is magical.

One morning we saw an eagle pull a fish out of the river with its talons just a few feet away – watching, swooping and making the strike with precision and total accuracy. Then ten minutes later it was back for another!

There are large herds of buffalo and seriously big menacing crocodiles. Colin said they had more teeth than they knew what to do with, but my guess is that these prehistoric predators know exactly what to do with their teeth. Our guide Samuel proudly told us that a human bite is about 150 pounds per square inch, a lion or tiger around 1,000 psi but that a crocodile has around 4,000 psi. Its bite would go clean though your arm or a leg. No one was fancying a refreshing dip in the cool water! The charm of the river was the profusion of colourful birds and abundance of graceful butterflies of all sizes and colours. Any big cats must have been hiding, but a well chewed carcass in the fork of a tree suggested that leopards were not far away.

On board the food was delicious and the camaraderie continued to grow. Enjoying our first spectacular sunset together with Moses keeping our glasses refilled was a delight and we were soon exchanging stories. Kay and I had come from a very comfortable stay at the Victoria Falls Hotel where we had lunched the previous day with the GM, our ever happy friend Julio, who we named *Julio the Jovial.* Emma and Tim were heading to the very same hotel from the boat so I phoned Julio and asked if he'd look after our new friends.

The last night on board arrived all too soon and we regretfully said goodbye to our chums on the Chobe, both our fellow guests and those who had worked hard to ensure we had such a memorable cruise. We had a feeling that the ship's ladies would sing for us again and perhaps dance, so we decided that we'd surprise them by joining in. Well, it was more of a shock for them to be honest – Emma and Sharon led us bravely, and any natural rhythms that we Brits and white Africans had must have deserted us when we boarded, but we did cause some raucous laughter with our bouncing out of time and out of tune efforts.

Moses was not to be left out as Nicki, who I would insist on calling Vicki for no explicable reason (like a biblical character, *Nicki* who shall be called *Vicki*) said, "Wasn't there a funny song in that old musical *Singing in the Rain* about a fellow called Moses?" She and Jonathan googled it, and up it came – the first verse was easy to remember and, sounding nothing like Gene Kelly and Donald O'Connor, the newly formed "English speaking sextet" serenaded him with:

Moses supposes his toeses are Roses,
But Moses supposes erroneously,
Moses he knowses his toeses aren't roses,
As Moses supposes his toeses to be!

Needless to say *our* Moses was quite bewildered by all this attention, but took it, together with a decent tip all in good heart, and made a good fist of joining in with our final rendition.

A few days later I had a text from Tim and Emma saying they had indeed been well looked after by *Julio the Jovial*, personally greeted and given a suite. Nice! They wanted to invite us to dinner as a thank you once we were all back in England – and may they have our address. Something to look forward to, to get us reminiscing about happy times afloat!

The Baroness

Our dinner invitation duly arrived but it was on House of Lords stationery from Baroness Piddling – or as we called her, Emma from the boat. Looking back to those evenings drifting on the Chobe, I had no idea that Peers could be such fun!

On arrival at the Lords and having cleared security, we were directed to the waiting area for guests, which is adjacent to where the Peers hang their coats, so with a few minutes to kill I strolled around the rows noticing that each hook is individually named: Baroness Garden of Frognal; Lord

Snape (no dark arts in the Lords surely?) Baroness Young of Old Scone, The Earl of Sandwich; and Baroness Bakewell of Hardington Mandeville. I was loving the food theme. These are all genuine names, just so you know. There hung some very finely tailored coats and a few quite shabby garments that would have looked more at home in a jumble sale. I smiled when I saw the name plate at the nearest hook to the exit which simply stated *Wellington*. Well, why wouldn't the Duke of Wellington have his own coat peg?!

We enjoyed a lovely evening with Emma and Tim in the Peer's Dining Room – which is a bit like The Ivy for spotting familiar faces. And Emma knew *everyone*.

At the time I was working on an idea for a speaker dinner to raise money and profile for the plight of the homeless in London, and also to get donations of warm clothes which could be distributed to people sleeping rough ahead of the next winter. I'd met a chap called James Bowen who had emerged as an ambassador and spokesperson for the homeless. James and his distinctive ginger cat Bob had become well known through their book, *A Street Cat named Bob*. James had been homeless, a busker and a recovering drug user who found purpose and new direction in life thanks to a stray cat befriending him and giving him a worthwhile focus. With Bob on his shoulder James developed new strength and became confident enough to be able to face just about anything. The book was made into a film also named *A Street Cat named Bob* which proved to be extremely popular, making both James *and* Bob very well known.

I wondered – might Emma like to co-host an evening with me at The House of Lords, and might James enjoy speaking in such a prominent and revered place or would the pressure be too much? And could we sell enough places to make it work?

Yes! Emma liked the idea. "Very worthwhile, and would be a very different to what we usually have here!" she responded. Yes! James wanted to be involved, saying "if you would interview me Clive I know I can handle the pressure." James being a busker we thought it might be fun to have some music too and we invited Henry Facey a fellow Covent Garden guitarist to join us for a musical interlude.

As you would imagine that there is much formality and fine detail to be shared and agreed in setting up even a simple speaker evening at The Lords, including special permission to have people bring their donations of clothes. However, there was no way I could have foreseen just how many rules, regulations and unforeseen obstacles the powers-that-be in the House of Lords would throw in my path!

A few days before the event we had a call to say that we could no longer ask people to bring their donations of clothes. They would be forbidden to bring them through the airport style security walk through, and also they "didn't want the foyer looking like a jumble sale!" My mid went back to some of the Peers own coats, but I said nothing. We had asked guests for heavy winter items which we would now have to collect or ask people to send by post. We wondered if they would.

A cat named Bob

We held the event on a Friday evening actually *in* the Peers Dining Room. We discovered only when James and Bob arrived that apparently animals are banned from the Houses of Parliament. House of Lords admin had known for months that for our *"Evening with a cat named Bob"* that Bob was both *a cat*, and *an integral part* of the evening. THE CLUE WAS IN THE TITLE but Security were having none of it and just wouldn't let him in. This was a disaster beginning to unfold before my eyes.

In order to save a guest mutiny and to stop James turning tail and heading home (he now has one), *Baroness Brilliant*, moving at the speed of a heat seeking missile and with the powers of Wonder Woman, somehow persuaded the security people to see sense. After a short delay which felt to me like hours, they were *finally* in!

This event was a big deal. Some of our star clients were supporting us. James has a great following and some of his supporters swelled our number. People had come from three European countries especially for the evening, and one lady wearing a most beautiful kimono had come from Japan, bringing special food for Bob which she had to smuggle in because (naturally) tinned food is banned in Parliament. At least when carried by visitors.

We'd built a little stage on which sat three chairs, for James, Bob and me. Seriously. Bob sits and observes, taking it all in. The Baroness received polite applause for her welcoming words and then James appeared with Bob on his shoulder and the ladies of the crowd swarmed forward, all wanting to get as close as possible to Bob. They were as wild as a Tom Jones concert (except thankfully no knickers were thrown skyward in Bob's direction as this would probably have broken even more Parliamentary rules).
The adulation went on and on. And even though the caterers had hot food standing by and were very keen to serve it, and James had set Bob down on the middle chair, the phones and cameras were still clicking and flashing and I just could not cajole people back to their seats.

But then it was Bob who decided enough was enough and he stood and turned around facing the back of his chair, his tail toward the assembled throng.

I asked people again to please be seated and this time they instantly evaporated back to their tables. I was beginning to understand about Bob being a *very* intuitive and clever cat.

If Emma wasn't already wondering at this stage if she hadn't been a bit hasty agreeing to host this event, she soon would be. James whilst mercifully no longer needing to ingest anything illegal, was suffering from extreme nerves and was in dire need of cigarettes to calm him. But Parliament (obviously) has a strict non-smoking rule. Moreover as a visitor you are only permitted to be where you are designated to be. You do not have liberty to roam, say from the dining room, down to the

outside terrace which is a bit of a route march, but is where you would need to be – outside – to light up a fag. But there is an exception to the having-to-stay-put rule which is that if you are accompanied by a Peer and *only* a Peer you may roam. Sadly for Emma, she was the *only* Peer and James had need of *many* cigarettes. *Very* many.

But he did make it through – I teased out of James in interview the things he told me he wanted to talk about, emotionally recalling his depths as a sometimes suicidal homeless person trying to get clean, the abuse he took from vile thugs, drunken passers-by and sometimes even the police, the massive difference that choosing to care for Bob had made, and his journey to now. After the depths have come the highs of a more comfortable life after the achievement of his book, and the unanticipated worldwide success of the film. He appreciated the privileges that becoming an unexpected celebrity had brought him. His life was now stable with Monika, his girlfriend by his side, on his wavelength and most importantly who had earned Bob's approval!

Henry had become an accomplished guitarist and singer who had by then progressed from busking and we could understand why when he dueted with James and then enthralled us with a solo set finishing with *Streets of London* – most apt. The audience joining in was spontaneous and poignant after all we had heard. Bob had settled comfortably on a plump cushion on a House of Lords monogrammed chair and presided over the proceedings with an air of *catisfaction**.

Emma rung me the next day to say "*What* an evening! I loved the singing but come to think of it don't think we are allowed music in that room. Good job I didn't know about it beforehand" and "Yes, of course we can talk about another one, but let's leave it a few weeks, months, or even years. I need some recovery time!"

I think that once again, I got away with it. Just! Only just!

Footnote:
**catisfaction.* *The contentment of a satisfied feline.*

AFTERWORD

The Starfish Principle - making a difference where we touch

It is said that travel broadens the mind and I believe this to be true. If you *travel*, rather than simply *holiday* abroad, and engage with local people, you can learn, help where you connect, and in the process of making other people's lives easier you become so much more grateful for the things you take for granted back home. Basic things, like breathing fresh air, access to clean water, and living without fear and anxiety. Because it's a sad truth that not everyone enjoys even these basics.

I have become acutely aware through my travels that we all share the same traits. We all love our children, want somewhere to sleep and to keep clean, and we all need something to eat, and to drink. I believe that our political leaders should focus much more on what unites us all – what *we have in common*, no matter our faith, economic situation or colour of skin. Decisions about so much of what happens seem to be based on what divides us. And usually those divisions are most often caused by those same things, religion, money and colour. Sometimes envy and greed.

One of my negotiating tactics, especially if I know the people can be a bit tricky, is taking cake to the meeting! (Why are you not surprised?) It can only help. But, sadly, with or without cake, you and I cannot solve the problems of the third world. But as individuals, we can make a *huge difference* to ordinary everyday people like ourselves when we travel in poorer countries.

By directly supporting and helping the local people we engage with, through donations of money, food, clothing, shoes or whatever is needed which is sometimes just a few kindly words of encouragement, we can *make a real difference where we touch*. Our immediate natural reward is the wonderful feeling of *confelicity** which cannot fail to warm our inner soul and make us feel better about ourselves.

At my 50th birthday celebration at Pinewood Studios when I launched my Charity Bursary Fund, I told a story which I'd like to repeat here. I think it's a Buddhist fable and it goes like this:

One day, an old monk asked his pupil to meet him on the beach for his next lesson. During the night there had been a huge storm and thousands of starfish had been washed up onto the beach, as far as the eye could see stretching in both directions. As the young monk approached he could see his Master struggling to bend his aching joints so that he could reach down and pick up a starfish and throw it back in the sea.

"Good morning Master!" The Novice called out. "May I ask what it is that you are doing?"

The old man paused looked up and replied, "I am throwing starfish back into the sea. The storm has washed them all up onto the beach and they can't return to the sea by themselves. When the Sun gets high they will die unless we throw them back into the water!"

The young man replied "But Master there must be tens of thousands of starfish on this beach. You will not be able to make a difference."

The old monk slowly bent down once again, picked up yet another starfish and threw it as far as he could out into the sea. Then he turned, smiled and said, **"I made a difference to that one!"**

It has been said that one of the most common reasons people don't get involved in helping others is that they see the challenge is overwhelming. They feel that they can't make a difference. But I've always found that a good way to overcome the procrastination is to break a big challenge down into many smaller undertakings and then tackle them one at a time. I call this approach the *starfish principle*, after the old monk on the beach. And the help you give doesn't have to be anything huge or life-changing.

A random act of kindness from a stranger can make a person's day.

To offer help rather than criticism, praise rather than indifference, or just smiling and being a friendly face, can lift a person's spirits. Your kindly word or a single smile can transform a person's mood in an instant.

We don't ever know what is going on behind a stranger's façade. What pain they are having to cope with, what injustice they may be trying to come to terms with, or what unhappiness time just won't heal.

It undoubtedly helps to have a secure foundation in your own life, to be able to be that ray of sunshine for everyone else. And this is where I am so very lucky. I've lived with Kay since shortly after we enjoyed the day together at *Live Aid* in 1985, and although she's still not convinced I'm the right man for her to marry, (some girls do take a while to make their minds up), she's been an inspiration to me. Certainly in the kindness stakes – being naturally able to see the other persons point of view, and being quick to sympathise and slow to judge. *She* is naturally kind. I have had to work at it.

My other pillar of stability is my pesky little brother Peter. Aren't *all* little brothers pesky? He is always in my corner, ever helpful and always willing to listen. I might be more well travelled, but he often has wise words well worth *listening to*. With these two completely dependable loved ones in my life, I am blessed in ways that I could never have imagined.

I've become reflective about myself as I come to the end of writing my first book. I try to be agreeable, I answer letters promptly, arrive without too much luggage and I'm happy to contribute some banter and opinions in the bar, at the dining table or indeed where ever I find myself in the company of people.

But I realise that I am of the old world. My ambitions were for that time, and I achieved many of them which I have shared with you on these pages.

I yearn for the return of good manners being woven into our everyday lives, rather than just an occasional pleasant surprise. To being greeted in shops, restaurants and hotels by well trained people who are there because they love dealing with their fellow man. People who take a pride in giving good service, a feat which is becoming increasingly rare and is often now referred to as *old fashioned service*.

Although smart phones, computers and meeting via zoom rather than via British Airways or even British Rail have their place, I have no desire to be reliant upon them, and I certainly *don't want to live my life through a screen*. Booking tickets, paying bills and now even shopping; remote, tapping away devoid of human contact and conversation, not knowing who I'm dealing with. I like to touch and *be in touch*; to see people's faces, brush their hand or sleeve in a gesture of support, squeeze their arm or hug them in affection or in sympathy, and feel the warmth of *their* hugs and smiles mirroring mine.

I'll finish our time together by telling you what I always tell my guests at the end of every event I host.

My words are inspired by Dave Allen's familiar farewell to his audience *May your God go with you.* I say to mine,

please always remember to drive just a little slower than your Guardian Angel can fly!

Footnote:
Confelicity. A much underused word which conveys the feeling of delight and joy in the happiness of others.

A bonus chapter

My editor had taken his shears to this chapter, but I have put it back now, as my tribute to a friend who loved football, but who we lost to the great stadium in the sky on the eve of the *Final of Euro 2020* in July 2021.

1966 *and all that:*

Dedicated to my friend, client, business genius and most generous of philanthropists Bill Blevins.

Bill was at Wembley on that great day in 1966, and years later took a table at my tribute dinner to that England team. He had been a football referee, and lived long enough revel in England reaching the Euro 2020 Final, but sadly not long enough to see it played out.

I was just eight years old when England won the World Cup in 1966. I remember it well, sitting on the floor of my Mum and Dad's front room, watching the match on a black and white television with a small square screen hired from Radio Rentals, as people did in those days. I was sitting on the floor because the neighbours had crowded in and were filling every chair, as we were the only family in our street with a television.

I still clearly remember the moment when the wondering: *can we do it, will we do it? it **looks like we're going to do it!*** came to an end as commentator Kenneth Wolstenholme, barely able to contain his excitement, uttered that phrase, now enshrined in history; "There are people on the pitch. They think it's all over", and at that moment Geoff Hurst blasted in the third goal of his hat trick, England's fourth, and the immortal words *"It is now!"* tripped from Wolstenholme's lips.

44 years later I decided I'd like to organise a tribute dinner to the "lads of '66" on the eve of the 19th playing of the World Cup, to be hosted by South Africa. The 'lads' were now the 'granddads of '66' but we couldn't call them that, so we named the event *"The Legends of '66"*.

I knew I could sell tickets if only I could get hold of few of the legends and persuade them to turn up. Luckily, a friend of mine knew Gordon Banks, our goalie that day, and gave me his phone number. I rang him and he was not only delighted to be asked to be part of the celebration but also gave me the direct phone numbers of our goal scorers that day, Martin Peters and of course, Sir Geoff Hurst. They both said yes, and I could feel another of my *touching history* moments coming on!

On the night we were expecting our capacity crowd of 300 guests at the Marriott Grosvenor Square and the plan was to follow my now successful *entertainment between courses* format. For the assembled guests there were to be TV monitors around the room so that snatches of the play, featuring each of the three legends, could be shown. Each would speak between courses and at the end I was to have the privilege of sitting on stage interviewing those gentlemen and taking questions from the audience.

What a thrill it was for me to meet and chat with my childhood idols! I even sat myself next to Geoff Hurst at dinner. Organiser's privilege. He lit up the room that night with his toothy grin, just as he had at Wembley Stadium all those years ago.

I told Gordon, Martin and Geoff that because what had happened on the pitch that great day was so well documented, I thought it would be much more interesting for the guests to hear about things that they still remembered from *before* and *after* the game, that hadn't been part of the media coverage. I wanted the guests, most of whom wouldn't actually meet the speakers for long enough to have a chat, to feel that they had at least made a connection with them, leaving with some golden nugget of a story that they hadn't heard before.

The team had been staying not far from Wembley at the less than luxurious Hendon Hall Hotel in North London, and Martin Peters told us that the night before the Final, Alf Ramsey, England's Manager had laid on a trip to a local cinema to see *Those Magnificent Men in their Flying Machines*. He said, "The cinema people knew we were the England team, but none of us thought it was strange that Alf had to pay *4 bob** each for us to get in!"

Gordon commented that they walked back to the hotel and not a single person asked for their autographs.

Martin went on "Geoff didn't know if he was going to play the next day as Jimmy Greaves might have been fit, and we thought he'd be Alf's first choice. Alf only told me that I was in the team in the reception of the cinema as we were leaving. Geoff and I were room-mates and he waited till we got back to the hotel to tell me that he was in the team as well – we were like two big kids, jumping about, dancing round the room, cheering and hugging each other!"

Martin went on "I remember on the morning of the final seeing Nobby (Stiles) going out of the hotel. I asked him where he was going and he said to find a catholic church to put 10 bob in the collection box, pray and confess. He told me he was off to Golders Green. I didn't have the heart to tell him! He came back two hours later a whole £1 lighter, complaining that the only holy man he could find had given him a Breakha (Jewish blessing) and that *his church* didn't give change!"

Gordon recalled the amazing atmosphere in the streets. "On the way from the hotel to the stadium there seemed to be a flag hanging from every house, supporters along every inch of the way dressed in red white and blue, and even a banner proclaiming *Bobby Moore* for Prime Minister!*

Although the final had been watched by millions none of the team were any richer. There were no such thing as player's match fees for international matches in those days. Geoff Hurst told us "We were honoured to pull on our England shirts, and were *really proud to play with those three lions on our chests.*"

One of our audience asked Martin - if he had the choice of playing when he did or in the modern game which he would choose, hastily following with, "I'm sorry that was probably a stupid question because you would be a multimillionaire by now if you played today, so the choice would be easy."

Martin said without hesitation, "No. I'm pleased I played when I did. For me playing football wasn't about the money, and if I played in the modern game I wouldn't have my World Cup Winners medal."
Then almost at a whisper, *"It means the world to me."*

Gordon Banks, acknowledged to have been one of the world's greatest goalkeepers couldn't help but mention his *miracle save* against Brazil in the Mexico World Cup four years later. We let him – it was after all his finest moment! He revelled in reminding us that the goal *scorers* get all the glory, whilst the goal *stoppers* rarely make the headlines unless they pull off something spectacular. His glory moment came when Pele, *the* undisputed king of world football, had directed a powerful and lethal header towards the England goal. It looked certain that Pele would score, but Gordon launched himself across the goalmouth, seeming to defy all the laws of physics, and almost unbelievably flipped the ball over the bar. Gordon told us "Pele said afterwards at that moment he hated me. As he hugged me he told me '*I just couldn't believe it. It was the greatest save I have ever seen!*' Coming from one of the greatest if not the greatest player of all time, that made me happy."

Gordon is a most modest man for it needed a prompt from both his old teammates for him to tell us, "For winning the World Cup the FA had given Alf Ramsey an unexpected £22,000 for the team and told him to divide it up, giving the lion's share to the players who had played in the most matches."

"And who were they Banksy?" asked Geoff.

"Well" he replied, "Bobby Charlton and me were the only two who played in every game."

"So what did you and Bobby do?" prompted Martin.

"Bobby and me went to Alf and said that this was a team effort.

There are 22 men in the squad and we say that everyone should get the same. Alf disagreed, but we said we wanted it to be that way."

Doesn't that gesture speak volumes about the integrity of those two men? Incidentally, £1,000 in 1966 would be the equivalent of over £16,000 today.

I was fascinated to hear these stories of what happened before the match, then Geoff followed up with a good one from some years later.

Of the three of them Geoff was by far still the most recognisable. Still slim, had not lost his hair and although a little greyer was still very much looking like the Geoff Hurst of yesteryear. He told a story of getting into a London taxi, asking to be taken to Heathrow and being left to settle and read his newspaper, as most unusually the cabbie had no interest in taking the opportunity to chat with the footballing legend in the back of his cab.

Geoff went on "We were close to the airport exit on the M4, and the driver fixed me with a stare via his rear view mirror and said *go on then, give us a clue?"*

"So, I put down my paper and said,

OK, I played over 500 games for West Ham, scored the winner when England won the World Cup, and I was recently honoured with a knighthood by her Majesty the Queen.

To which the cabbie replied *"yeah yeah, cut the bol*ocks! Which **terminal** do you want?"*

When it came to me to interview them, I couldn't resist asking Geoff about his controversial second goal that many said didn't cross the line, and should have been disallowed. On the day 11 players on the pitch were screaming at the ref *der ball uberquerte die linie nicht!* (which roughly translated means ze ball dit not kross ze line)

"Well," said Geoff confidently, "the Russian linesman said it did and the Swiss referee agreed, so it was a goal."

"Yes Geoff," I continued, "we all know what they said but what did *you think* at the time?"

"I thought that it was at least a yard over the goal line!"

The enormous salaries paid to today's Premier League stars means that when they finish playing few will ever have to work again. The 1966 team didn't have that luxury. Gordon earned his living as a printer and Geoff and Martin went into the insurance business. Geoff had some very good stories, telling us that at an insurance conference he attended some years later, there was chat in the bar with a couple of delegates from the USA about how Americans say everyone remembers where they were when President Kennedy was shot. Someone said, *"But that's American history – here we all remember where we were when England won the World Cup."*

Geoff went on, "they went round the table, each person saying where they had been, and when it got to me I said I was at Wembley that day. *So you got a ticket you jammy devil* said one of the delegates. I said no, I was lucky enough to be on the pitch. Silence. The same guy asked me if I used to play for West Ham? When I said I did, and that it was nice to be recognised, he stood up and said, *"Let me shake your hand, this is a proud day for me, I never thought I'd meet **Bobby Moore!**"*

To finish I asked if they had any regrets. They hadn't really. Which was good to know. Geoff did tell the tale though, of how his wife Judith has never forgiven him for a missed invite on the night of Final. The victorious England team and their wives went off to a swanky dinner organised by the FA at the Royal Garden Hotel in London to celebrate. But the organisers had failed to invite the wives to the main event, putting them in a small anti-room somewhere else in the hotel. How times have changed!

Geoff recalled, "We had no say at all in the arrangements and were appalled that our wives were separated from us and treated like that. But what could we do? In those days you didn't argue with the Manager, and you certainly didn't question the FA. But the wives were furious and blamed us for not kicking up a fuss at the time.

And the thing that doesn't change for all of us husbands is when your wife isn't invited to something she thought she should have been invited to, she doesn't let you forget about it for the next 40 years!"

Well, I didn't know that Lady Judith Hurst had something in common with Kay!

Footnotes:

*4 shillings, or "bob". As shillings were colloquially known, is the equivalent of 20p - but at today's value would have been around £3.20. Nobby's £1 would have cost him £16.

*Bobby Moore. Just in case you don't know, Bobby Moore was England's much loved Captain. A most modest man who almost missed his debut first team appearance for West Ham as the bus was late.

*1966 and All That. Is the title I cheekily borrowed for this chapter. It was first the title of Sir Geoff Hurst's book, which is a wonderful read and contains many great stories and memories which I have not talked about here. So do add it to your collection.

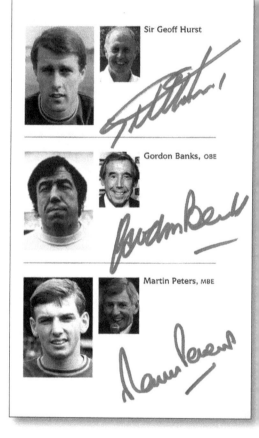

Sir Geoff Hurst

Gordon Banks, OBE

Martin Peters, MBE

We created this *Then and Now* page in the souvenir menu booklet. The Legends pre signed it, but that still didn't save them from being mobbed for personal dedications!

Clive's Scrapbook

A few final personal happy memories to share

It is always special starting the day in a hot air balloon in Africa.

With Murray in Casino Square Monte Carlo.

An off duty moment on safari with Jonathan Truss.

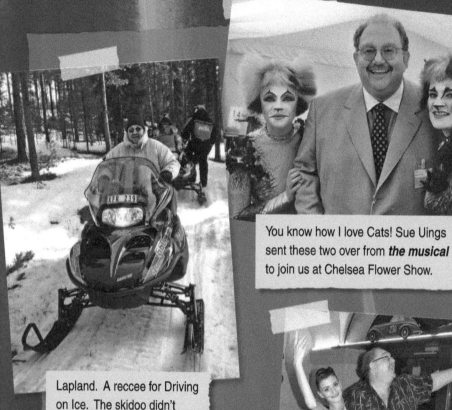

You know how I love Cats! Sue Uings sent these two over from *the musical* to join us at Chelsea Flower Show.

Lapland. A reccee for Driving on Ice. The skidoo didn't understand speed limits!

I invited a ballet dancer to entertain us during dinner at Italy's Mille Miglia Museum. How could I resist when she invited me to join her performance?

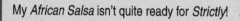

My *African Salsa* isn't quite ready for *Strictly*!

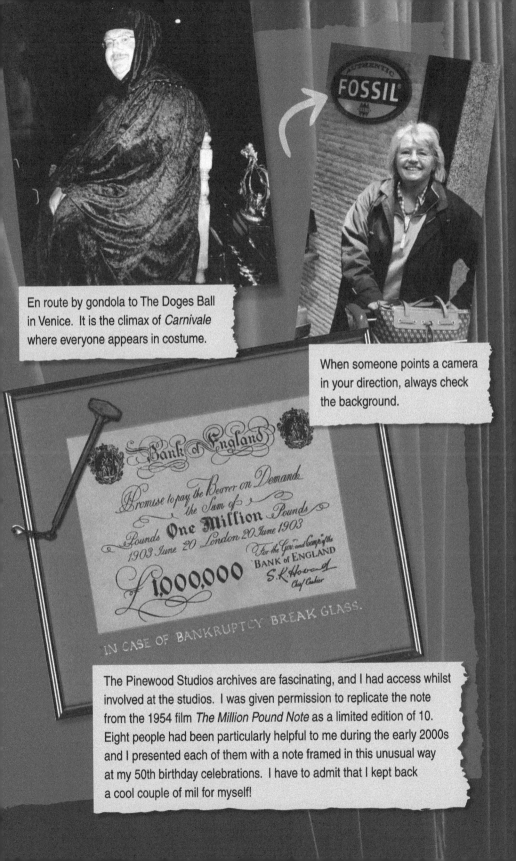

En route by gondola to The Doges Ball in Venice. It is the climax of *Carnivale* where everyone appears in costume.

When someone points a camera in your direction, always check the background.

Bank of England

Promise to pay the Bearer on Demand the Sum of

Pounds **One Million** Pounds

1903 June 20 London 20 June 1903

For the Gov: and Comp: of the
BANK of ENGLAND

£1,000,000

S.K. Howard
Chief Cashier

IN CASE OF BANKRUPTCY BREAK GLASS.

The Pinewood Studios archives are fascinating, and I had access whilst involved at the studios. I was given permission to replicate the note from the 1954 film *The Million Pound Note* as a limited edition of 10. Eight people had been particularly helpful to me during the early 2000s and I presented each of them with a note framed in this unusual way at my 50th birthday celebrations. I have to admit that I kept back a cool couple of mil for myself!

Halloween with my nephews Flynn (F.T.) and Brody (B.T.) in arms.

At our own Venice Carnival dinner on the last night of the Rally. Masks and specs don't really complement each other!

With pesky little brother Peter. Mum and Dad's greatest gift – friends for life.

Larking around in Galapagos with Jonathan Scott.

Getting around in India. I didn't so much get into this Tuk Tuk as "put it on".

Up front with the pilot, who let me take control of the Cessna for a few minutes just before landing.

I always enjoy the banter with Rick at our special accasions.

This is special. With Benjamin who looks after Sheldrick's elephants out in the wilds of Tsavo East at Ithumba. He calls the orphans *his elephant family*.

The theme for my 50th birthday BBQ was *reincarnation, come as you were.* Ray came as a Milk Sheik, and is here seen reciting the very funny *Ballad of Daniel.* You may know it? Ray ended up in the pool with the rest of us, but still in his hired costume. I don't think he ever recovered any of his £400 deposit from up-market theatrical costumiers Nathan & Berman! Here seen next to Maurice, who came as Hooray Henley.

KENYA
THIS SIGN IS ON THE EQUATOR

EQUATOR

NANYUKI
ALTITUDE 6389 FT.

I'd never stood in both hemispheres at the same time. Bit touristy I know, but had to be done.

Kay after a few too many "No Clives!"

Granddaughter Scarlet was a just little older than here on the beach, when she uttered those now immortal words "It's not *really work*, **is it Papa?!**"

Thank yous

I love this Charles Dickens quote from *Nicholas Nickleby*

"Family not only need to consist of merely those with whom we share blood, but also those for whom we'd give blood."

So let me begin this rather self indulgent chapter by thanking those few friends of whom I think as family, and to whom the quote applies. The reason *I think I got away with it* is that I've been very fortunate to have found many great people who have been by my side and have shared my journey. Some of their names follow.

My great mate **Ray Jones**, for always being in my corner and for being a constant *Ray of sunshine* in my life. We have adventures yet to come! My wonderful unflappable loyal and hardworking p.a. for much of my career **Sue Miles** (neé Stratton), who I still miss. Two former General Managers at Prestige, **Jo Teague** who has since built up an exceptional event catering company called The Merry Kitchen, and **Becky Knight** now in education management and also a fine actress who would make a success of whatever she turned her hand to.

Maureen (Morzie) Hunniford my bookkeeper for over 20 years, who took great care of me and my money. **Karen Barnes** who came to Prestige to sort out a mess and thankfully decided to stay.

Glenys Groves and **Scilla Stewart**, the main stay of my opera nights for a quarter of a century – come on girls, let's make some more memories! **Gary Williams** the most polished of performers and a true gentleman, who with **Glenn Macnamara** are right up there as two of the UK's finest voices, and people I feel proud to call my friends. **Maureen Rowlatt**, my Grandma on my Yorkshire side who is the best adopted Grandma a chap could wish for, and who still makes *the best* breakfasts! **Colin Ensor** and **Chris Collett** for their warm friendship and for being my wing men on so many rallies. **Sharon Collett** for the same reasons, and for being a shoulder to cry on when I most needed one. **Richard** and **Pola Long** for doing probably more to help underprivileged children in Kenya than the

Kenyan government. **Tanya** and **Robert Lewis** for always being so willing to share with us what makes them happy. **James Lacey** for coming into my life at just the right time, and feeling just the right collar. **Andy Hindle** for our long friendship and for being the only person in my industry older than I am! **Jack Katz** a great friend and support through *all times*, not just good times. Business coach and my new friend **Gavin Ingham** who helped me stay sane during covid lockdown. **Peter Thomas**, my brother and therefore of course he *is* family, but I love him for who he is, and not just because we share blood.

Kay deserves a special mention here. I am focussed and single minded when I'm on a mission to meet a deadline, preparing for an event, a speaking engagement, or finishing a project like this book. Shutting out distractions can be an asset, but it doesn't help domestic harmony. I know I could be more focussed on home. She says to me *Clive there are just two things wrong with you. Number one you don't listen. And number two... ... ... I don't know!* Some other stuff she bangs on about! But seriously my darling, I'll try to be better. There. I've gone public with that now.

I have dined in some "great little find" cafés, bars and fine Michelin restaurants, but some of the *best meals* I've enjoyed have been in people's houses, and the best of the best are where preparation and cooking is done with passion. I've often returned the compliment by *preparing* with an empty stomach *dining* with passion from the kitchens of **Jayne Smiles, Carole Edgley, Hilary Mackinnon, Clive Travers, Celia Burnett, Shona Muir, Joyce Sinclair**, and of course my own dear **Kay** who still makes her *legendary* shepherd's pies. **Maurice Godden** and **Scarlet Smiles** are right good bakers too!

Overseas I much rely on my local partners. It's not the companies but the *people* who matter most and I single out a few people on whom I can rely totally, and would not want to come to their country and work without. In India **Manoj Pamneja**, who also takes me to some of the best (safe) street food places. In Africa, **Dominic Grammaticas, George Murray** (despite being a Scot he is a great ambassador for Kenya), **David Kimani, Anthony Muli, Katrina Dingley** (neé Patterson) **Dave Richards** and **Collin Welensky**. In Thailand **Bruce Haxton** (even if he is a Leeds Utd supporter) who taught me to drive a Tuk Tuk. In Spain and Portugal the ever efficient and supportive **Gary Drewett**. In Mexico **Michael Fishbach**. It was from Michael's research boat in the Sea of Cortez that I actually stroked the back of a baby grey whale. Just astonishing! In Monaco, **Vanessa Ilsley**, one of the most respected and well connected people I know. In Italy **Francesca Blench** and **Nicola Appuzo**, both helpful and consummate professionals. In Galapagos and Ecuador **Rosario Arroyo**, whose charm has opened many doors for us.

Sadly there are some who are no longer with us; dear friends who added to my life's pleasures, making the music sound sweeter, the wine taste richer, the laughter ring louder – just because they were there. I try remember them in my prayers and highlight my affection for them here so that their families and surviving partners will know in what high esteem I will always hold them.

Mike Pavitt, whose noble example, wonderful stories and good humour live on in me. **David Tilley** the gentleman hotelier and quiet benefactor. **David Bulstrode**, who believed in my judgement and helped me on my way. **Leonard Rossiter** and **James Hunt** who trusted me when I was just a kid really. **Jim Murchie** whose kindness to anyone who needed help was and is an inspiration. **Peter Short**, who led by fine courteous example and was always kind. **Athena Tulba** whose beautiful flower arrangements almost matched her own grace and charm. **Richard Webb, Bob Sinclair Tony Chandler, Robert Hardie, Sharon Godden** and **Audrey Chandler**, playmates who left us with yet more playing still to be done.

Jean and **David Thomas**, my Mum and Dad who I wish I'd known better.

Book Thank Yous

No book can ever be completed without team work. A team is only as good as its weakest link, and all of mine were strong and steadfast. My humble and most grateful thanks are due to:

Kay: Who was read every word hot off the keyboard. She gave me honest opinions, often jogged my memory and kept me grounded.

David Spicer: My editor and writing coach who succeeded in coaxing the best out of me. He deserves a medal for his patience, especially towards the end.

Chris Collett: Chris and his colleagues at Pen & Ink Graphics have made the pages come alive with their creativity and clever designs. Chris wishes he had rationed the number of amends I was allowed!

Francesca Blench: My proof reader and critic. In one of her emails back with comments she added: *p.s. Please excuse any typos.* She made me laugh!

Sue Oldershaw: My second proof reader.

Jasper Carrott: For generously writing the thoughtful and original Foreword, which *almost* made me laugh.

Gyles Brandreth: Who shared with me his knowledge of the world of publishing, and encouraged me to keep writing.

Charlotte Ballard: I spent hour upon hour day after day at my keyboard and regularly visited this great osteopath in St Albans, to have the tension and knots in my neck shoulders and back stroked, stretched and pummelled away. I referred to my visits to her as "going for a good Ballarding" I commend a Ballarding to anyone!

Gaynor Volpi: An animator at both Walt Disney and Hannah Barbera, well known for penning the Pink Panther, Scoobie Doo and Yogi Bear, and now for illustrating this cover, and some "little Clives" within.

Charles Honeywell: at Golden Bee Publishing, who invited me to join them.

Nick Singh: at Ingram for book printing and distribution.

Patrick Ensor: Who gave David and I the private room in his outstanding pub, the Fox & Hounds at Rickmansworth, in which to hone the manuscript. Most apt, doing a write up in a pub, after a life time of organising pi*s ups not always in breweries.

Photography and copyright. I am indebted to friends and contacts who have given me photographs to use. I've also used a few photographs from our archives dating back over 40 years which I cannot now attribute, in the belief that the photographers will understand that I have not deliberately not sought permission or failed to credit their work.
I have also conducted on line research to support some of my stories and have included facts about incidents, people, places, and snippets of recipes. If I have inadvertently infringed anyone's copyright, I sincerely and most unreservedly apologise.

Thank you to everyone, and particularly:
Chris Collett, Dave Richards, Collin Welensky, Richard Long,
Tom Littlejohns, Jonathan Truss, Mfuwe Lodge, Governor's Camp,
Angie and Jonathan Scott, Peter Gill, David Newton and me,
Clive Thomas.

Extra special thanks must go to *Tom Littlejohns* for a significant number of his excellent wildlife images for which I am most deeply indebted; and *Jonathan Truss* for brightening many of our safaris with his warm and sunny way, and superb Whicker impersonations - usually better than mine dammit!

If you want to you can now make me feel like The Rhinestone Cowboy! I'd love to be getting cards and letters from people I don't even know, and offers comin' over the phone!

If you need a raconteur to bring some of these stories to life in an afternoon or after dinner talk, or you'd like to know about the next book, working title *"Expensive Habits according to Clive Thomas"* or you'd just like to share some thoughts or feedback with me, then I'd be delighted for you to contact me here **clive@clivethomas.me**

I've talked about some **charities whose work I care about deeply.** Let me know if you would like to know more about the work and current needs of: **The Mara Rianda Trust** (children in South West Kenya); **The Mae Vang Elephant Home** (elephants in Northern Thailand); **Saving the Survivors** (saving injured Rhinos mainly, but other injured animals too in East Africa); **Sheldrick Wildlife Trust** (elephants, mainly orphans, in Kenya); **Cheetah Conservation Fund** (cheetahs generally, mainly Namibia & East Africa); **Helping Rhinos** (Kenya and beyond) and **Help for Heroes** (retired and injured service people in UK).

About the Author

Clive was born in Edgware, North London in 1958, grew up in Stanmore and went to local primary and secondary schools. He loved 'Whicker's World' on television and wanted to become a journalist and travel the world like Whicker. After a short time at The Harrow Observer, he talked his way first into the Daily Mirror and then the Daily Mail where he was asked to join as a freelance. It was there he was exposed to the world of sports sponsorship which set him on a course of sponsorship broking, hospitality management and unique event creation, which has occupied most of his time ever since.

Despite also being a tennis coach during his formative years, Clive has always battled with his weight. He did try serious dieting once, but it was the most miserable afternoon of his life! Clive is a deal maker and a front man, and loves anything creative. A natural performer he never misses an opportunity to pick up a microphone to personally introduce his audiences to singers, speakers, members of the Royal Family and from now on, to tell people tales from this book.

He has an easy style of writing with a light touch, often with humour and always with sincerity and warmth for his subjects, whether they be people or wild animals. He lives happily in Bedfordshire with Kay, his partner of many years, assorted cats, and a life's accumulation of CDs and photos which he hopes to now have time to listen to and sort out, while simultaneously working his way through his wine cellar.

Before it's all too late.

Lightning Source UK Ltd.
Milton Keynes UK
UKHW021606020222
398044UK00006B/111